THE
BITCOIN
GUIDEBOOK

THE
BITCOIN
GUIDEBOOK

HOW TO OBTAIN, INVEST, AND SPEND THE WORLD'S
FIRST DECENTRALIZED CRYPTOCURRENCY

IAN DEMARTINO

Skyhorse Publishing

Skyhorse Publishing books may be purchased in bulk at special discounts for sales promotion, corporate gifts, fund-raising, or educational purposes. Special editions can also be created to specifications. For details, contact the Special Sales Department, Skyhorse Publishing, 307 West 36th Street, 11th Floor, New York, NY 10018 or info@ skyhorsepublishing.com.

Skyhorse® and Skyhorse Publishing® are registered trademarks of Skyhorse Publishing, Inc.®, a Delaware corporation.

Visit our website at www.skyhorsepublishing.com.
10 9 8 7 6 5 4 3 2 1

Library of Congress Cataloging-in-Publication Data is available on file.

Cover design by Rain Saukas

Print ISBN: 978-1-63450-524-6
Ebook ISBN: 978-1-5107-0148-9

Printed in the United States of America

To my parents, Jon and Tamah, for always supporting me.

To my girlfriend, Laura, for teaching me how to work and live.

To my editors, Jon, Erica, Olga, and Joe, for putting up with me.

And to all the freaks and geeks on the Internet for being the world's greatest teachers.

Thank you.

CONTENTS

SECTION II: HOW TO INVEST IN BITCOIN

SECTION III: WHAT CAN BITCOIN DO FOR ME?

SECTION IV: THE FUTURE OF BITCOIN

Foreword

This is my first book, so I can't pretend to be an expert on how these things are supposed to go. What I do know is that when you sit down to write a book, you should make sure you know who your audience is. This is true about writing anything, but it is particularly true when you sit down to write 80,000 words. No one wants to look back on all that work and think to themselves, *What was it all for?*

So I spent some time thinking about whom this book should address. I knew right away it wouldn't be for programmers; I am not a programmer and they understand what is "under the hood" of Bitcoin better than I, so there is no point in me trying to speak to them. *Mastering Bitcoin: Unlocking Digital Cryptocurrencies* by Andreas M. Antonopoulos is a much better book for programmers. I also knew it wouldn't be targeted at investors. I have never had the kind of disposable income to get serious about day-trading cryptocurrencies. There are dozens of ebooks by former Wall Street investors and current Bitcoin day traders who have far more experience in that field than I do.

I decided to write the kind of Bitcoin book I would want to read, had I been picking up a book about Bitcoin in 2012, before I started writing about it professionally.

What I would have wanted back then was a book that explained Bitcoin to me in terms that I could understand, but didn't hold back on letting me know what is possible. I also would have wanted to be informed about both the good and the bad of cryptocurrencies. It seems to me that Bitcoin evangelists too often gloss over the negative aspects of the community and with this book I intended on covering everything, warts and all.

One book, *BitCon: The Naked Truth About Bitcoin*, touched on some of these subjects, but it was rather short and seemed determined to make an ideological point rather than giving an honest look. It was all warts, nothing else.

This book doesn't shy away from the bad things Bitcoin is doing and the pitfalls it faces, but neither does it ignore the light that appears to be just over the metaphorical horizon, giving reason for hope.

By the end of this book I want you, the reader, to be able to discuss Bitcoin's ins and outs with anyone—from its past to its present to its potential future. You won't go from reading this book to programming the next great Bitcoin service, but the next time you hear someone mention Bitcoin at a dinner party, I guarantee you will be able to keep up in the conversation.

This book won't make you excel at any one aspect of Bitcoin. Rather, it is designed to make you a "Jack of all trades" or a "B student" in Bitcoin. You will understand it, you will understand how to use it, you will know where it came from, and you will have an idea of where it is going.

However you have obtained this book, I thank you for taking the time to read it and I hope you find it helpful in some way. If you would like to donate to the author, you can do so with the following QR code:

Bitcoin Address: 3Bi1fhng5LfoDzue5MTfGw9PgHNKKgRkVt

Disclaimer: Although I have attempted to make this book as accurate as possible, cryptocurrencies are complex and constantly evolving. So it is worth mentioning right off the bat: do your own research—things can change from month to month and week to week. I also make no claim to the legitimacy of the companies mentioned in this book, as their status can change at any time.

Keywords

altcoin: Short for "alternative cryptocurrency"; another crypto-currency similar to Bitcoin. There are more than a thousand alt-coins currently in existence; most are nearly exact copies of more successful cryptocurrencies, but some very innovative ones have been produced as well.

ASIC: Application-specific integrated circuit. A piece of hardware designed to do one thing and one thing only. In the cryptocurrency world, it mines for a specific algorithm (SHA256, Scrypt, etc.).

BFGMiner: The second most-popular Bitcoin-mining software.

Bitcoin/bitcoin: Bitcoin with a capital B refers to Bitcoin the system, the network or the currency as a whole; bitcoin with a lower-case b refers to individual bitcoins, as in, "I have five bitcoins."

Bitcoin-Qt: Also called Bitcoin Core, it is the primary implementation of Bitcoin and what all other wallets and services are based on.

Bitcoin XT: An alternative implementation of the Bitcoin code, compatible with the current main implementation of Bitcoin, that was pushed primarily by Gavin Andresen and Mike Hearn. It is used to test new features and entered the public consciousness as a possible replacement for Bitcoin-Qt if the various factions in the block size debate could not reach a compromise. It offered 20MB-sized blocks as a primary feature.

block: Transactions on the blockchain are grouped into blocks, confirmed by miners roughly every 10 minutes. They are currently limited to 1MB in size but that is likely to change in the near future.

blockchain: The decentralized public ledger that makes Bitcoin work. Every transaction and account is kept track of here. Not to be confused with Blockchain.info the website or its parent company, Blockchain. Also used to refer to any upcoming technology that uses a public ledger to keep track of digital value; *i.e.*, "They are developing their own blockchain technology."

block explorer: A website or piece of software that allows users to observe and follow Bitcoin transactions through the blockchain. Can also be used to describe similar systems for altcoins' blockchains.

CGMiner: The most popular Bitcoin-mining software.

cold wallet: A wallet on a computer or storage disk that is not connected to the Internet and must be momentarily connected to the Internet and turned into a hot wallet in order to sign transactions. Can then be turned back into a cold wallet.

core developer: Developer of a cryptocurrency who has access to git commits in the site's GitHub page.

cryptocurrency: Any digital currency that uses cryptography to secure its system or users' identities and account holdings.

Dark Web: The part of the Deep Web that is built from specific services. Including but not limited to drug activities but also where journalists can meet sources anonymously and securely, anonymous meetup groups and any other activity that might require the protection of anonymity.

decentralization: The idea that a network, service or company ownership could be distributed among a large group of people without a central point of failure, *e.g.*, "The Internet is a global, decentralized communication network."

Deep Web: All data on the Internet not visible by regular web browsers, from banking information to illegal drug markets.

ecash/emoney: Any kind of digital money separated from the fiat world; typically used to refer to pre-Bitcoin digital currencies.

faucet: Services on the web that will give users a small amount of Bitcoin for free for completing small tasks such as viewing ads. When Bitcoin was inexpensive, they gave out full bitcoins.

Today they give tiny fractions of bitcoins that, like full bitcoins previously, are worth fractions of a cent.

51% attack: Proof-of-work is used in Bitcoin to validate the blockchain. It takes computational power to validate and confirm transactions. Changing one transaction will change the verifiable data in all subsequent transactions. Therefore, if there are two competing blockchains with different transaction histories, the one that is longer will be considered the "true" blockchain because it has the most computational power behind it. Since malicious actors usually work alone, it is unlikely that any one group could put more computational power behind its modified blockchain compared to the real blockchain. However, if someone did control a higher hashrate than the combined hashrate of all of the miners working on the true blockchain, that group would be able to outwork the valid chain and get its blockchain confirmed as valid. This is called a 51% attack.

fork: Copying an open-source code and making modifications to it. In the context of cryptocurrencies it can also mean when miners either accidentally or maliciously start mining a false blockchain.

full node: A local Bitcoin wallet that stores the entire blockchain and helps validate and spread confirmed transactions from miners. Unlike miners, full nodes do not require any specialized hardware and do not receive any reward.

git commit: A possible change to the open-source code on the website GitHub.

GitHub: A website that hosts open-source code for collaborative work on that code.

GUIMiner: The most popular Bitcoin-mining software with a graphical user interface.

hard fork: Changes to a cryptocurrency's code that requires participants to upgrade their software in order to be able to continue functioning with the upgraded clients. If the majority of users do not upgrade, the older software will continue mining on its own blockchain; since that blockchain will be longer with a higher hashrate, the coin's network will split in two and potentially be disastrous. However, successful hard forks are often the only way to make significant changes to a cryptocurrency's code.

hash: A unit of measurement for how much computational power is being put toward a network.

hashing power: Another way to say hashrate.

hashrate: The total number of hashes being put toward a network. The total number of hashes equals the number of computational equations taking place on the Bitcoin (or other cryptocurrency) network. 1/THs hashrate means the network is capable of one trillion calculations per second.

hot wallet: A wallet connected to the Internet. Bitcoins are at risk of being stolen if the computer or password for the wallet is insecure. Suitable for spending money and short-term storage. All web wallets are hot wallets.

lead developer: Developer who decides which developers have git commit access.

local wallet: A wallet, either hot or cold, that is stored on your computer.

miner: A participant of the Bitcoin network who does the complex mathematical computations that secure the Bitcoin network while also confirming every transaction through cryptography. Can refer to either the actual computer hardware doing the work or the individuals or companies that own the hardware.

mining: The process of confirming Bitcoin transactions in groups called blocks by solving complex mathematical computations and then sending the transactions to the rest of the network. For doing this, miners are rewarded with a small amount of Bitcoin, which is how new bitcoins are made. Miners also receive the small fees attached to each transaction, which is what they will have to subsist off of when all 21 million bitcoins are mined, estimated to occur around the year 2140. Miners are in constant competition with each other.

Mt. Gox: An online site that was originally intended to trade Magic: The Gathering cards but eventually became the first and largest Bitcoin exchange, creating the first centralized open marketplace. After a multitude of security failures and accusations of fraud, it collapsed in early 2014, tanking the price of Bitcoin, which had been higher than it ever had been before. Bitcoin's price still has not recovered completely.

node runner: A participant in the Bitcoin network who downloads the entire blockchain and double-checks the miner's work but does not compete in the mining race and does not receive any reward but is nevertheless an important part of securing the Bitcoin network. Developing incentives for node runners has been considered as the blockchain grows in size and fewer people want to download the entire thing.

open source: Any code that is open and can be modified by the public.

paper wallet: Your private or public key, printed out or written on a piece of paper.

pre-mine: When some altcoins are created for the first time, the creators will sometimes generate a number of coins before the network is turned on and people are able to mine them in a fair way. Generally indicative of a scam, it can be a part of an honest coin's program if it is a small number of coins and is done in a transparent way or if the coin requires it because of its type.

proof-of-burn (PoB): Using the blockchain to prove that Bitcoin or another cryptocurrency has been sent to an unspendable address, effectively removing it from the system.

proof-of-stake (PoS): The type of cryptographic proof that secures a coin's blockchain that weighs votes based on coin holdings rather than computational power.

proof-of-work (PoW): The type of cryptographic proof that secures the blockchain that measures votes based on computational power.

public-key encryption: A method where information can be verified by an outside party without revealing that information through the use of a publicly identifiable key. That key can be used to confirm that a message came from someone holding its related private key without revealing the specifics of that private key.

Scrypt: The computer algorithm used by Litecoin and many other alternative cryptocurrencies to secure their networks. It was designed to be more resistant to ASICs.

SHA256: The computer algorithm that Bitcoin and many other cryptocurrencies use to secure their networks.

sidechain: A possible solution to scaling Bitcoin. Blockchain-like ledgers that will keep track of a large number of transactions that will be added to the final blockchain in a compressed form.

soft fork: A significant change to a cryptocurrency's code that, while perhaps "requiring" an upgrade to wallet software for security or another reason, older software will be able to send, receive, and validate transactions and won't accidentally start validating an alternative blockchain.

wallet: General term for the software that communicates with the Bitcoin network to sign transactions using your Bitcoin address.

web wallet: A wallet controlled and held on a website hosted by another company. It is only as secure and trustworthy as the company hosting it. Generally suitable for spending money only, but some services pride themselves on extra security and have multisig technology with off-line key generation that is suitable for short- to medium-term storage.

X11: The algorithm used by Dash and several other currencies. It utilizes 11 different algorithms, hence the name.

Who's Who

Gavin Andresen: The core developer to whom Satoshi Nakamoto handed the keys to Bitcoin.

Andreas Antonopoulos: Author, Bitcoin advocate, and security expert.

The Bitcoin Foundation: A trade organization that once was the primary funder of core developments.

Chamber of Digital Commerce: A pro-Bitcoin lobbying group.

Hal Finney: Early cryptographer who helped create PGP. An early Bitcoin supporter, he received the first Bitcoin transaction.

Mike Hearn: Bitcoin developer and Google employee; he created Lighthouse and is an advocate for Bitcoin XT.

Olivier Janssens: An early adopter of Bitcoin who has become an angel investor in the space. He funded the creation of Lighthouse, a program that had been designed to crowdsource upgrades to

Bitcoin's core code but so far is mostly used to crowdfund unrelated projects.

Mark Karpelès: CEO and owner of Mt. Gox when the exchange crashed.

Wladimir van der Laan: Current lead developer of Bitcoin.

Jed McCaleb: Founder and former owner of Mt. Gox, cofounder of Ripple, and cofounder of Stellar.

Satoshi Nakamoto: The anonymous creator of Bitcoin, suspected to be one person or several people.

Dread Pirate Roberts: The leader of the infamous Silk Road underground marketplace. May be a group of people or a name passed from person to person.

Amir Taaki: Dark Wallet co-creator and lead developer of Darkmarket, later forked to Open Bazaar.

Peter Todd: Bitcoin core developer.

Ross Ulbricht: Was accused and convicted of being Dread Pirate Roberts; his case is under appeal.

Roger Ver: Angel investor and Bitcoin evangelist; CEO of Memorydealers.com, one of the first sites to accept Bitcoin, and founder of the company Blockchain.

Cody Wilson: Dark Wallet co-creator and 3D-printed gun designer.

Craig Wright: A recent addition to the search for Satoshi Nakamoto. *Wired* magazine recently reported he was "probably" the creator of Bitcoin (or wanted the world to think he was). In May 2016, he attempted to prove that he had created Bitcoin by signing a message using an account associated with Satoshi Nakamoto. Many were convinced at that point, including Gavin Andresen. However, much of the community remained skeptical. After promising to provide even more evidence, Wright backed out. These developments came too late to allow for a proper discussion in this book, however.

Section I:
What Is Bitcoin?

Chapter 1:

Bitcoin 101: Blockchain Technology

> This is what we've been waiting for, this is the cyberchryst moment. This is when the activists that have been pushing against the FED are going to win.
>
> —Max Keiser, journalist, *Russia Today*

There are two aspects to the question "What is Bitcoin?" that are connected but distinct: first, what Bitcoin actually is, and second, what Bitcoin can do. Additionally, what people often mean when they ask that question is "How does Bitcoin work?" I will attempt to answer all three questions in this book.

Simply put: Bitcoin is a new form of currency—like the familiar euro or dollar—and it is the digital equivalent of cash. Any person can digitally "hand" someone a bitcoin, multiple bitcoins, or a fraction of bitcoin, across the world or in the same room. Like handing someone cash, and unlike older digital financial systems, the money doesn't have to go through an intermediary like a bank or another company. The advantages of using Bitcoin, which I will get to later, are what gives it its value.

Bitcoin is also a distributed ledger, *i.e.*, a record of every transaction and every Bitcoin wallet's balance (you can think of a wallet as something akin to an account for now). This ledger is also called a blockchain. Every wallet, rather than being stored in a bank's database, exists on this ledger; each wallet has its own private key and public key. The public key is also called the Bitcoin address. It is between 25 and 36 alphanumeric characters and begins with either a 1 or 3. This address can be shown to the public and will allow anyone to send you bitcoins. Like an email address, Bitcoin wallets can be created almost instantaneously and disposed of just as quickly.

The private key will look something like 5JJqKVLu29gfaf XvCjva9zBtVapjrE8qNerXWt9RTAv4ebbDX4E and needs to be protected at all costs. It is often said that possession is nine-tenths of the law. In Bitcoin, the private key is the entirety of the law. Whoever holds the private key can send the bitcoins in the corresponding wallet at will. There is no way to reverse a Bitcoin transaction, so securing the private key is the most important tenet of Bitcoin. You might be a bit confused at this point; it might be easier to understand if you are put into a hypothetical situation in which you have to create a new currency without a physical presence.

Imagine being stuck on a deserted island with 19 other people. There is enough food and fresh water to survive, but rescue or escape is out of the question. You would all need to work together to survive; and to distribute your resources fairly, you might want to keep track of who worked for whom and for how long. If this were the case, you would need to come up with some kind of monetary system. You could use seashells or shiny rocks or something similarly rare, but undoubtedly someone would have the ability to cheat the system. Why help your friend build his hut for two seashells when you can simply walk on the beach until you find two seashells of your own? How, in an environment where people could easily simulate work, do you create a system that allows them to honestly exchange hours of work for payment?

One solution might be to create a ledger or list. This ledger could keep track of how much work everyone has done and quantify it in "work units." The ledger would record what each person has and allow them to deposit that into another participant's account. If the ledger kept track of every person's supply of units and every trade that happened, no one would be able to inflate their balance by adding shells or shiny rocks or any other "work unit" from outside the system. The problem with the ledger solution is that all the participants have to trust the person with the ledger to play fair. If only one entity or group has the ledger, they ultimately control how much money everyone has, and that is a tempting position for even the most benevolent of people.

Decentralization is the solution to this problem. You can give two copies of the ledger to two trusted people in the group. They would then be able to cross-check each ledger and make sure the records match up. Still, participants are now asked to trust two entities rather than one. Although it is better than entrusting all of the power to one ledger-holder, it still is not an ideal arrangement.

The best solution would be to write out 20 copies of the ledger and distribute it to everyone on the island. At the end of the day, everyone could cross-check the transactions that took place with everyone else and a consensus could be formed without a central authority. Eventually, the survivors on the island might realize that the seashells themselves are unnecessary and that it is actually the ledger that is important. You could remove every seashell from the island and it wouldn't matter; the ledger would remember who had what and could track who traded what. One could even argue that the seashells are an impediment to trade since gathering, securing, and keeping track of which ones are legitimate would take work that could be focused elsewhere. The seashells, like all currencies, are meant to track work. If a ledger is already doing that, the seashells themselves become extraneous. The actual currency are the "work units" on the ledger—the seashells or any other physical object are just something meant to keep a record of the work, but it is the work itself that is the actual currency.

You can think of Bitcoin as being that currency and the blockchain as being that ledger. The nearly instantaneous communication made possible by the Internet opened the door, but it wasn't until an anonymous entity known as Satoshi Nakamoto implemented a decentralized ledger that anyone walked through it. Every full participant in Bitcoin has a copy of the ledger; anyone can check their copy against every other ledger and be confident in its accuracy. It gets a bit more complex than this when discussing how that accuracy is verified, but this is the basic principle.

The obvious difference between our example and Bitcoin is that Bitcoin operates on a global scale and the island was limited to 20 people; it is only through computers and the Internet that Bitcoin is possible. Additionally, there is no physical space on the Internet; you can't send seashells through a fiber optic cable. Therefore, a digital currency can't have physicality.

That is the primary challenge in creating a workable digital currency: it doesn't really exist, at least not in the way we are accustomed to thinking about existence. The concept of existence was more easily defined in the past. Something either existed or it didn't. You could hold it or you couldn't. But with the creation of the virtual world, what defines existence? Does a book become more real when it is printed on paper? Is its existence more valid than an electronic version of that same book? Certainly, it "exists" in a more tangible way in the physical world, but few would argue that the physical version of the book is more valid than the electronic version. They both tell the same story.

In a sense, money represents its own story—the story of work. But money isn't printed on a piece of paper in order to tell that story. It is printed on a piece of paper or engraved into a piece of metal or stored on a computer server for convenience. The vast majority of money, from dollars to euros to yuan, exists electronically. No one would say someone is poor because they don't have a lot of cash while they have millions of dollars in their bank account. If an electronic representation of physical cash is just as valid as physical cash, then how does a currency that is only represented electronically fit into that equation? And since we already have digital representations of traditional money, do we really need a digital-only currency like Bitcoin?

Online shopping is a recent phenomenon. While $289 billion was spent in e-commerce in 2012,[1] in the early 1990s buying something online was unthinkable for the majority of consumers. The birth of online commerce can be traced to 1994 when

---

[1] "Statistics and Facts about Online Shopping." Statista. June 2014. Accessed May 19, 2015. http://www.statista.com/topics/2477/online-shopping-behavior/.

the first "secure" transaction—a $12.48 purchase of the Sting album *Ten Summoner's Tales* on the website Netmarket—took place.[2] The credit card number used to purchase the CD was encrypted and the consumer public slowly began to realize that the Internet was a viable marketplace. The following year, both Amazon and eBay were launched, and the rest is history.

And yet, people were theorizing about the logistics of the Internet economy well before any of those events took place. While it could be argued that these questions can be traced to Nikola Tesla's discussion of global wireless "central nervous centers," it is ultimately Marshall McLuhan who should be credited. In his 1964 book *Understanding Media*, McLuhan described an interconnected and interactive form of media that sounds shockingly similar to the Internet and, one might argue, virtual reality. Earlier, in *The Gutenberg Galaxy*, he had coined the term "global village," which is still used to describe the Internet today. McLuhan also coined the phrase "The medium is the message," meaning that the way information is conveyed in society has a more profound effect than the actual information. These concepts are starting to engage with the question of how culture would work in an electronically connected society, but McLuhan was primarily concerned with communication and media, not economics. That wouldn't come until later.

Older readers might remember the in-home shopping networks of the late 1970s. Users would fill out electronic menus on early home computers and transmit them over the phone to the pharmacy or convenience store of their choice. Though not

---

[2] Lewis, Peter H. "Attention Shoppers: Internet Is Open." Editorial. *The New York Times*. August 12, 1994: n. pag. Accessed May 19, 2015. http://www.nytimes.com/1994/08/12/business/attention-shoppers-internet-is-open.html.

a bad idea at the time, these early networks became obsolete as use of the Internet grew. Still, this precedent shows that the idea of ordering things through your computer wasn't new even in 1994. It was just that no one had yet figured out how to do it in a safe and convenient way.

When Netmarket made that first sale, everyone who was paying attention seemed to know they were witnessing the dawn of a new era. It wasn't just that someone had purchased something via the Internet. It was the fact that it was the first sale where the buyer could be reasonably confident that his credit card information would be secure. Before Netmarket, anyone buying something online simply had to trust that the person on the other end wouldn't steal this information.

With Netmarket, customers were required to download special software based on the even-then-legendary PGP program. PGP, which stands for "Pretty Good Privacy," is a technology that enabled private and secure communication between two parties on the Internet using encryption. A major milestone for cryptography, its encryption algorithms would serve as the basis for the industry for decades; open-source software based on it is still in use today.

Buying things online got easier after the Netmarket transaction but it did not always have the same level of security. As it turns out, simply encrypting a credit card isn't the most secure way of transacting online. Early ecommerce was rife with scams and credit card hacks. Netmarket itself would be embroiled in controversy when it accidentally leaked information on nearly a million orders in 1999.[3] Personal information leaks continue to

---

[3] Wolverton, Troy. "Netmarket Exposes Customer Order Data." *CNET News.* CBS Interactive, May 10, 1999. Accessed May 19, 2015. http://www.cnet.com/news/netmarket-exposes-customer-order-data/.

this day. It was this fear that forced futurists and developers alike to wonder, before that sale and way before services like PayPal, if the Internet needed its own currency.

The idea isn't as insane as it might sound. In the past, currencies were generally limited to certain nations or regions. This arrangement worked fine for centuries because it was relatively rare that someone from one side of the world, holding the local currency, would need to transact with someone on the other side of the world who was holding a different currency. The advent of the Internet, however, allowed people to transcend not only political borders but geographic ones as well. Suddenly, it became commonplace for a person on one side of the planet to communicate with someone on the other side. And once people began to communicate globally, they inevitably wanted to engage in some sort of commerce.

The problem was that no one had solid grounds for trusting the party on the other end of the computer screen. Simply handing your credit card number to an unknown person in a different legal jurisdiction didn't make sense. In addition to the financial-institution compatibility issues—would your US credit card work with the merchant's Russian bank?—the process was extremely unsafe. It consisted of sending your credit card number, unencrypted in most cases, to an anonymous person who could be located anywhere. While online shopping has undoubtedly gotten safer since the early days of the Internet, security has remained a major concern and has become one of the primary motivations for the use of Internet currency or "emoney." Although remittance, distributed funding, micropayments, and accessible investing are often pointed to as the areas where Bitcoin can make the most headway today, the original motivation behind the early iterations of electronic cash was primarily to address these security concerns.

In his 1994 book *Out of Control: The New Biology of Machines, Social Systems, and the Economic World*, *Wired* magazine editor Kevin Kelly outlined what he thought was needed for an Internet economy to fully take off. Kelly argued, "A pretty good society needs more than just anonymity. An online civilization requires online anonymity, online identification, online authentication, online reputations, online trust holders, online signatures, online privacy and online access. All are essential ingredients of any open society." What the Internet needs, according to Kelly, is both anonymity to provide privacy and identification, verification, reputation, and signatures to provide security. The two desires seem to be fundamentally at odds. How can you have both privacy and identification?

The answer lies in cryptography and encryption, as Kevin Kelly and the "cypherpunks" of the time had correctly predicted:

[I]t seems to me that encryption technology civilizes the grid-locking avalanche of knowledge and data that networked systems generate. Without this taming spirit, the Net becomes a web that snares its own life. It strangles itself by its own prolific connections. A cipher is the yin for the network's yang, a tiny hidden force that is able to tame the explosive interconnections born of decentralized, distributed systems. Encryption permits the requisite out-of-controlness that a hive culture demands in order to keep nimble and quick as it evolves into a deepening tangle.

It was specifically public-key encryption that would have this effect. Public-key encryption allows users to be verified without being identified. Traditional encryption relies on an agreed-upon key that decrypts a message. That works with a trusted second party but obviously isn't ideal when dealing with large groups or anonymous sources because the key could easily be compromised. With public-key encryption, every user has two keys: a public key and a private key. The public key is shared openly and allows anyone to encrypt a message that only your private key can decrypt. The public key can't be used to discover the private key, so it is safe to share, but the process does work in reverse, with a technique called digital signing. By encrypting a message using your private key—instead of another user encrypting a message using your public key—you create a message that can only be decrypted using your public key. This allows users to digitally sign a message or document in a way that can't be counterfeited. More importantly for the development of Bitcoin, however, it makes it impossible for someone to claim that they did not send or post something if they digitally signed it. This added layer of verifiable security is essential to making any digital currency function properly.

To go back to our previous example about the 20 survivors on the deserted island, let us suppose a disagreement pops up. One individual claims that he paid another individual for goods or services but the second individual denies that the exchange took place. No one else was around to record the alleged transaction so no one can tell which ledger is the accurate one. In our scenario, it would be hard to determine who is telling the truth and who is lying. The Bitcoin network makes this process much more reliable by forcing every participant to digitally sign every time they make a transaction, not unlike how your "signature" secures a credit card transaction or a check.

In the Bitcoin world, the public ledger is called the blockchain. Each account on the Bitcoin network, called a wallet, is tracked on the blockchain. Every time a transaction is sent to the network, the sender digitally signs it and a timestamp is made of the transaction. It is then included in a group of transactions that get processed together, and a condensed version of the previous group of transactions is added into the group. Since every new group of transactions includes the prior group in a condensed version, changing anything along the line would alter the transaction history and invalidate the chain. If someone wanted to go back and erase or change an older transaction, they would have to redo the mathematical computations that make up the ledger until that point.[4] What this means is that the blockchain is practically immutable.

When a transaction is sent to the network, it is recorded on the blockchain forever. The rest of the community doesn't need to depend on the word of either of the two participants. Either the transaction was recorded on the blockchain and the condensed version—called a hash—can be cryptographically verified or it can't. There is no room for debate.

For this network to run properly, someone has to process the complicated mathematical equations that verify the hashes for each transaction. These participants are called miners, and in exchange for performing these transactions and adding to the blockchain, miners are rewarded with newly created bitcoins as well as the proceeds from a small miner fee attached to each transaction. We will talk about mining in more detail in a

---

[4] Nakamoto, Satoshi. "Bitcoin: A Peer-to-Peer Directory System." *The Cryptography Mailing List* (2008). Accessed May 18, 2015. https://bitcoin.org/bitcoin.pdf.

later chapter, but it is important to note that the blockchain is recorded in roughly 10-minute segments called blocks. Each time a miner correctly confirms a group of transactions, the miner will be rewarded.

The blockchain enables every transaction and balance to be recorded, tracked and verified. Meanwhile, cryptography and decentralization allow users with fairly basic skills to remain reasonably anonymous in their transactions, combining security with privacy. Bitcoin enthusiasts, eager to discredit perceived slights related to the sale of illegal goods online, will point out that Bitcoin is not anonymous but rather pseudonymous. The difference is that "anonymous" means you lack any identifiers at all, while "pseudonymous" implies an identifier that doesn't directly give up your real-life identity, like an online handle or a Bitcoin address.

That debate boils down to semantics, because with some just-above-beginner-level Bitcoin techniques, pseudonymity easily becomes anonymity. Nevertheless, Bitcoin is essentially what those early 1990s futurists and economists both desired and feared. There were dissenting opinions on whether the Internet's currency—or currencies, as it turned out—would be anonymous or traceable, and the answer turned out to be both: everything is tracked, but users have the ability to keep their real-life identity hidden.

Long before a workable form of emoney was invented, however, there were warnings about the potential dangers of digital currencies. Some feared that these currencies would aid terrorists, drug dealers, extortionists, pedophiles, and other criminals. In her 1994 article in the *Journal of Criminal Justice Education*, Dorothy Denning, then a chair of computer science at Georgetown University, wrote about one of these dangers: "[Cryptography] can be used to implement untraceable cash and anonymous, untraceable transactions. While such services can offer many privacy benefits, they also could facilitate money laundering and fraud."[5]

Denning wasn't the only one to express such misgivings. In a December 1994 *Wired* article, Steven Levy quotes a member of the American Bankers Association, Kawika Daguio, who writes:

> Speaking for myself, it would be dangerous and unsound public policy to allow fully untraceable, unlimited value digital currency to be produced. . . . It opens up opportunities for abuse that aren't available to criminals now. In the physical world, money is bulky. In the physical world, it is possible to follow people, so a kidnapper can potentially be caught if the currency is marked, if the money was being observed on location, or if the serial numbers were recorded. Fully anonymous cash might allow opportunities for counterfeiting and fraud.[6]

Daguio's criticism of the potential of anonymous digital currencies sounds exactly like the criticisms Bitcoin faces today, namely that it is used by criminals, kidnappers, and extortionists. I won't deny that these things are happening. I won't even make

---

[5] Denning, Dorothy E. "Crime and Crypto on the Information Superhighway." *Journal of Criminal Justice Education* 6.2 (1995): 323-36. Accessed October 28, 2015. http://www.tandfonline.com/doi/abs/10.1080/10511259500083501?journalCode=rcje20.

[6] Levy, Steven. "E-money (That's What I Want)." *Wired* 1 Dec. 1994: n. pag. Wired.com. Accessed October 28, 2015. http://www.wired.com/1994/12/emoney/.

the argument that cash has been used for criminal activities far more often and for far longer than digital currencies, because the truth is that digital currencies are better suited for certain criminal activities than even cash is. Bitcoin is a useful tool and people will find uses for it, both good and bad. I suspect criminal activities surrounding digital currencies will only get more advanced in the future, but at the same time, so will legitimate investments and innovations.

Bitcoin is many things. It is an online currency, a distributed ledger, and a decentralized network. And yet it may also become the fulfillment of the predictions, desires, and even fears of the early pioneers of the Internet.

Chapter 2:

A Practical Guide on How to Buy, Save, and Spend Bitcoins

> We have elected to put our money and faith in a mathematical framework that is free of politics and human error.
>
> —Tyler Winklevoss, entrepreneur and Olympian

So you've decided you want some bitcoins. Sounds simple enough, but what now? An important decision to make is what, exactly, you want to do with the bitcoins you obtain.

First things first: forget about getting a significant number of bitcoins for free. For reasons I will explain in an upcoming chapter, it is no longer feasible for the average user to obtain bitcoins through mining—the process that creates more bitcoins. There are things called faucets that will dole out small numbers of bitcoins for free or in exchange for watching ads, but they only provide fractions of a cent at a time.

It is a far better idea to simply buy the bitcoins. The question then becomes: where and how do you buy them and what do you want to do with them once you have them?

Let's tackle the first question. You can buy bitcoins either directly from another person or from an exchange. Currently, the most reputable exchanges in the United States are Circle and Coinbase. Signing up with these exchanges means you will have to follow the relevant regulations, namely the Know-Your-Customer (KYC) and Anti-Money Laundering (AML) regulations. This means there will be some level of identity verification, typically a scanned government ID and a bill that proves your place of residence.

Either exchange, Circle or Coinbase, will link up to your bank account, credit card or both. Once verified, you can then purchase bitcoins. They are usually delivered into your account almost instantly, though it has been known to take a few days if either exchange finds the purchase suspicious or if it is a large amount.

Both exchanges—and most others that enable fiat-to-bitcoin transactions—will provide you with what is called a web wallet. In the case of these kinds of exchange, they are acting as Bitcoin banks. They will hold your private keys—the unique and randomized set of characters that allows the holder to send bitcoins from a particular wallet—for you, and although you are free to send the bitcoin wherever you like, either exchange could theoretically lock your account. If either exchange goes insolvent, then your bitcoins are likely lost.

Despite that remote possibility, many users still hold their coins on these exchanges. Coinbase and Circle don't appear to be going anywhere soon. Both have had millions in venture capital cash funneled into them and both aim to be the leaders in the Bitcoin space for decades to come.

In any case, the benefit of web wallets is the convenience they offer. They are easily accessible from a PC or cell phone and both have very friendly UIs (user interfaces). The downside is a sacrifice in privacy and security. Two-factor authentication is available for both services and is highly recommended. "Two-factor authentication" is a term used to describe any security system that requires two pieces of information: a password and something else. That "something else" is often delivered via text messaging or through the popular cell phone apps Authy and Google Authenticator.

Now that we have bitcoins, what do we do with them? If you plan to buy a significant number of bitcoins, you will likely want to move them to someplace more secure than Coinbase and Circle. There are multisignature web wallets out there that provide a bit more security while still being convenient to users. Coinkite and BitGo are two popular ones that have impeccable security measures. BitGo, which is what I have experience with, will give you several options on how to determine your key. It can be randomly generated through your browser, a third party can generate it, you can have an app—currently iOS-only—generate it, or you can generate it yourself. Using the third-party service will mean you can recover the key if you lose it. However, this will require that you trust the third party to protect the key properly.

All of the above options are fairly straightforward, other than the offline generation, *i.e.*, generating an encrypted key while not connected to the Internet. In that case, you'll want to find some BIP32 key generator software. I suggest bit32.org. You generate your key following the instructions, grab the BIP32 extended key and copy it into BitGo. For best security, this last step should be done on a computer other than the one you normally use.

Now that you are armed with a multisignature web wallet and have some control over the private keys, the next step is sending that wallet bitcoins from your Circle or Coinbase wallet. Simply grab the "public key"—the key you are free to give out to the public and that allows people to send you bitcoins—which starts with a 3 and will look something like 3Bi1fhng5LfoDzue5MTfGw9PgHNKKgRkVt. (Your Circle or Coinbase public key, which by default is not multisignature, will look similar but will start with a 1.) Click "send" or "send bitcoins" in your Coinbase or Circle wallet, and then copy your BitGo, Coinkite, or paper wallet address into the "To:" space and click "send."

From there, you can send or receive bitcoins to any other Bitcoin address while still keeping your bitcoins reasonably secure. This is acceptable for medium-sized amounts of money— whatever amount that means to you—that you may want to spend but don't want to quickly turn back into fiat.

Recently, Coinbase started its own multisignature wallet service called the Vault. It is a user-friendly option that allows you to give keys to other people or yourself. BitGo has a few more years of experience—and reputation—in the space, but it is a viable option.

If and when you want to cash those bitcoins into fiat, your options will be to either sell them to a person directly for cash (I do not recommend accepting PayPal or any other reversible transaction unless you plan to sell bitcoins as a business) or to put it back into Coinbase or Circle and sell it there, where the cash will be put directly into your bank account after a few banking days.

I will cover the actual process of buying and selling bitcoin for cash—and other payment methods—in detail in Chapter 10.

For long-term savings, printing out a "paper wallet" is a good idea. To do this, the software with the best combination of security and usability is, in my opinion, bitaddress.org. It creates Bitcoin addresses based on random actions you perform in your browser—moving the mouse, typing keys, whatever—then allows you to create an address from that. For a more secure wallet, it is recommended that you download the software itself (a link is provided on the site that lets you do this).

After that, simply print out the wallet and use your previously created web wallet to send bitcoins to the public address that was created for your paper wallet using the QR code (or by manually entering the public address).

There is, of course, the option of doing everything yourself; that is what Bitcoin is all about, after all: money without third-parties. By downloading your own copy of Bitcoin Core—about which we will talk more in a moment—and the blockchain, you can have a Bitcoin wallet that is as secure as the computer you put it on and help secure the Bitcoin network while you are at it. This is called a local wallet. A local wallet that is disconnected from the Internet is called an offline wallet and is often referred to as "cold storage."

It isn't exactly a user-friendly process and is not something that I recommend someone does for their first Bitcoin wallet. That said, it is something every Bitcoin user should do at least once if they plan on holding Bitcoin long-term. Anyone planning on saving large amounts of money with an eye toward saving for retirement should absolutely create a local wallet and offline wallet—if not putting the long-term savings in a paper wallet.

Bitcoin Core and Armory, which offer multisignature services for offline and local wallets, are the two most popular local wallets. Download them from their respective sites—currently bitcoin.org and bitcoinarmory.com—and install the program. Upon launch, you will begin the long (more than 50GB) download of the Bitcoin blockchain. Once completed, you'll be a legitimate part of the Bitcoin network as something called a full node. You will keep a continually updated version of the blockchain and will propagate transactions confirmed by miners (more on mining in a later chapter). It isn't necessary to be a full node—and doing so will use significant bandwidth—but every node does help make Bitcoin's network move smoothly and securely. The software should handle everything on its own but if you run into issues, make sure port 8333 is open. You will have to check your individual router settings on how to do that.

From there, the process is again pretty straightforward and not unlike using a web wallet. If you'd like to turn the wallet into an offline wallet, find the "wallet.dat" file in the program's folder and move it to a USB stick or similar storage device.

One last option that bears mentioning is what is called a "hardware wallet." These are wallets created by various companies that allow people to hold and spend bitcoins with minimal connection to the Bitcoin network. Unfortunately, I haven't used one and can't speak directly on their effectiveness. KeepKey, TREZOR, and Ledger are the current leaders in the industry.

So now you know how to obtain, store, and spend bitcoins. But why would you want to? That takes a bit longer to explain. I'll start with a short history of Bitcoin.

Chapter 3:

Precursors, History and Creation, Satoshi's White Paper

I've been working on a new electronic cash system that's fully peer-to-peer, with no trusted third party.

The paper is available at: http://www.bitcoin.org/bitcoin.pdf

The main properties:

Double-spending is prevented with a peer-to-peer network.

No mint or other trusted parties.

Participants can be anonymous.

New coins are made from Hashcash style proof-of-work. The proof-of-work for new coin generation also powers the network to prevent double-spending.

—Satoshi Nakamoto's announcement of Bitcoin, The Cryptography and Cryptography Policy Mailing List, November 1, 2008

With this message, an anonymous person or group posting under the name Satoshi Nakamoto started the revolution known to the public as Bitcoin.

When the Internet first came into the public's consciousness, people instantly began wondering how Internet commerce would be handled. A lot of people could see the potential of selling goods through the Internet, since—as I noted earlier—systems that enabled home shopping through computer terminals had been around since the 1970s. The problem was that there wasn't a system that made transactions on the Internet secure. If you wanted to buy something from someone, you had to send them your credit card number through email, and hope that they wouldn't overcharge you and that the email would not be intercepted or compromised. This situation was not ideal—and without established, legitimate companies doing business online, the thought of handing out your credit card information to an anonymous individual on the Internet was seen as naïve at best and insane at worst.

Even before Internet usage became widespread, people were already working on a solution to this problem. A common proposal was to create a currency for the Internet that could operate separately from the fiat (or government-issued currency) world. Bitcoin was not the first attempt to create such a currency. Several other digital currencies were attempted before Satoshi Nakamoto published the Bitcoin white paper in 2008.

The primary goal of all digital currencies, including Bitcoin, is to make the transaction safe. There isn't much point to a digital currency if it can be replicated or spent in two places at once or anything else that would enable someone to spend more than they legitimately own. In order for a digital currency to function, people need to have faith in its value, and they won't if it has security flaws.

This concern can only be alleviated if there is some level of accountability for the participants. Something has to make sure that each user isn't acting maliciously. Not in a Big Brother sense with some entity looking over our transactions, but simply in that the network needs to make sure every account has the value it is trying to spend.

David Chaum created the first somewhat successful Internet-powered currency: Digicash. Chaum was an early Internet pioneer and had written about the electronic cash concept in 1983, years before the first web browser was released to the public. There were three features that Chaum saw as critical to an electronic cash system and they would eventually be incorporated into Digicash. In his 1983 paper "Blind Signatures for Untraceable Payments," published in *Advances in Cryptology: Proceedings of Crypto 82*, he laid out what he saw as the core requirements of an electronic cash system:

1) Inability of third parties to determine payee, time, or amount of payments made by an individual
2) Ability of individuals to provide proof of payment or determine the identity of the payee under exceptional circumstances
3) Ability to stop use of payments media-reported as stolen

What is missing from these core requirements is the concept of decentralization. Indeed, Bitcoin would become the first electronic cash system that relies on a decentralized system rather than a centralized one. Digicash, Chaum's invention, relied heavily on centralized structures.

The blinded signature function Chaum wrote about in 1983 worked as follows. A user would request a digital token, basically a string of code with a unique identifier that would be redeemable at a bank for some predetermined value. The bank would digitally hand the token to the user, who would attach a blind serial number (or signature) to it that the bank would not see. The bank would then sign the token without seeing what the serial number was. The user would then reveal the serial number before sending it to a merchant. The merchant would take the token to the bank that issued it, which would have a ledger of all claimed serial numbers.

Unfortunately, this process could not reliably prevent the dreaded double-spend attack. A user could, in theory, spend a token at one merchant and then spend that same token at another. If the user could get away with the item he or she purchased before the merchant was able to send the token to the bank and find out whether it was on their ledger, the user would have successfully spent that coin twice.

When the company Digicash went live in 1990 and launched Chaum's "ecash," the proposed solution to this potential problem was to eliminate the anonymity of the payee if that payee was acting maliciously. The user would send personal information to the bank, which would then be encrypted and attached to the token. The merchant would be unable to see the information but if a token were spent twice, the second token would become slightly different. The bank could use that information to unmask the double-spending user. One flaw of this system was the payee's vulnerability. In cases of a hacked account or a fraudulently acting bank, a completely innocent party could not only have their money stolen but also suffer the public shame of being accused of stealing.

Since it was not distributed and David Chaum was publicly known, Digicash had no choice but to operate within the boundaries set by the legal system. Making ecash traceable was essential in gaining the support and approval of governments and banks. There were concerns about blackmail, money laundering, and terrorism funding, so Digicash had to make its ecash work in a way that would allow for the removal of anonymity in certain circumstances.

The idea that any third party with authority could strip anonymity away is sacrilegious in the Bitcoin community today. But Chaum should be cut some slack—it was a different time. Anonymity was secondary to making sure Digicash's ecash worked at all. And it would not be able to work without support from banks and governments, who wanted some recourse in case of criminal activity.

Digicash and its ecash lasted a while but never caught on, though it did come close multiple times. According to reports, it was close to signing deals with Citibank, Visa, and Microsoft.[1] It has even been said Microsoft was offering $180 million to put Digicash into Windows 98, but I could not find any reliable sources to confirm this. In the end, those deals fell through, due more to business failings than technical ones.[2]

Whatever the reason, Digicash's ecash never took off. Not enough merchants accepted it, not enough banks utilized it, and as encryption methods started allowing people to conduct

---

[1] Vigna, Paul, and Michael J. Casey. *The Age of Cryptocurrency: How Bitcoin and Digital Money Are Challenging the Global Economic Order*. New York: St. Martin's Press, 2015. 56-59.

[2] Clark, Tim. "Digicash Files Chapter 11." CNET News. November 4, 1998. Accessed June 21, 2015. http://news.cnet.com/2100-1001-217527.html.

business online with credit cards, consumers didn't see much use for it. Digicash toiled in obscurity, remaining stagnant and overconfident in the superiority of its technology to all others. The Internet, meanwhile, went ahead and grew up without it. By the time Digicash had filed for bankruptcy and was liquidated in 1998, ecommerce had become big business and web wallets similar to PayPal were well on their way to prominence.[3]

After the failure of Digicash, not much happened in the cryptocurrency space. Instead, services like PayPal arose, giving users the ability to send money to each other without having to interact directly with a bank. They still had to go through PayPal, but that process seemed less intrusive and PayPal made it easy. You didn't have to write down a long string of random digits to record the bank's routing and account numbers; you just needed an email address. And you didn't need to expose personal details to other parties. The emergence of PayPal was crucial, because even though the number of companies you could trust with your credit card information online was expanding, it was already apparent that smaller vendors would remain a force on the Internet, especially through rapidly growing services like eBay.

There were a few other cryptocurrency attempts, however, the most prominent of which was E-gold. E-gold was a digital currency backed by—you guessed it—gold. The company held actual gold bullion that backed its digital currency. It was started in 1995 by a former oncologist named Douglas Jackson;

[3] "E-Stats." United States Department of Commerce. March 7, 2001. doi:10.1021/cen-v077n034.p028.

it breathed its last in 2009.[4] Before Bitcoin, E-gold was undoubtedly the Internet's most successful currency, but it all depended on Jackson. When he pleaded guilty to money laundering and running an unlicensed money-transmitting business, the currency was dead. He tried to revive it after getting released from house arrest by falling in line with regulations, but by that time it was too late.

A *Wired* article from 2009 describes Jackson's vision for the currency:

As Jackson envisioned it, E-gold was a private, international currency that would circulate independent of government controls, and stand impervious to the market's highs and lows. Brimming with evangelical enthusiasm, Jackson proclaimed it a cure for the modern monetary system's ills and described it at one point as "an epochal change in human destiny" and "probably the greatest benefit to humanity that's ever been thought of."[5]

This doesn't sound all that different from what Bitcoin enthusiasts say about their currency. Indeed, the crowd that was first attracted to E-gold was quite similar to the people who first adopted Bitcoin: gold bugs, libertarians, privacy advocates and, yes, criminals.

---

[4] Jackson, Douglas. "E-gold Update: Value Access." e-gold Blog. November 2, 2009. Accessed June 21, 2015. http://blog.e-gold.com/2009/11/egold-update-value-access.html.

[5] Zetter, Kim. "Bullion and Bandits: The Improbable Rise and Fall of E-Gold." Wired.com. June 6, 2009. Accessed June 21, 2015. http://www.wired.com/2009/06/e-gold/.

E-gold was mentioned in a 2005 article in the *New York Times* about online criminals selling stolen credit cards. According to the article, they were using E-gold as their preferred method of payment because of its global reach and anonymous accounts.[6] By this time, E-gold had become the second-largest online payment service, second only to the rapidly growing PayPal.

It wasn't just card thieves who were attracted to E-gold. Ponzi schemes were common with E-gold. Jackson worked with authorities and complied with government requests for information on user accounts—as it turned out, E-gold was not very anonymous if Jackson wanted to reveal a user's identity. But the Secret Service, which was investigating the stolen credit card numbers, decided not to work with Jackson and sought to bring E-gold into the regulated space along with the likes of MoneyGram and Western Union. Jackson, meanwhile, didn't think his company should be subject to those kinds of regulations.[7]

The government thought otherwise and he was charged with conspiracy to operate an unlicensed money-transmitting service and conspiracy to commit money laundering. And that was the end of E-gold.

It was at this time that a little upstart technology was emerging on the scene: Bitcoin. Before Bitcoin could be created, though, there were a few issues that needed solving. In 2008, months before Nakamoto would publish his white paper describing Bitcoin, Nick

---

[6] Zeller Jr, Tom. "Black Market in Stolen Credit Card Data Thrives on Internet." Nytimes.com. June 21, 2005. Accessed June 21, 2015. http://www.nytimes.com/2005/06/21/technology/black-market-in-stolen-credit-card-data-thrives-on-Internet.html.

[7] Condon, Stephanie. "Judge Spares E-Gold Directors Jail Time." CNET. November 20, 2008. Accessed June 21, 2015. http://www.cnet.com/news/judge-spares-e-gold-directors-jail-time/.

Szabo had proposed something quite similar, which he called bit gold. Bit gold was never actually created. Instead, it was a proposal that incorporated nearly all of Bitcoin's major characteristics.[8] This similarity, it should be noted, is why Nick Szabo is one of a handful of credible candidates as the real identity of Satoshi Nakamoto.

Unlike E-gold, Digicash and the other early attempts at electronic cash, bit gold would have been decentralized. It would have had a time-stamped public ledger and a limited hard set quantity. The problem that no one had been able to solve with a decentralized ledger is called the Byzantine Generals problem. I find its traditional explanation to be unnecessarily complex.[9] The problem boils down to this: a network in which information has to be propagated by its participants relies on the honesty of these participants. If they are not honest, incorrect information could be propagated through the network by honest actors who had been fed incorrect information by the dishonest ones.

Proof-of-work, pioneered by Nick Szabo and perfected by Nakamoto, addresses this problem. Every transaction is time-stamped and includes a hash of the transaction before it, which, again, includes a timestamp and a hash of the transaction before it. Therefore, if a malicious actor wanted to propagate a new chain, he or she would have to go back in the ledger to the transaction they wanted changed and then remove the subsequent transactions and recalculate all the work that happened after that point. Otherwise, the hash of each subsequent transaction would

---

[8] Szabo, Nick J. "Unenumerated." December 27, 2005. Accessed June 21, 2015. http://unenumerated.blogspot.com/2005/12/bit-gold.html.

[9] Lamport, Leslie, Robert Shostak, and Marshall Pease. "The Byzantine Generals Problem." In *Programming Languages and Systems. 3rd ed. Vol. 4.* Association for Computing Machinery, 1982. Accessed June 21, 2015. http://research.microsoft.com/en-us/um/people/lamport/pubs/byz.pdf.

not match mathematically. So if that malicious party wanted to catch up to the legitimate chain, he or she would have to be faster at mathematical equations than the group of people working on the legitimate chain together.

In real-world terms, this means a miner trying to issue a false blockchain and have it accepted would have to have more computational power than the miners working on the legitimate chain. In order to remain secure, there needs to be more computational power working on the legitimate blockchain than there are malicious actors working on any single false chain. This is where something called the theoretical "51% attack" comes in, which I explain below.

The one problem with the bit gold solution was that it would have used the number of participants rather than the amount of computational power behind a ledger to determine its validity. This would have made any currency based on the bit gold proposal vulnerable to a so-called Sybil attack,[10] in which a malicious actor could make multiple pseudonyms and then use all of them to propagate a modified ledger. Bitcoin, instead, relies on how much computational power is put behind the ledger, meaning it is only vulnerable to a 51% attack, in which a malicious actor would have to be responsible for more than 51% of the network's hashing power in order to propagate an incorrect ledger. Putting together this kind of computational power is a virtual impossibility and would cost hundreds of millions of dollars. In addition, the hashing power on the network is growing all of the time, making a 51% attack less likely as the network grows.

---

[10] Tschorsch, Florian, and Björn Scheuermann. "Bitcoin and Beyond: A Technical Survey on Decentralized Digital Currencies." The Digital Currency Challenge. Accessed June 21, 2015. doi:10.1057/9781137382559.0014.

Despite this one relatively minor difference, Nick Szabo's bit gold is sometimes called the genesis point for Bitcoin. In his original 2005 blog post, Szabo did not mention anonymity but he did mention two ideas that are now considered the main tenets of Bitcoin's economic philosophy: decentralization and resistance to inflation. The post starts and finishes with these ideas:

> A long time ago I hit upon the idea of bit gold. The problem, in a nutshell, is that our money currently depends on trust in a third party for its value. As many inflationary and hyperinflationary episodes during the 20th century demonstrated, this is not an ideal state of affairs. [. . .] In summary, all money mankind has ever used has been insecure in one way or another. This insecurity has been manifested in a wide variety of ways, from counterfeiting to theft, but the most pernicious of which has probably been inflation. Bit gold may provide us with a money of unprecedented security from these dangers.

In fact, while he did not use the actual term "bit gold" in his previous non-mailing list writings, Szabo did get close to the concept even before 2005. In 1999, he posted about the "God Protocol," a concept that borrowed heavily from Wei Dai's B-money proposal.[11] This was offered by Dai on the Cypherpunk

---

[11] Dai, Wei. "Bmoney." Weidai.com. 1998. Accessed June 21, 2015. http://www.weidai.com/bmoney.txt.

mailing list in 1998.[12] It suggested using hashcash—a system that prevents email spam by requiring extra computational power to be used to send emails, making spam too expensive—to create rarity in cryptocurrencies, one of the most important features used in Bitcoin today. It is rarity that allows Bitcoin to have a supply-and-demand dynamic.

The God Protocol was a proposal to replace a third-party central server with an automated virtual third party. It used early concepts of cloud computing and, had it been implemented, would have likely become a proto-version of today's autonomous corporation—a digital corporation that can function with little or no human input—which many people imagine is *next* in Bitcoin. The God Protocol was intended as a solution for smart contracts—another concept later revived by Bitcoin. Szabo writes in his blog:

[Network security theorists] have developed protocols that create virtual machines between two or more parties. Multi-party secure computation allows any number of parties to share a computation, each learning only what can be inferred from their own input and the output of the computation. These virtual machines have the exciting property that each party's input is held in strict confidence from the other parties. The program and the output are shared by the parties.

For example, we could run a spreadsheet across the Internet on this virtual computer. We would agree on

12 Dai, Wei. "PipeNet 1.1 and B-money." November 26, 1998. Cypherpunks. Accessed June 21, 2015. http://marc.info/?l=cypherpunks&m=95279516022393&w=2.

a set of formulas and set up the virtual computer with these formulas. Each participant would have their own input cells, which remain blank on the other participants' computers. The participants share output cell(s). Each participant inputs their own private data into their input cells. Alice could only learn as much about the other participants' input cells as she could infer from her own inputs and outputs.

You can see how that concept could have evolved into something not unlike the blockchain. When you add the cryptography of PGP, Digicash's tokens and the B-money concept of using the CPU computational power to create scarcity, you start to see something approaching a cryptocurrency similar to Bitcoin.

It wasn't until Nick Szabo's bit gold post that all those ideas were brought together. But there were still some issues. The aforementioned potential Sybil attack had not been addressed, nor had anyone conceived of the idea of putting the "unforgeable chain" (as Szabo called it) onto every client's (or at least, enough clients') individual computer. Instead, he envisioned "several different timestamp services," perhaps automated as described in the God Protocol, and there was no mention of a pure peer-to-peer system.

Overall, there wasn't a lot of progress in the cryptocurrency space from the mid-1990s to the mid-2000s. This lack of progress is not unreasonable. There simply weren't a lot of people working on it at the time. Many saw it as a pipe dream, having been let down by Digicash or E-gold. Others thought that a currency couldn't survive unless it was backed by a commodity like gold or silver. Still others feared that any attempt would be met with strong government resistance.

They weren't wrong about that last point. E-Gold was eventually shut down by the US government. Digicash was not, but consumer demand never kept up with its lofty goals and the issues related to its centralized aspects made it unattractive to many cryptographers as a concept—so even if it could have been revived, very few people were working on it.

On November 1, 2008, the cryptocurrency/electronic cash movement was reborn with Bitcoin. It was initially met with skepticism. The Bitcoin community is far from unified today and that was the case from the get-go. Satoshi Nakamoto, whoever he, she, or they are, did a great job calmly replying to each question and criticism.

I do not want to get too deep into speculation about Satoshi Nakamoto's real identity, because it has been written about *ad nauseam* already. No conclusions have been reached and the mystery will likely persist until and unless Nakamoto reveals himself. And even then, I presume the debate will continue in some corners of the web.

The prime suspects include Hal Finney, a cryptographer who was influential in applying the idea of reusable proof-of-work to emoney, which was cited in Szabo's bit gold proposal. He was also the recipient of the first-ever Bitcoin transaction. The aforementioned Wei Dai was still involved in cryptography after the B-money proposal and so is a prime suspect. There is, of course, the long-held theory that Satoshi Nakamoto is/was Nick Szabo, who wrote publicly about concepts very similar to Bitcoin. There is also David Chaum, who certainly had the necessary experience and perhaps wanted to show the world that electronic cash was viable. Adam Back invented hashcash and commented on the B-money proposal when it was first proposed in the Cypherpunk mailing list, so he can't be ruled out either.

A man named Dorian Prentice Satoshi Nakamoto, who was living in a small house in California, was once "outed" as the real Satoshi Nakamoto by *Newsweek* in a highly controversial cover story.[13] When the article came out, Satoshi Nakamoto's email came back to life, only to post on the Bitcoin developer mailing list that he was "not Dorian Nakamoto." It wasn't digitally signed, however, so the email was likely from someone with Nakamoto's email account and not Nakamoto him/her/themselves.

All of the popular candidates have denied being the real Satoshi Nakamoto.

Of the main suspects, I think Szabo is the most likely candidate and Dorian Nakamoto is the least likely. But I believe it is more likely that Nakamoto is some sort of combination of Szabo, Finney, Dai, and Adam Back. I'm not saying they are the creators of Bitcoin, only that those individuals were the ones most active in working toward something akin to Bitcoin and had the tools to do it. It is just as possible, however, that it wasn't any one of them, as there were numerous anonymous people posting on the Cypherpunk mailing list at the time and a few of them expressed an interest.

The identity of Nakamoto pales in significance to the fact that the Bitcoin white paper was published. Not long after the 2008 post, Bitcoin was launched. Nakamoto already had the code

---

[13] Goodman, Leah McGrath. "The Face Behind Bitcoin." *Newsweek*, March 6, 2014. Accessed June 21, 2015. http://www.newsweek.com/2014/03/14/face-behind-bit-coin-247957.html.

ready and claimed that he had worked on it for two years prior to the release of the white paper.

On January 3, 2009, the genesis block (*i.e.*, the first block in a blockchain) of Bitcoin was established. On January 9, v0.1 of Bitcoin was released through the cryptography mailing list. On January 12, the first transaction took place between Satoshi Nakamoto and Hal Finney, and the Bitcoin revolution was underway.

There were a few more milestones that are worth mentioning. On October 5, 2009, the first exchange rate for Bitcoin was established by the New Liberty Standard website based on the cost of electricity it took to create a bitcoin during the mining process with the "difficulty level" at that time. (The difficulty level refers to how hard it is for a computer to solve the computations that run Bitcoin; more on this in the mining chapter.) One dollar equaled 1,309.03 bitcoins (BTC) so that each bitcoin equaled approximately $0.00076, according to their algorithm. Some Bitcoin users objected, saying that the price was too high.

On May 22, 2010, the first public exchange of Bitcoin for a physical good occurred in what has affectionately been named "pizza day" in the Bitcoin community. BitcoinTalk user laszlo sent 10,000 BTC to user jercos, who used his credit card to have approximately $25 worth of pizza delivered to laszlo.

In July 2010, the soon-to-be-infamous Mt. Gox exchange was launched, giving users a central place to buy and sell bitcoins quickly, eventually leading to a massive price increase to $0.06 per bitcoin. Less than a year later, on February 9, 2011, Bitcoin reached parity with the US dollar, causing multiple media outlets to report on the new currency and bringing in a tidal wave of new users.

On July 26, 2011, a bar in Berlin called Room77, which advertises "warm beer, cold women, and fast food made slowly," started accepting Bitcoin, which it continues to do to this day. By March 2013, the price of a bitcoin had reached $100 and Bitcoin had a market cap of more than $1 billion. No one was sure of Bitcoin's future at this point but most enthusiasts were fairly confident it was not going away anytime soon.

Eventually, the price skyrocketed again. Unfortunately, this event coincided with the infamous Mt. Gox failure—more on this in a later chapter—which brought the price down once again. Since that time, Bitcoin has been more stable than it was during the Mt. Gox era, but it also declined steadily until late 2015 when a consistent rise in Bitcoin's price began. The price briefly dipped under $200 in early January 2015 but has since rebounded, holding at around $220 to $250 for months before suddenly skyrocketing to more than $450 in early November 2015. The current rally will undoubtedly have passed by the time you read this book but as I write, everyone is wondering if this might be the next massive jump.

But if Bitcoin's history can tell us anything, it is that it can function at any price level. People are invested in Bitcoin and they are going to see that it is used in the future, even if only by tiny niche economies that the likes of PayPal and Apple Pay are unable to touch. That idea won't please investors; they want Bitcoin to be used by everyone, everywhere. That could happen. It seems almost inevitable that Bitcoin or some sort of block-chain technology will be used to modernize the financial world, but it could also go the opposite way and only be used by the people who absolutely need it. In that case, the price may never reach the lofty predictions of the Bitcoin faithful. However, the technology itself will go on; it is just as easy to send a bitcoin worth a dollar as it is to send one worth $1,000.

In either case, the technology will be up to the task. It has proven to be extremely versatile and there are very few reasons to think this will change.

Chapter 4:
Who Runs Bitcoin?

Bitcoin is not "unregulated." It is regulated by algorithm instead of being regulated by government bureaucracies. Uncorrupted.

—Andreas Antonopoulos, author,
Bitcoin evangelist, and security expert

There are a lot of misconceptions about Bitcoin. Especially early on, media outlets had a tough time reporting on Bitcoin accurately because of its unconventional origins and existence. As I discussed in the previous chapter, there were several attempts to create a currency for the Internet in the past. These iterations had the fatal flaw of being issued by a central power. When Bitcoin first gained media attention and for years afterward, news outlets erroneously referred to a "Bitcoin CEO." For instance, when Autumn Radtke, CEO of the Bitcoin exchange First Meta, committed suicide, the *New York Daily News* reported that Bitcoin's

CEO had committed suicide.[1] Such a notion is impossible because Bitcoin has no CEO.

The straightforward answer to the question in the title of this chapter is that no one "runs" Bitcoin. Bitcoin is not dependent on any one organization for its existence and no one is "in charge" of it. When Satoshi Nakamoto launched Bitcoin in 2008, he essentially gave birth to an independent entity that has lived and grown and evolved not unlike any other organism. Like a good parent, Nakamoto stuck around and guided Bitcoin, but when he disappeared, Bitcoin remained. Nakamoto's final post on the Bitcoin Talk forums (as of this writing) transferred lead developer status to Gavin Andresen.

That title doesn't mean that Andresen was in charge of everything. No one can control who joins Bitcoin or how many bitcoins someone has or who can send what to whom or anything like that. There is only one thing that can directly affect Bitcoin and that is its code. Andresen—and later his successor, Wladimir van der Laan—was given control over that code but his changes don't have to be adopted by the community at large, and if they aren't then they will be forgotten.

There are several groups of people who have influence in the Bitcoin industry because of their various roles. The people who use the currency (the average Bitcoin user), the people who keep the network running (the miners), the people who provide services on top of Bitcoin (corporations and websites that offer Bitcoin services), the people who maintain Bitcoin's code (the

---

[1] Moran, Lee. "Bitcoin CEO Researched Suicide before Taking Her Own Life: Coroner." *NY Daily News*. September 16, 2014. Accessed June 21, 2015. http://www.nydailynews.com/news/world/bitcoin-ceo-researched-suicide-life-coroner-article-1.1941010.

developers), as well as the people who pay the developers to maintain the code, all have influence over Bitcoin's direction.

The most popular answer from Bitcoin evangelists for the question "Who runs Bitcoin?" would be "the community," and the community does hold significant sway. This term is generally used to refer to the people who use Bitcoin, either through spending or investing. If they move to another chain or coin, the rest of the industry would have to follow them. The community is obviously not unified in its views, however, so any real direction or change is unlikely to come from this sphere with the exception of preventing an unpopular change.

The miners, meanwhile, are the group of people who make things work. If the miners don't confirm transactions on the blockchain, everything comes to a screeching halt. This group is a little more unified than the community because all its members share a similar interest: they want Bitcoin mining to be as profitable as possible. Like the general community, though, miners are spread across the world, with much of the network's hashing power originating in China. It is tough to get a read on how they feel about particular issues or changes. Nevertheless, they represent a huge potential power structure in Bitcoin. They don't hold the keys but they are the only ones who can turn them.

As is the case in any industry, companies have influence simply because of how successful they are. Companies such as Coinbase, Bitstamp, Circle, and Blockchain.info all have massive user bases and where they go, the industry tends to go. But saying they "run" Bitcoin or are in charge of it would be like saying Apple or Samsung are in charge of the cell phone industry. They set trends but they don't enforce standards.

We are left, then, with the two most influential and powerful groups in the Bitcoin ecosystem: the developers and the groups that pay the developers. Gavin Andresen and Wladimir van der Laan are the two most prominent core developers of Bitcoin. It could be said that they are the most influential individuals in the Bitcoin world, though Bitcoin would continue even without them.

As is the case in all open-source projects, Bitcoin's code is ultimately controlled by one person. Van der Laan has held that position since Andresen handed him the keys to the GitHub page in early 2014.[2] (GitHub is a forum for collaborative open-source projects.) This doesn't mean he has complete control, however, as anyone can split and copy the code—an act called forking—at any time; and if he or she could get Bitcoin miners and users to switch to that new version, it would become the accepted one. Although van der Laan does have control over what changes are pushed to the Bitcoin core code (*i.e.*, the code that Bitcoin functions on, and that every other Bitcoin wallet is in some way based on and compatible with), he is dependent on the community to support those changes.

It should also be noted that core developers, at least those who work full-time, don't work for free. They have to be paid and the question of who pays them is not always easy to answer. In theory, they should be paid by Bitcoin users, but direct donations to core development have been underwhelming and the developers have instead been funded by other means.

Andresen and other core developers were previously paid by the Bitcoin Foundation, a trade group dedicated to the continuation

---

    [2] Shubber, Kadhim. "Gavin Andresen Steps Down as Bitcoin's Lead Developer." CoinDesk. April 8, 2014. Accessed June 21, 2015. http://www.coindesk.com/gavin-andresen-steps-bitcoins-lead-developer/.

of Bitcoin's adoption, acceptance, and development. In the heady days of 2013 and early 2014, the Bitcoin Foundation found itself flush with cash. Previously small donations had by then appreciated greatly thanks to the increase in Bitcoin's value.

By that point, however, the Bitcoin Foundation was already reeling from scandal. The Mt. Gox fiasco was in full swing by late 2013 and former Bitcoin Foundation CEO Mark Karpelès still sat on the Foundation's board of directors. Reports at the time seemed to indicate that Karpelès had a nonchalant attitude as his company burned to the ground and he had to be encouraged to step down from the Foundation.[3] Shortly after the embattled and nearly universally hated CEO stepped down, Charlie Shrem, another Bitcoin Foundation board member and the CEO of BitInstant, was arrested. He was accused of using his company to help the users of the underground marketplace Silk Road launder money using Bitcoin. Shrem eventually pled to a lesser charge and was sentenced to two years in prison.[4]

By mid-2014, it was difficult to find anyone who truly supported the Foundation. The scandals had done irreparable damage to its image and there was a growing concern about a perceived centralization of Bitcoin core development. This development was primarily funded by the Foundation and some in the community were concerned it would provide an avenue for someone to influence development in a less-than-benevolent way.

---

[3] McMillan, Robert. "The Inside Story of Mt. Gox, Bitcoin's $460 Million Disaster." Wired.com. March 3, 2014. Accessed June 21, 2015. http://www.wired.com/2014/03/bitcoin-exchange/.

[4] Cook, James. "'Bitcoin Millionaire' Charlie Shrem Sentenced To 2 Years In Prison." Business Insider. December 22, 2014. Accessed June 21, 2015. http://www.businessinsider.com/bitcoin-millionaire-charlie-shrem-sentenced-to-2-years-in-prison-2014-12.

One attempt to respond to the situation came from Olivier Janssens, a venture capitalist, early Bitcoin adopter, and, one could argue, a crypto-philanthropist. Concerned about the Bitcoin Foundation's potential control over Bitcoin core development, he offered a $40,000 prize—plus another $60,000 in other prizes—for anyone who could offer an alternative way to fund core development. The incentive resulted in the creation of Lighthouse, which was developed by former Bitcoin developer Mike Hearn.[5] It allows people to donate to projects on the Bitcoin platform, the idea being that developers could make posts describing an issue they need to fix or feature they need to add and Bitcoin users or companies could fund those projects.

Lighthouse never replaced the Bitcoin Foundation as a reliable way to fund core development. It has instead been used to crowdfund mostly crypto-related projects. Its creation has nevertheless kicked off a debate about how much control the Bitcoin Foundation should have over core development.

Gavin Andresen has contended that the Bitcoin Foundation has no control over Bitcoin's core development.[6] According to Andresen, it did not attempt to influence his decisions on what code was included in the core code of Bitcoin. Despite these assurances, much of the community wasn't convinced. It wasn't so much that they didn't believe Andresen's statements; it was more of an issue about the potential for misuse rather than actual misuse that had already occurred. A trade institution, the

---

[5] Higgins, Stan. "Mike Hearn Wins $40k Bounty for Bitcoin Core Crowdfunding Platform." CoinDesk RSS. July 02, 2014. Accessed June 21, 2015. http://www.coindesk.com/mike-hearn-wins-40000-bounty-bitcoin-core-crowdfunding/.

[6] Higgins, Stan. "Gavin Andresen: Bitcoin Core Development." CoinDesk RSS. November 20, 2014. Accessed June 21, 2015. http://www.coindesk.com/gavin-andresen-bitcoin-foundation-pivot-centralize-development/.

Bitcoin Foundation depended on funding from corporate partners. These partners were likely to have ideas on how they would like to see Bitcoin's code evolve.

Andresen himself seemed incorruptible and the Bitcoin Foundation's Board of Directors seemed to understand the importance of core code independence, but what about future lead developers? Would they be as incorruptible as Andresen? What about future Bitcoin Foundation board members? Would they always be so benevolent and concerned about Bitcoin's health, above all else, forever?

As user donations dried up due to the scandals and debate over their influence on development, the Bitcoin Foundation became increasingly dependent on corporate donations. Its reserve also started to run low as the price of Bitcoin was rapidly falling due to the Mt. Gox scandal and the subsequent panic. Ironically, Bitcoin's current high-water mark—$1,124.76, set on November 29, 2013—had been reached just before the Mt. Gox exchange collapsed. Although people were ecstatic about the four-figure bitcoin price, it was tempered by the fear of what was about to come. The Bitcoin industry had never experienced anything quite like Mt. Gox. What happens when the biggest centralized point of a decentralized system falls apart?

With so much uncertainty in the community, the Bitcoin Foundation could not allow itself to be perceived as abandoning Bitcoin, so it could not sell its reserves. If word got out that the Foundation had cashed out its bitcoin holdings, it could have caused a massive panic in the industry.

In addition, with so much confusion in the mainstream media about who was in charge of Bitcoin, if an organization named the Bitcoin Foundation were perceived as abandoning the currency, one could anticipate the negative headlines that would follow.

Perhaps the Foundation should have hedged its bets a little bit and put more of its holdings into fiat, but this couldn't have been an easy decision to make. Most observers would have said that the price of Bitcoin was bound to decline, as it had after previous jumps, but there was also a sense that this might be the time Bitcoin would "break through" and gain mass acceptance. That hope was naïve—as the Foundation likely knew—but doing anything that would cast doubt on that possibility would have been a bad PR move both for the Foundation and for Bitcoin itself.

By the start of fall 2014, the Foundation was running on fumes. Donations had mostly dried up. The Foundation's public donation address only received around 0.3BTC in October 2014,[7] although this figure does not reflect corporate donations and member dues.

The price of Bitcoin was way down from its late winter 2014 high and it was rare to find people who were enthusiastic about the Foundation.

This is when the Bitcoin Foundation started to reform. It determined that core development was the most important task it had. At the time, the hope was that the community would get behind a narrowing of its focus and maintaining Bitcoin's core code seemed like a cause anyone could get behind.

Yet much of the community didn't get behind it and donations did not increase significantly, at least not enough to solve the Foundation's financial woes. Meanwhile, concerns about the

---

[7] https://blockchain.info/address/1BTCorgHwCg6u2YSAWKgS17qUad6kHmtQW.

Bitcoin Foundation's potential control over core development were increasing.

The community got a chance to express its discontent when the Foundation held an election to fill the seats vacated by Karpelès and Shrem. Among the candidates was Olivier Janssens, the same Olivier Janssens who put up $100,000 of his own money for the development of an alternative to the Foundation's funding. Only paying members of the Bitcoin Foundation could vote but their opinion seemed to reflect what was being expressed on the public forums, such as Reddit and BitcoinTalk. After a highly contested election, Olivier Janssens and Jim Harper—another candidate who was against the Foundation's practice of funding core development—were elected to the two open spots. In addition to transitioning away from core development, the two candidates promised to bring transparency to the Foundation's finances.[8]

The election was a clear sign that the Foundation members were no longer comfortable with the Foundation board holding the purse strings to development. Not much happened publicly for a few weeks after the election. Then, Janssens dropped a bombshell. Posting on Reddit and in the Bitcoin Foundation forums, Janssens asserted that the Foundation was completely broke. He also revealed to me in an interview that paychecks for Andresen and other core developers had already stopped arriving.[9]

---

[8] Englund, Jinyoung Lee. "Election Runoff." The Bitcoin Foundation. February 20, 2015. Accessed June 21, 2015. http://blog.bitcoinfoundation.org/election-runoff/.

[9] Janssens, Olivier. "The Truth about the Bitcoin Foundation." Reddit. April 4, 2015. R/Bitcoin. Accessed June 21, 2015. http://www.reddit.com/r/Bitcoin/comments/31e6jh/the_truth_about_the_bitcoin_foundation/.

The Foundation went into damage control mode, writing in a now-deleted post that it was planning on releasing the same information that Janssens had just revealed in a week or two, after it created a plan for addressing the problem. The Foundation also insisted the situation wasn't as bad as Janssens claimed.[10] These statements might or might not have been true but it is easy enough to say you were *just about to come clean* when you have already been exposed.

There were two immediate issues to address after Janssens's post. The first and most urgent was how to keep core development funded. Janssens offered to fund development himself until another solution could be devised.[11] The second issue was how the Bitcoin Foundation could move forward from this point and whether it should continue to exist at all.

The second issue still hasn't been resolved completely. The Bitcoin Foundation still exists and now has a greater focus on adoption rather than development, but it is unclear how funding has been going and it is unknown at this time whether it is financially solvent. The Foundation's new executive director, Bruce Fenton, who is now working in a voluntary capacity, has promised reform.[12]

---

[10] "The Facts About the Bitcoin Foundation." The Bitcoin Foundation. April 7, 2015. Accessed June 21, 2015. https://web.archive.org/web/20150407230759/https://blog.bitcoinfoundation.org/the-facts-about-the-bitcoin-foundation/. (Since deleted, accessible only through archive.org)

[11] DeMartino, Ian M. "First Interview With Olivier Janssens After 'The Truth About BTC Foundation' Post." Mining Pool. April 6, 2015. Accessed June 21, 2015. http://www.miningpool.co.uk/first-interview-with-olivier-janssens-after-the-truth-about-btc-foundation-post/.

[12] Rizzo, Pete. "New Bitcoin Foundation Director Bruce Fenton Pledges Fiscal Reform." CoinDesk RSS. April 13, 2015. Accessed June 21, 2015. http://www.coindesk.com/bruce-fenton-bitcoin-foundation-executive-director/.

The bigger issue has been solved for the time being but some people still have concerns. The core developers never publicly responded to Janssens's offer to fund core development, partially because another solution presented itself fairly quickly. The MIT Digital Currency Initiative announced that it would begin funding core development, and it has been partially doing so since then, with the rest coming from the community and various companies.[13]

Most seem to agree that the current situation is an improvement over the previous one. Having Bitcoin's core code maintained and updated by an academic institution has obvious advantages over having it maintained and updated by a corporate trade group. It seems less likely that an academic institution would be influenced by outside sources into pressuring developers to code based on what the big corporations in Bitcoin would prefer.

There are many who still have concerns, however. Development funding is still centralized. It may be centralized in a better place than it was before but it still is centralized. The concern about future MIT project directors and their influence over future developers is still valid. The people involved in Bitcoin now will undoubtedly be considered the early adopters of the currency and human nature tends to lionize those who came before us.

The mechanisms that control Bitcoin are not yet set in stone. There isn't even a consensus among core developers about what should be done and who should be in charge. At the time of this writing, there is a significant debate taking place in the community

---

[13] Prisco, Giulio. "Gavin Andresen and Other Core Developers Join MIT's Digital Currency Initiative." Bitcoin Magazine. April 22, 2015. Accessed June 21, 2015. https://bitcoinmagazine.com/20132/gavin-andresen-core-developers-join-mits-digital-currency-initiative/.

over how Bitcoin will scale in the future. This debate has threatened to cause a split among the core developers and could cause Bitcoin as a whole to fork. On one side are the miners, who will have to process bigger blocks and store a larger blockchain in order to mine. On the other are the payment processors who argue that they need larger blocks to handle the growing demand for Bitcoin transactions. The outcome of the debate will show where power really lies within the politics of Bitcoin.

The reason why the debate is taking place is that there is a limit to the number of transactions that the network can handle at a time. Each block is currently 750KB to 1MB in size and can only hold a certain number of transactions. This was never meant to be a hard limit but Satoshi Nakamoto built it that way so that malicious actors would have a tougher time trying to spam the network with a bunch of meaningless transactions. It wasn't a problem at first because Bitcoin wasn't popular enough to necessitate larger or faster blocks. 1MB at roughly 10-minute intervals was more than enough for the volume the network had to deal with at the time.

Today, Bitcoin is much more popular and the block size limit is becoming a problem. While most blocks still aren't filled, some have been, and during transaction spikes some users have complained about abnormally long transaction times. If Bitcoin is going to scale to the level of Visa or MasterCard, it is going to need to handle far more transactions than it can now. If transactions start stalling, users may panic and attempt to spend those same coins again before they are sent, not only adding to the backlog but potentially causing mining conflicts and slowing things down even more.

The debate continues. Most likely, we will see some sort of compromise. But the point is, who decides what happens in

Bitcoin isn't completely settled and the current situation is confusing even to insiders. And when you are talking about billions of dollars, the answer to "Who controls Bitcoin?" is an important one. It is easy for Bitcoin enthusiasts to say, "The community decides," but the community doesn't really decide what changes are made. How much input have they had in the block size debate?

Bitcoin users could theoretically jump onto a new fork and anyone is technically capable of making their own, but that is unlikely to happen anytime soon. Bitcoin's core code is coded by a group of developers who are beholden to the community, but the community doesn't order them around. No one holds votes on which features are added next or what bug fixes are most critical. Yes, the community votes by its participation on the network but that is where its control ends. How the current chain is modified and who decides on these changes is still up in the air. The lead developer ultimately makes the final decision, but how much control should they have and how much should they listen to their community? Andresen argues that he should be like any other lead developer on any other open-source project and take charge. Van der Laan disagrees. What we settle on, however, could have implications lasting far longer than the involvement of either of those two in Bitcoin.

Even if you haven't jumped into Bitcoin yet and do so after you read this book, you will still be considered an early adopter by the people of the future. If Bitcoin really is the currency of tomorrow, then it has a massive amount to grow. Those who adopted it in 2015 or 2016, a mere eight years after Satoshi's white paper was published, will seem like daring risk-takers who jumped at the opportunity to harness an emerging technology.

Americans have long idealized their Founding Fathers and still look to them for guidance on issues those eighteenth-century men could not possibly have understood. Likewise, people in the Bitcoin community idealize Satoshi Nakamoto and it is not uncommon to see an argument end with a quote from him or for a new Bitcoin alternative to claim to be a purer version of Nakamoto's creation.

In the future, it won't just be Nakamoto. The thoughts of the core developers and other influential members of today's Bitcoin community will be quoted as gospel. This is unfortunate—because they are fallible people like everyone else—but seems unavoidable. The best we as a community can do is give the Bitcoiners of the future a good example to follow but nearly everyone disagrees on what that might entail.

If we set the precedent that centralized funding of core development is okay, Bitcoin users of the future will point to that and continue to say it isn't a problem. In 20 or 30 years, someone may try to influence the Bitcoin core development team by threatening to pull funding. What recourse will we have then? Development funding has always been centralized, people will say. It won't be much of a stretch to turn funding into influence. Rules can be turned on their head slowly over time without anyone noticing but only if someone works toward that. The people who do that kind of work usually have ulterior motives.

It stands to reason that the precedent we set now will be used in the future. It also stands to reason that in the future there will people trying to turn that system to their advantage. The current arrangement might be the optimal one but there hasn't been a vigorous public debate about it. The election of Janssens and Harper proved that the community—even those who paid to be

Bitcoin Foundation members (and who were the only ones who could vote)—did not want them to hold the purse strings to core development.

How does the community feel about the MIT Digital Currency Initiative funding development? I don't know; I don't think anyone asked them.

Chapter 5:
What Gives Bitcoin Its Value?

> Economists and journalists often get caught up in this question: Why does Bitcoin have value? And the answer is very easy. Because it is useful and scarce.

> —Eric Voorhees, cofounder of the Bitcoin company Coinapult

Many people wonder what gives Bitcoin its value. The first question many people ask is whether Bitcoin is backed by anything. The answer: Bitcoin is backed by its code as well as its utility—that is, what it can do. If Bitcoin stops being useful, it will lose its value.

People will often argue that Bitcoin's value comes from what people think it is worth. This statement can be made about anything, yet it is not quite accurate. You may be willing to pay a dollar for a bottle of Aquafina, or two dollars, depending on what you perceive that bottle of water to be worth. So yes, our perception of a thing's value does have a direct effect on that value. But if Aquafina started putting out water that was unfiltered and partially filled with mud, it would be less refreshing and people would not be willing to pay as much because it wouldn't be as useful.

The utility of Bitcoin is the foundation on which everything else is built. Without this utility, everything else falls apart. All the speculative day trading is just noise. Its scarcity is a big factor but ultimately that also goes back to utility. Bitcoin has a hard cap on the number of coins that will be created. There will only ever be 21 million bitcoins in existence. New bitcoins are created when miners solve a new block and are rewarded for their trouble through a combination of new coins and the miner fee. (You "solve a new block" when your computer—or more often, dedicated mining software—figures out the complex mathematical problems that confirm the accounts sending bitcoins have the bitcoins to send and have digitally signed their transactions. Each block currently has 750KB to 1MB worth of transactions.) Roughly every four years, the number of new coins created per block will be cut in half, until 21 million are eventually created— and at that point, miners will have to sustain themselves entirely on fees. This is forecast to occur sometime in the next century. Knowing the parameters of Bitcoin in advance makes Bitcoin more useful as a speculative investment and as a currency.

When proponents of the gold standard make their pitch, they often point out that gold has utility. A dollar is simply a piece of paper. Gold, they argue, holds real value as a commodity, as a valuable mineral for electronics, and—as it has been for thousands of years—as an attractive material for jewelry. Yet even a commodity-backed currency is dependent on the word of the issuing body. Although gold and other precious materials will likely always hold some value, if every government office shuts down, a piece of paper that says it is worth an ounce of gold is still just a piece of paper. If you are living in the United States, the thought of the government disappearing overnight might not seem like a realistic fear, but for citizens of third world countries, or even traditional first world countries with economic problems, such as Greece, that fear is a bit more palpable.

Bitcoin gets its value from what it can accomplish without any issuing body. This is different from saying that is where it gets its *price*. Bitcoin's price is influenced by a lot of things: adoption, speculation, and value all make up major pieces of the equation. But its actual value comes from its utility. In a theoretical world where speculation doesn't affect the price of Bitcoin, the price of one bitcoin would be whatever it is because of its value and scarcity, and that value is made up entirely of its utility. Furthermore, without that value, everything else would collapse like a house of cards.

What that utility is, is still being developed. Bitcoin already has many uses and I will cover them in a later chapter, but let me briefly run through some of the more obvious ones. First, Bitcoin can be sent anywhere in the world for an extremely small fee—generally around $0.02—opening up huge opportunities for remittance.

Bitcoin and other technologies based on blockchains are also programmable, giving them utilities that haven't even been thought of yet. For example, people have been able to use Bitcoin to invest in securities, stocks, valuable materials, and even other currencies from around the world, without the fees and high cost of entry typical of traditional methods for investment in those areas.

For the economically paranoid, Bitcoin also offers a store of value outside the direct influence of governmental organizations as well as offering the possibility of anonymity for embarrassing or illegal services.

From a merchant perspective, Bitcoin also has the advantage of not having large fees from credit card companies that cut into their profits. Credit card companies typically charge between three to four percent for each transaction, a fee the merchant normally takes on themselves. For merchants with small profit margins, that fee could eat up half or more of their profits for each credit or debit card transaction. As noted earlier, Bitcoin, by contrast, has a miner fee of around $0.02 and could therefore greatly increase merchants' profit margins.

Early in the life of the Internet, many pioneers envisioned an economy run entirely online. In the early 1990s, author Bill Eager was writing books about marketing on the Internet before marketing on the Internet was something most companies spent much time thinking about. At the time, buying something online, particularly physical goods, wasn't just rare. For most items, it was impossible.

In 1994, Eager made a striking prediction. In his book *The Information Superhighway Illustrated*, he wrote, "Online shopping is a $200 million business that has the potential to increase to $4.8 billion annually by 1998."[1]

As it turns out, Eager's prediction was too conservative. The year 1998 ended up being a pivotal one for online shopping as it transitioned from technology-minded consumers to mainstream

---

[1] Eager, Bill. *The Information Superhighway Illustrated.* (Indianapolis, Que Pub, 1994)

consumers. According to a report by the Boston Consulting Group released in December 1998, online shopping generated $4.4 billion in the first six months of the year alone. That number was expected to jump to more than $13 billion by the time the year was out and holiday shopping was factored in.

The late 1990s and early 2000s are remembered as the era when the dot-com bubble finally popped. But that wasn't the case for online retail shopping, which continued to grow every year. There was a lot of blood in the water as traditional retail businesses came online and challenged the web-only sites for market share, but total spending grew and continues to grow today at a rate that would have been unfathomable to most of us just 20 years earlier. By 1999, online spending had doubled to $27 billion and grew again to $45 billion in 2000.[2] By 2013, business-to-consumer online retail sales accounted for $803.76 billion in total revenue, a figure that is doubled when you account for online business-to-business transactions.[3]

The early visions of an Internet economy have been fulfilled. We buy everything from clothes to music to cars, even our pets, online. Buying something online is no longer a novelty; it is expected. People who haven't bought anything online are an increasingly rare breed—even a sizable portion of the elderly have purchased something online.[4]

---

[2] Abdelmessih, Nina, Michael Silverstein, and Peter Stanger. "Winning The Online Consumer: The Challenge of Raised Expectations." The Boston Consulting Group, 2001. Accessed March 15, 2015. http://www.bcg.com/documents/file13692.pdf.

[3] "Statistics and facts about Online Shopping" Statista. Accessed March 15, 2015. http://www.statista.com/topics/871/online-shopping/.

[4] "E-COMMERCE: Evolution Or Revolution In The Fast-Moving Consumer Goods World?" Nielsen. August 2014. Accessed May 19, 2015. http://www.nielsen.com/content/dam/corporate/us/en/reports-downloads/2014%20Reports/nielsen-global-e-commerce-report-august-2014.pdf.

Many of the early Internet pioneers envisioned an Internet with its own currency. "The Internet is global," they argued. For a global, instant, and digital economy to run correctly, we need a global, instant, and digital currency to go along with it. If Bitcoin doesn't evolve any further, it will still be all of these things. It already is a global currency that is instant and, like the Internet, open for use by nearly everyone. Early Internet pioneers did not talk about the speculative possibilities that the Bitcoin ecosystem is so obsessed with today. That unfortunate aspect of the Bitcoin culture only arose after the wild price swings.

Kevin Kelly, the first executive editor of *Wired* magazine, predicted the development of an electronic money system and the effect it would have on our world in his 1994 book *Out of Control: The New Biology of Machines, Social Systems and the Economic World*. Kelly wrote:

> By its decentralized, distributed nature, encrypted emoney has the same potential for transforming economic structure as personal computers did for overhauling management and communication structure. Most importantly, the privacy/security innovations needed for emoney are instrumental in developing the next level of adaptive complexity in an information-based society. I'd go so far as to say that truly digital money— or, more accurately, the economic mechanics needed for truly digital cash—will rewire the nature of our economy, communications, and knowledge.[5]

---

[5] Kelly, Kevin. *Out of Control: The New Biology of Machines, Social Systems and the Economic World*. (New York, Basic Books, 1994, Reprint 1995)

Although predictions related to how much time and money we would spend online were fulfilled, the Internet never got its own currency. There were attempts but the centralized nature of the currency issuer always made emoney incompatible with the decentralized nature of the Internet. Some currencies failed because the company issuing them merely acted as money transactors themselves, adding an unnecessary middleman instead of eliminating one. Others failed because the issuer abused their power and scammed those who had bought in. Yet others ran afoul of government regulations.[6] These issues are avoided with decentralization.

When Satoshi Nakamoto invented the blockchain by combining the distributed ledger and proof-of-work concepts, he fulfilled the long-held vision of a workable, distributed, decentralized currency for the Internet. With it, anyone can transfer virtually any amount for a few cents or less. The blockchain tracks every transaction and its distributed nature ensures that no government agency can shut it down. The details of how this works will be covered in another chapter but the first use case of Bitcoin and the blockchain is the ability to transfer value on the Internet as easily as sending an email and almost as cheaply. More uses for the blockchain are being developed every day but this is the most obvious. Many experts have called money transfer the first "application" of the blockchain; however, even that one application has near-endless uses.

Using the QR code found in the front of this book, any reader with a Bitcoin wallet can send bitcoins to me, the author. No

---

[6] Zetter, Kim. "Bullion and Bandits: The Improbable Rise and Fall of E-Gold." Wired. com. September 6, 2009. Accessed May 20, 2015. http://www.wired.com/2009/06/e-gold/.

banking institution needs to approve it; it doesn't matter where you are or when you are reading this. If I still have access to the wallet, I can receive the money. In fact, regardless of whether I have access to that wallet, any user can send money to that address at any time for as long as the Bitcoin blockchain is in existence.

This might not sound impressive. After all, banks can transfer money. The banks will take their cuts but there are ways people can send money digitally using the legacy system. However, the difference between having to ask for permission and not having to ask for permission is not a small one. Using Bitcoin, any user can send any amount of money to any business or any individual in the world with a Bitcoin wallet, without restrictions.

If someone in Russia wants to launch a crowdfunding project, he or she has to find a service that can deposit money into a Russian bank account and then move it to a crowdfunding site that will either deny or approve his or her project. Then that site will take its own cut simply for connecting investors and inventors. Bitcoin can cut out those middlemen. Using Bitcoin, people can send someone money without asking for permission from anyone.

This is also a freedom issue. Centralized and legacy systems have the ability to prevent users from sending money to certain entities. At the height of the controversy over a leaked video showing American helicopter pilots joking while shooting people who seemed to be civilians, for instance, whistleblower site Wikileaks lost PayPal and credit card support.[7] Although there might not be any legal basis for this type of ban, individual

---

[7] Barnes, Julian and Jeanne Whalen. "PayPal Drops WikiLeaks Donation Account." *The Wall Street Journal*, December 4, 2010. Accessed March 10, 2015. http://www.wsj.com/articles/SB10001424052748704767804575654681242073308.

companies can decide to prevent individual people from sending money to support causes they believe in. Bitcoin, along with a strong legal defense, has helped these individuals get around such bans. With no central power to prevent users from sending money to a specific entity, users can send their bitcoins to whatever cause they fancy.

Bitcoin has the potential to cut out not only Internet-based middlemen but real-world ones as well. Walmart buys a lot of goods from China. There is significant markup added to the items in order to keep Walmart's profits high. But do we really need them? Using the Internet and Bitcoin, I can easily send money to anyone in China. The recipient doesn't have to worry about setting up a system that accepts American credit cards and can make deposits into a Chinese bank account. I can simply buy bitcoins with dollars and send them to a business owner in China, who then converts them to yuan. The fees, if any, could be much lower than sending money via Western Union or credit card. In fact, the biggest potential for fees comes when interacting with the legacy banking system—converting from dollars to bitcoins and then from bitcoins to yuan.

Think about how this can change the global economy. In the past, world leaders—for better or worse—have been pushing us toward globalization. With free trade eliminating tariffs, the workforce moved from regional to global at a rapid pace. This, few would deny, has been less than favorable for many American workers. Those workers are getting beat out by cheap labor in Latin America and Asia, and the profits are increasingly being passed on to the middlemen who facilitate deals between sweatshop laborers and American consumers.

Whatever your view on free trade, the hurdles that increase costs—what is often called friction by economists—are not helpful. If we are to have a global economy, we need a global currency. Removing middlemen and enabling money to be transferred directly from producer to consumer can greatly expedite this process. It also enables cottage industries by allowing them to sell directly to consumers worldwide without intermediaries. Hopefully, these will turn into sustainable industries that treat their employees fairly, increasing worker leverage in their region and eventually worldwide.

On a more basic and immediate level, Bitcoin allows for low-cost remittance. Sending money from first world countries where banking is relatively accessible to third world countries where it is not can be very expensive. The highest fees are nearly 50 percent and average around nine percent. With $316 billion sent from migrant workers to their home countries in 2009, those fees add up to billions of dollars sucked up by middlemen that could otherwise contribute to local economies.[8] Bitcoin can replace those middlemen.

Lending is another example of how Bitcoin can make a big difference. Microloans are becoming more popular online as a way for small-time investors to grow their money while helping individuals by allowing them to avoid exorbitant interest rates charged by loan companies.

BTCJam and similar services allow investors to fund borrowers for everything from business plans to personal projects. Loans can be denominated in both Bitcoin and dollars. While BTCJam is a middleman, cutting out the credit card and money-transferring

---

[8] "Transfer fees." *The Economist.* December 15, 2010. Accessed March 15, 2015. http://www.economist.com/blogs/dailychart/2010/12/remittances.

middlemen enable it to operate while only taking a one to five percent fee from the borrowers. This removal of friction enables more investments and more payments.

Another service cryptocurrencies can theoretically provide is the role of arbitrator in any transaction. BitHalo, the Bitcoin half of BlackHalo, was the first instance of workable smart contracts, which are regulated by computer code rather than legal force. Smart contracts enable the sale of physical goods without either party needing to trust the other. BlackHalo was designed for Blackcoin, an alternative cryptocurrency that I will discuss in Chapter 21. BitHalo has the same functionality but works with Bitcoin. It enables quick transfers between the two currencies.

More importantly, BitHalo allows for a decentralized marketplace without the need for a third-party arbitrator like eBay or PayPal. While Bitcoin on its own allows for the direct sale of goods and services from merchant to buyer, there is no way for anyone to settle disputes. Once Bitcoin is sent, it is under the control of the recipient and if a seller neglects to send the product or provide the service, there is very little the buyer can do about it. BitHalo fixes this problem by taking human nature into account. Each party is expected to put down a deposit separate from the actual transaction. Both deposits and the buyer's money are held in escrow controlled by the program itself. Once both sides approve the transaction, the buyer's money will be transferred to the seller and deposits will be returned to both users. If both users agree to cancel the transaction, the money will be returned to the buyer and both deposits will be returned to their respective owners. However, when both parties can't agree to cancel by a predetermined date, their deposits are lost and sent to a wallet with no retrievable address. The funds are essentially removed from the Bitcoin ecosystem.

Used properly, BitHalo gives sellers and buyers confidence that the other party is dedicated to making sure the transaction comes to an agreeable end. If the deposit is worth three times the actual transaction, neither side gains by trying the scam the other. Although scams and intimidation tactics might still be used on occasion, this system provides a workable method of ensuring trust in a decentralized marketplace.

The problem with BitHalo, however, is that no one is using it. With no one filling the marketplace, there is little reason for buyers or sellers to download the software. Beautiful ideas are not always beautifully implemented. This has been an issue with a number of Bitcoin-related projects.

OpenBazaar is a promising project that has been explained as Bittorrent to the Silk Road's Napster. Unlike the Silk Road, OpenBazaar is decentralized, like Bitcoin itself, meaning there is no one server that the government can shut down to close it. It is based off the code called Darkmarket that was created by Amir Taaki and a team of other developers. Brian Hoffman forked Darkmarket and turned it into OpenBazaar, which uses the same principles but on the surface seems to be distancing itself from the Silk Road. At the same time, there are no rules in place preventing the sale of anything, nor can there be with the software. What OpenBazaar ultimately becomes—be it a decentralized Amazon or eBay, or something edgier, like a decentralized Silk Road—remains to be seen. The project is in alpha right now and cannot be used by the average consumer, though this may no longer be the case by the time this book hits store shelves.

Still, there is more to Bitcoin than transactions between parties. As mentioned, Bitcoin doesn't just bring basic banking to those without banking access; it also has the potential to bring advanced banking abilities to users around the world.

Bitcoin 2.0 projects, as they are often called, can involve Bitcoin or other cryptocurrencies. The main idea behind these projects is that the blockchain and blockchain technologies can be used to transfer and keep track of holdings of valuables other than Bitcoin or other digital currencies. Even if a 2.0 project is not built off of Bitcoin, like Ethereum, increased investment and interest in cryptocurrencies as a whole tend to increase Bitcoin's value as well. Since Bitcoin is currently the most successful, secure, and popular cryptocurrency, any increased interest in cryptocurrencies as a whole has a positive effect on Bitcoin's price.

The first example of a "2.0" cryptocurrency was Namecoin, which, in addition to being a currency, acted as a distributed domain name registrar free from the control of any government, individual or group. Users need to download the Namecoin blockchain in order to view sites registered using the Namecoin protocol. Sites on the Namecoin network use the .bit domain extension. Unlike .com, .net, .org, or other domain extensions you normally see on the web, .bit registrations are not issued or controlled by a central entity. Instead, they are issued by the Namecoin network and no entity has the power to seize a .bit website registration.

Namecoin was the first example of a Bitcoin 2.0 project but there have been others. Counterparty, Ethereum, Masterparty, and Nxt are on the forefront of crowdfunding and crowd-investing. While all these platforms are different, they essentially allow the same thing: users can issue their own assets that can represent various things other than money, including ownership in a company.

Although most assets have so far been used in a way similar to traditional crowdfunding or investing, there are many other possibilities. Distributed Automated Corporations (DACs) are something nearly the entire cryptocommunity is excited about. Like all corporations, DACs are entities that exist to make money. Unlike most corporations, however, DACs don't have any employees. Instead, a DAC runs itself using code. It finds an activity online that can create profit, such as watching advertisements, and performs it over and over again. Its ownership is cryptographically linked to the individuals who hold the DAC's assets through Bitcoin or another cryptocurrency and its profits are distributed to them. A DAC can be many things; the only qualification is that once it is set up, it has to be able to run with minimal or no outside influence. As the technology evolves, it is feasible that a great number of people could own DACs and that these could provide a secondary and passive stream of income for their owners. If this is sustainable remains to be seen—"free" money is rarely free and I don't think our society is ready for a world without real work, but DACs still present some interesting possibilities.

It is not only Internet-created corporations that Bitcoin and blockchain technologies have given us the ability to invest in. Traditional finance is also being opened up to those who previously lacked the connections and funds needed to invest. Uphold (previously known as Bitreserve), BitGold, and several other services allow users to invest and hold precious metals or even other fiat currencies. In the case of Uphold, 27 different fiat currencies and precious metals are supported in addition to four digital currencies (Bitcoin, Litecoin, Ether, and Uphold's own Voxelus). Uphold opens up investment opportunities that would otherwise be unavailable to the average consumer without enough disposable income to make a large initial investment and deal with significant fees. Uphold has recently removed fees for all verified customers—those who prove their identity by uploading personal documents—for fiat currency conversion.

The two services described above allow the quick transfer between precious materials or fiat and Bitcoin. Other companies allow users to trade stocks using Bitcoin as collateral. The stock market is no longer limited to investment bankers and those who can afford high minimum deposits required by various sites.

Bitcoin gives users an investment vehicle that was previously reserved for those in the upper middle class and above. Bitcoin users can invest their spare change into a range of commodities almost instantly. If a user decides they want to get rid of their investment or simply spend some of it, they can also do so almost instantly without incurring exorbitant fees. It is also possible to "invest" less than a penny.

The uses I've described so far, while not all strictly involving sending money back and forth, are still financial in nature. But the blockchain can do much more than that. It can store documents in a secure cryptographic manner. A user could encrypt a digital copy of their passport, store the hash of that file on the blockchain and then use that copy as a backup. Two users could record their marriage on the blockchain; in fact, this has already happened.[9] Nearly every official document or contract that needs a notary could be stored on the blockchain and while it might not be recognized legally as such, it is far harder to forge a blockchain transaction than a notarized document.

---

[9] Vigna, Paul, and Michael Casey. "BitBeat: Wedding Bells on the Blockchain." MoneyBeat. September 26, 2014. Accessed May 20, 2015. http://blogs.wsj.com/moneybeat/2014/09/26/bitbeat-wedding-bells-on-the-blockchain/.

The utility could potentially go beyond the financial. Decentralized cloud storage is also a possibility using blockchain technology. Storj doesn't run on the Bitcoin blockchain; it runs on the CounterParty system, a coin and set of financial services built on top of but separate from the Bitcoin blockchain. Storj intends to create a storage system using the public ledger and cryptographic tools pioneered by Bitcoin.

Meanwhile, the infamous Kim Dotcom, known for his previous Megaupload.com and his current Mega.co.nz, has been teasing an "IP-less" Internet that will use blockchain or Bitcoin technology in some way, though news has seemingly slowed on that front.[10]

It is impossible to name all the uses of Bitcoin, just as it is impossible to name all the uses for the computer. Just as a computer has unlimited uses because it is programmable, Bitcoin, as programmable money, is very versatile. By the time you read this, there will undoubtedly be more uses for Bitcoin.

New tools are being created for use on the Bitcoin blockchain or a related technology every day. And Bitcoin is just one of the thousands of cryptocurrencies in existence. It was the first, however, and it remains the most valuable, popular, and useful of all digital currencies. Bitcoin's utility is limited only by the talent of its developers and the funding that gives them the time to work on it. Ultimately, this is also what determines its value. If Bitcoin wants to compete with Apple Pay, PayPal, Google Wallet, and the rest, its open-source developers—I don't just mean the core

---

[10] Cuthbertson, Anthony. "Kim Dotcom's Blockchain MegaNet and Bitcoin ATMs Stolen." International Business Times RSS. February 17, 2015. Accessed May 20, 2015. http://www.ibtimes.co.uk/cryptocurrency-round-kim-dotcoms-blockchain-meganet-bitcoin-atms-stolen-1488393.

developers but all developers working on related projects—need to provide more utility for Bitcoin than is currently available, in whatever form is important to the consumer. That is what it always comes down to in technology. There is no reason to think Bitcoin is any different.

Chapter 6:

Bitcoin: Anonymous or Pseudonymous?

There's going to be so much information about individuals floating around, that we want to protect privacy as much as we can. . . . But some of the bankers feel that an anonymous system is never going to make it, or even be something that they can get behind.

—Early cryptographer Ernie Brickell, December 1994, *Wired*

Bitcoin is often referred to as an anonymous digital currency, which isn't the worst way to describe it. However, every wallet is given a public key or identity. Therefore, it would be more accurate to call the network "pseudonymous" rather than anonymous. This is an important distinction and I will get into why and what it could mean in a legal sense in this chapter.

As I mentioned in Chapter 1, the blockchain tracks all transactions and balances on the network. Each wallet is identified by a long string of numbers that acts as the user's Bitcoin identity or pseudonym. As long as that identity is kept separate from your real-life identity, transactions can't be traced back to you in the way a credit card statement can.

The issue is that there are a lot of different ways to link a Bitcoin account to an online identity. And from there, it is usually only a small jump from "online identity" to "real-life identity." Getting onto the Bitcoin network is the biggest hurdle to remaining anonymous on the Bitcoin network. If you don't work for Bitcoin or can't find someone who will sell you bitcoins for cash, you will eventually have to make a wire transfer, use a credit card or PayPal account, or do something else that will allow any enterprising third party to figure out who you are, how much Bitcoin you purchased, and what wallet you put it in.

Once someone does that, they can simply follow your transactions on the blockchain. Although there aren't actual pieces of data or any other "physical" thing moving through the network, the blockchain records every subtraction from your account and its corresponding deposit on the network.

If Bob gives Jack five bitcoins, the network will see that there were five bitcoins subtracted from Bob's account and added to Jack's account. Nothing actually "travels" through the Internet; there are just five fewer bitcoins in Bob's wallet and five more in Jack's. If Jack is a disreputable person, Bob might not want the whole world to see that he is giving Jack five bitcoins, but the transaction will be recorded on the blockchain for anyone who cares to look. As mentioned, the Bitcoin network doesn't track transactions by individuals' names; it only tracks wallet addresses.

A typical Bitcoin transaction will look something like this: 18xAMYmeDHqmtPvM76VwECqzcEC7oCST15 0.02BTC---> 38ccq12hPFoiSksxUdr6SQ5VosyjY7s9AU

That means nothing to you or me. All you might see is that wallet 18xAMYme... gave 0.02BTC to wallet 38ccq12.... However, if you knew that I controlled that first address and that the second address is controlled by the Bitcoin homeless outreach charity Sean's Outpost, then you can easily figure out that I sent 0.02 bitcoins to Sean's Outpost on June 22, 2014.

Now let's say I want to hide my charitable transaction from the public. It isn't enough to simply buy bitcoins with a credit card and then send that money to another user; there needs to be an intermediary, and that intermediary needs to behave in specific ways.

If wallet A sends five bitcoins to wallet B and then wallet B sends five bitcoins to wallet C, you can be reasonably confident that it was wallet A's intention to send wallet C five bitcoins. This is especially true if wallet B didn't have any bitcoins to begin with or had only received bitcoins from wallet A during its entire existence.

If an interested party knows that I own wallet A and wallet C is owned by Sean's Outpost, then they can be reasonably confident that I was intending to send the bitcoins to Sean's Outpost.

In a legal sense, there is some question when the level of reasonable doubt would exonerate someone in the case of a crime being committed. If I send bitcoins to another wallet that had no bitcoins previously and then that wallet sends that same amount of money to an account associated with a drug dealer, is that a reasonable level of evidence to convict me of buying drugs? What if the intermediate wallet, wallet B in this case, already had some bitcoin in it? What if that bitcoin came from a variety of sources? What if I send it three bitcoins and it sends two to wallet C? What if it then sends me back the remaining one? What if it doesn't? These types of questions, I suspect, will be answered by the courts in the coming years.

When it comes to personal privacy, however, legal questions aren't always the issue at hand. The court of public opinion can often be harsher than the legal one, and how and when you spend your money could be information used by advertisers or worse—scammers, stalkers, and psychopaths.

There has been a concerning trend in the media to portray any attempt to preserve personal privacy as a criminal act. Somehow, not wanting to broadcast everything to everyone has become associated with the criminal element. There are plenty of logical reasons to want to keep your personal transactions private—reasons that have nothing to do with criminal activity.

I write for CoinJournal, which pays me in Bitcoin. I also ask for donations on my personal blog, so my Bitcoin address is public information. If a competing website wanted to try and poach me from CoinJournal, it could look at how much money is sent every week from CoinJournal and offer me more money.

Competitive employee poaching is a serious concern for a lot of businesses and having employee salaries publicly available might not be an ideal situation.

There is also the concern of becoming a target. If people can publicly see that you have just come into a large amount of money, this presents its own set of problems.

Beyond that, privacy is just a human-rights issue. In an article about Digicash, the pre-Bitcoin attempt at a digital currency I talked about in an earlier chapter, *Wired*'s Steven Levy quotes the cryptographer and then-Digicash employee Niels Ferguson:

> Oh, the number of times I've had to argue with people that they need privacy! They'll say, "I don't care if you know where I spend my money." I usually tell them,

"What if I hire a private investigator to follow you around all day? Would you get mad?" And the answer always is, "Yes, of course I would get mad." And then my argument is, "If we have no privacy in our transaction systems, I can see every payment—every cup of coffee you drink, every Mars bar you get, every glass of Coke you drink, every door you open, every telephone call—you make. If I can see those, I don't need a private investigator. I can just sit behind my terminal and follow you around all day." And then people start to realize that, yes, privacy is in fact something important. Any one part of the information is probably unimportant. But the collection of the information, that is important.[1]

The point is that there are few things more private than your finances, so how do you deal with the fact that Bitcoin uses a public ledger? How do you keep your pseudonymous transactions on the Bitcoin network truly separate from your real-life identity?

It is important to remember that bitcoins don't actually exist other than in the code that makes up the Bitcoin network. It is impossible to track bitcoins because there is nothing differentiating one bitcoin from another. They are just variable balances in individual wallets. When a transaction is sent from wallet A to wallet B, nothing actually moves; wallet A just has fewer bitcoins while wallet B gains the corresponding amount.

---

[1] Levy, Steven. "Emoney (That's What I Want)." *Wired*. December 1, 1994. Accessed June 22, 2015. http://archive.wired.com/wired/archive/2.12/emoney_pr.html.

It is the transactions themselves that are tracked. If you simply vary your transaction amounts and split them up among many addresses, you can make these transactions much harder to follow than if you were simply sending money from point A to point B directly. Still, this technique only adds one more layer of complexity. Anyone willing to do the work should be able to connect the dots.

There are services that make Bitcoin transactions virtually impossible to track by today's technology. They accomplish this by mixing transactions together. If you take a bunch of different people's transactions, send them to a single wallet and then redistribute them to addresses the original contributors control but aren't linked to, it is virtually impossible to prove who owned what using the blockchain alone.

There are several ways to achieve this. The most obvious way, one that appeared as soon as Bitcoin started drawing mainstream attention, is a coin "laundry" service. These are groups of people who will take transactions from various users, mix them together, and then send them out to whatever addresses the customers ask for. In order to increase anonymity, the coins are typically held for a minimum of several hours, and the fee involved is variable and random in order to make it harder for interested parties to match up transactions.

This method has some disadvantages, however. You have to trust someone who by the nature of their business has to stay anonymous and is able to close up shop at any time.

Altcoins also offer an unintentional "washing" service. Someone wishing to disassociate their public identity from a certain transaction could always "jump blockchains." Altcoins, which will be discussed in a later chapter, are digital currencies that are separate from Bitcoin and have their own public ledger. A user could buy some altcoins on an exchange, move them out of the exchange into their own wallet not controlled by the exchange, then move them back onto a different exchange, sell them for bitcoins, and then move them to a new, separate wallet.

This approach is effective in that it can't be tracked on a blockchain but connecting with exchanges often requires some sort of personal identification and a possible log of IP addresses. This same method, however, can be applied to gambling sites, which rarely ask for identification and have also been offering an unintentional mixing service for years.

Recently, this service has become codified into software, eliminating the need to depend on sometimes untrustworthy third parties. The concept came to life in a technology called CoinJoin, which is now used by many services. CoinJoin, when used properly, mixes coins to increase anonymity automatically. However, depending on the parameters set by the user, CoinJoin doesn't necessarily make transactions anonymous because successful mixing depends on following the process described above. Users will often, either knowingly or through ignorance, choose convenience over privacy and opt to not mix their coins thoroughly enough to provide true anonymity.

Think back to the example above. If wallet A sends wallet B five bitcoins and then wallet B sends five bitcoins to wallet C, it is easy enough to assume wallet A was sending wallet C five bitcoins using wallet B as an intermediary.

Combining several Bitcoin users' transactions makes it more difficult to track but not impossible. If wallet A, wallet B, and wallet C send bitcoins to a mixing service (wallet D) and then pass that money onto wallets E and F but don't want outside sources knowing who sent what to whom, simply sending their bitcoin to wallet D is not enough.

If wallet A puts two bitcoins, wallet B puts six bitcoins, and wallet C puts nine bitcoins into the CoinJoin wallet—and then two bitcoins are sent to wallet E in one transaction, another six are sent to wallet E in a second transaction, and nine bitcoins are sent to wallet F—then we can safely assume that wallet A sent two bitcoins to wallet E, wallet B sent six to wallet E and wallet C sent nine to wallet F.

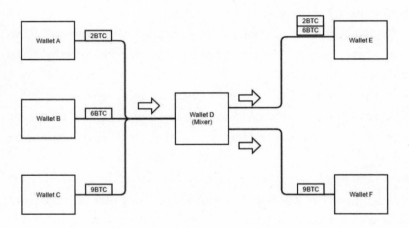

This is what was happening to users who tried to harness the CoinJoin feature on Blockchain.info's popular Bitcoin web wallet.[2] Blockchain.info is not a privacy-focused company; it

2 Southurst, John. "Blockchain's SharedCoin Users Can Be Identified, Says Security Expert." CoinDesk RSS. June 10, 2014. Accessed June 22, 2015. http://www.coindesk.com/blockchains-sharedcoin-users-can-identified-says-security-expert/.

simply provides information on the Bitcoin wallet and Bitcoin addresses that are easy to obtain and discard. It added CoinJoin as a feature but gave its users free rein on how they use it. Many of them did not understand that the process of mixing transactions with similar transactions was not automatic and were upset when they noticed how easy it was for a third party to track their transactions.

Most Bitcoin transactions are based on the fiat price at the time. With a constantly changing exchange rate that varies depending on which Bitcoin payment processor is used, transactions tend to look like this: 0.04534051BTC, an amount that is not easily matched. In order to properly mix coins, there need to be identical amounts going in and out.

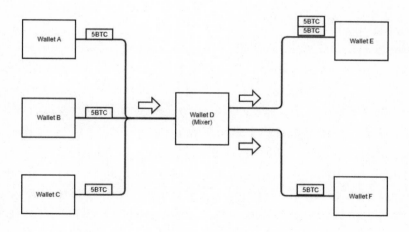

The diagram above shows a basic successful mixing. Although a law enforcement agency or other interested party might strongly suspect that wallet C sent five bitcoins to wallet F, it can't prove that wallet C didn't send those bitcoins to wallet E instead. The problem is that this method requires wallets A, B, and C to work together in order to send the same amount. This generally requires centralization in some way. There are popular services that will launder bitcoins and the more popular they are, the more powerful their mixing service is. The best services will establish rules for users to follow in order to maximize the effectiveness of their mixing services.

The above diagram shows the basic principles of mixing coins but most services take the process a step further by staggering transactions and randomizing the fee taken. Most mixing services take a small fee of between 0.1 and 0.25 percent but in order to illustrate this process simply, we will use round numbers. So let's assume that the mixing services take 0, 1, 2, or 3 bitcoins per mixing and this amount is chosen randomly.

Let's say the three wallets (A, B, C) want to send three different amounts to three other wallets (E, F, G) using a mixing service (wallet D). In this graph, I'm going to separate the transactions to illustrate that they were sent at staggered times.

Users are instructed to send Bitcoin in either 4BTC or 2BTC amounts and are told they will receive their mixed bitcoins in 1BTC or 3BTC increments. Users are also told to send three extra BTC for each mixing to account for the randomized 0BTC, 1BTC, 2BTC, or 3BTC fee. If they receive either a 1BTC or 2BTC fee, the extra bitcoins will be sent to the destination address— generally, the idea is to mix the coins into another account you own, not to send the bitcoins to their final destination through the mixing service.

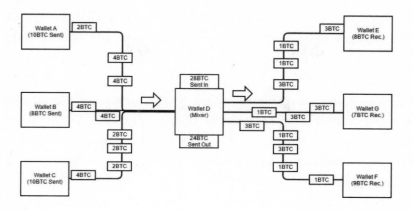

Things become more difficult for blockchain snoopers at this point. The only thing that could be determined from the above is that wallet B probably didn't send money to wallet F, because wallet B's total sent amount is lower than wallet F's received amount. However, it could be argued that perhaps wallet C wanted to send money to any of the three wallets E, G, or F, which would complicate things further.

But even discounting the possibility of wallets having multiple and shared destinations—because individuals acting independently of each other would be unlikely to send the same amounts at the same time—it becomes pretty tough to prove anything definitively using the blockchain. Wallets A and C might have been trying to send 7BTC to any of the three receiving accounts. Wallet B could have been trying to send 5BTC to either wallet G or wallet E and either paid a 1BTC fee or got lucky with no BTC fee.

With enough narrowing down and logical deduction, it might be possible to nail down one or more of the actors in this scenario.

Wallet B is at the most risk, because its total transaction amount didn't match that of wallets C and A. However, as things become more complex, it becomes even tougher to track down who did what. Mixing services become more effective as the number of users increases. Imagine the scenario above but with hundreds of input wallets and an equal number of output wallets. Wallet B would have hundreds of wallets with which to match up, not just three. Dozens of wallets could send in 8BTC over the same course of time that wallet B does.

As you can see, when people say Bitcoin is anonymous, they aren't exactly correct. It can be anonymous but it is more accurate to call it pseudonymous. Every wallet is given an identity and what that identity says about you can vary. Even if the wallet address itself is completely separate from its owner's real-life identity, a dedicated party could make a connection by watching a user's browsing habits, eventually matching up an IP address with a transaction. This is a vulnerability that comes from the way the majority of us browse the web—using the default settings that Microsoft or Apple or Google give us.

Careful Bitcoin users who are determined to hide their identity and transactions can use an anonymous web browser such as Tor. Tor, which was once short for "The Onion Router," is one of the few technologies out there that has a more nefarious reputation than Bitcoin.

When you connect to the Tor network, you go through an entry point called a node. There your request for information is mixed with the requests of every other user attempting to go through that node at that moment. This information is then encrypted together and then passed onto several other nodes before coming to what is called an exit node. The exit node decrypts the information and passes it along to the "regular" Internet. Tor then receives the requested information from the Internet, encrypts it, and sends it to an internal node, which then passes it to another internal node until it reaches another exit node, which decrypts the information and gives it back to the user.

This way, if the entry node becomes compromised, it will "know" who is requesting information but not what they requested. The exit node can figure out what everyone requested but not who it belongs to.

A Bitcoin address created and accessed by a computer using the Tor browser is virtually untraceable from the outside. If your computer is compromised by malware or viruses, no amount of precautions will prevent tracking. Popular operating systems, Windows in particular, are susceptible to snooping and attacks. Linux operating systems are generally more secure, but nothing is 100 percent.

Recent revelations have shown that the US National Security Agency and the UK's Government Communication Headquarters have built backdoors into consumer electronics. If that is the case with your equipment, there is unlikely to be anything you can do to prevent tracking.[3]

Whether you consider Bitcoin to be pseudonymous or anonymous, the fact is that it is possible to hide who you are giving bitcoins to on the network. Whether this is a good or a bad thing is open to some debate.

---

[3] Gallagher, Ryan, and Glenn Greenwald. "How the NSA Plans to Infect 'Millions' of Computers with Malware." The Intercept. March 12, 2014. Accessed June 22, 2015. https://firstlook.org/theintercept/2014/03/12/nsa-plans-infect-millions-computers-malware/.

Bitcoin is essentially the cash of the Internet world. If I hand someone cash and then I am unhappy with the product or service they give me in return, I am at their mercy when asking for a refund; there is no third party I can appeal to. There is also no way to prove a transaction took place.

Assuming the accounts involved aren't linked to any real-world identities, Bitcoin is the same way. The blockchain does make it possible to prove a transaction happened but without a link to real-world identities, there is no way to prove who sent what using only the data provided on the blockchain.

Ultimately, mixing services are only bringing the status quo of how cash transactions have worked in the physical world, to the digital realm. All sorts of escrow services exist to help provide trust. Ultimately, however, once the bitcoins leave your account, they belong to whomever you handed them to, just like cash—and there is very little that can be done to track cash transactions. Although regulators and fearmongers have attempted to paint Bitcoin as a tool that destroys the status quo, the truth is that it is only reestablishing the status quo that has existed for thousands of years before electronic transactions ever took place.

One of the most promising technologies in this specific niche of the Bitcoin ecosystem was Darkwallet, but it seems development has halted on the project as the developers ran out of money, despite having raised a lot of it. It is not currently in a usable state.

Co-invented by Cody Wilson, the creator of the 3D-printed gun, and Amir Taaki, the creator of Darkmarket, Darkwallet is a decentralized mixing service. Both of its inventors have anti-authoritarian, pro-individual freedom histories and politics. Nevertheless, their projects shouldn't be considered as radical as they are often painted by the mainstream media. Darkwallet has been portrayed as something designed to fund terrorism, buy drugs, and launder money.[4]

The truth is, Darkwallet is simply a tool, albeit one that can be used by criminals and innocent people alike. It can be used to obscure personal finances or purchases you'd rather keep private. Buying porn is a perfect example of a purchase someone might want to obscure for perfectly legal reasons. Porn isn't illegal—at least, most of it, in most territories, isn't—but a lot of people have plenty of reasons to want to keep that information private.

Bitcoin's blockchain is open for everyone to see. Mitigating the personal-privacy issues that brings is not necessarily a bad thing. Should I have to let Visa or MasterCard know what kind of images turn me on sexually? Is that anyone's business but mine? And does wanting to keep that information private make me a criminal? With the blockchain, the question isn't just about letting Visa and MasterCard see these things, but potentially, allowing the entire world to see them. That is one example why privacy-minded Bitcoin apps should not get the "criminal tools" reputation they often receive in the mainstream media.

Of course, Darkwallet can be used for all sorts of illegal purposes, including many of the things mentioned by the mainstream media. The developer's response would likely be that it is not as if those things didn't exist before. The fiat system served criminals perfectly fine. Drug dealers have always found a way to sell their wares and hide their profits. Terrorist organizations

---

[4] Copestake, Jen. "Hiding Currency in the Dark Wallet." BBC News. September 19, 2014. Accessed June 22, 2015. http://www.bbc.com/news/technology-29283124.

have always been able to find funding through traditional means, often from friendly governments.

As for laundering money, that depends on who is doing the laundering and how much of it they are doing. Getting money onto the Bitcoin network is really difficult to do without revealing your identity; making your identity disappear, as I covered, is relatively easy but it is also obvious when you do it.

If a CEO of a public company wants to embezzle funds using Bitcoin, he or she has to get the money onto the Bitcoin network; short of handing someone a stack of cash in exchange for Bitcoin, this would eventually require connecting a personal or company account to a company that sells Bitcoin. Since public company financial records are public and the Bitcoin blockchain is public, Bitcoin would be an incredibly poor tool for embezzling a large amount of funds. The money would disappear once sent to a mixer but red flags would instantly be raised once that happened. Mixing services are easy to spot because, by necessity, they have to have a lot of Bitcoin transfer in and out of them.

A traditional company putting a lot of money onto the blockchain and then making it disappear would make good reporters and investors ask why. Even if no one noticed, there would be a paper trail in plain view, never a good thing when it comes to crime.

This is a key point when it comes to using Bitcoin for criminal transactions: the record is there for everyone to see, forever. Current mixing techniques might be able to mask transactions on the blockchain, to the point where it's impossible to definitively tie transactions to a certain account. But this doesn't account for every other tracking technique outside of the Bitcoin blockchain nor does it account for techniques that will be developed in the future.

Bitcoin is not the only emergent technology currently being developed. Big data is another huge one and it is bound to incorporate the blockchain in some way. If one uses data from massive Internet tracking operations, it may become much easier to link someone's real-life identity to their Bitcoin wallet.

As Nathan Wosnack, the cofounder of Blockchain Factory (a B2B service that is primarily focused on extending the useful data found in the blockchain), has pointed out:

> I feel as though the statements about anonymity on an open and immutable public ledger that can be audited by anyone [like the blockchain] to be a completely ridiculous assertion and [a] modern myth. [. . .] Using mixers helps, but I'm still not convinced even those can save one from sophisticated forensic accounting tools likely being used and in development by law enforcement to analyze targeted [individuals] or even big data and figure out roughly who the parties are, where, and what they're buying or selling.

It is impossible to predict the future with 100 percent accuracy. We don't know what kind of tools will be combing through the blockchain in the future. For that reason, any serious crimes are probably better off being conducted in the fiat world with untraceable cash. It might seem advantageous to use Bitcoin rather than credit cards or wire transfers, and in many cases it could be, but the records of the latter form of transaction might eventually be deleted or buried. Banks are only required to keep records for five years. They might hold on to them longer than that but might not. With Bitcoin, those transactions are never going away. They are a part of Bitcoin's history forever, regardless of whether the people who participated in the transaction want them to be or not. It is not unreasonable to expect that in a cryptocurrency-powered future, political candidates will have their Bitcoin history pored over by their opponents and media sleuths.

The blockchain is not the only place they will look for hints. Interacting with the blockchain generally means interacting with the Internet. Every interaction holds the potential to reveal the user's identity through a leaky browser, an unmasked IP address, or via a dozen other ways. The Internet is not anonymous, so it is difficult to do anything—including interactions with the Bitcoin ecosystem—without compromising your identity. Even Tor nodes have been compromised in the past. Currently, the safest thing one can do is use TailsOS, an operating system that exists solely on a USB stick or other storage device and is reflashed (*i.e.*, erased of data outside the operating system itself) every time it is used. It is like having a brand new Internet identity every time you use it. When used in combination with other privacy techniques, TailsOS can even help circumvent government or other spying significantly. TailsOS was credited by Edward Snowden as being instrumental in helping him maintain his privacy while he leaked what are now known as the Snowden Documents.[5]

---

[5] Higgins, Parker. "The 7 Privacy Tools Essential to Making Snowden Documentary CITIZENFOUR." Electronic Frontier Foundation. October 29, 2014. Accessed June 22, 2015. https://www.eff.org/deeplinks/2014/10/7-privacy-tools-essential-making-citizenfour.

The people who can take advantage of Bitcoin in order to move money overseas without government approval are people who already fly under the radar. Preventing someone from moving their life savings out of a country before they emigrate elsewhere without paying taxes is not likely the kind of financial crime most of us worry about stopping. Yet those kinds of medium-sized transactions, as well as smaller ones, are likely to be the kind most enabled by the Bitcoin network. Bitcoin would be less effective than cash for the kind of multimillion-dollar transactions that regular people think of when they hear the term "money laundering." Certainly, once the money is laundered, it would be easier to transport than, say, a briefcase full of cash. But the question becomes how to get that money onto the network without it being linked to a real-life or corporate identity.

It's not as if there are plenty of people looking to sell hundreds of thousands of dollars worth of Bitcoin for cash. To find a whale like that you would need to go online and going online creates records.

Potentially, a Bitcoin-run world would be more difficult for big-time money launderers. If a currency such as Bitcoin ever replaces or significantly supplements traditional fiat currencies, it would only make sense that public companies would keep their public spending on the blockchain public. Given the choice, would you invest in a company that keeps all of its finances public or one that puts its money through a mixing service and hides its transactions from the public and its stockholders?

The same could be applied to charities. Would more people give to a charity that was upfront and open about how it spent its money or one that attempted to obscure the blockchain record?

Bitcoin ultimately is both pseudonymous and completely traceable. How easy a user is to trace depends on how hard that user works to obscure him or herself. Despite this seemingly contradictory nature, both Bitcoin's traceability and its increased privacy have roles to play in the technological future.

Chapter 7:

Bitcoin and the Criminal Element

Everyone knows that the Internet is changing our lives, mostly because someone in the media has uttered that exact phrase every single day since 1993. However, it certainly appears that the main thing the Internet has accomplished is the normalization of amateur pornography. There is no justification for the amount of naked people on the World Wide Web, many of whom are clearly (clearly!) doing so for non-monetary reasons. Where were these people fifteen years ago? Were there really millions of women in 1986 turning to their husbands and saying, "You know, I would love to have total strangers masturbate to images of me deep-throating a titanium dildo, but there's simply no medium for that kind of entertainment. I guess we'll just have to sit here and watch *Falcon Crest* again."

—Chuck Klosterman, *Sex, Drugs, and Cocoa Puffs: A Low Culture Manifesto*

You can't talk honestly about Bitcoin without talking about the criminal element. Although other advocates might downplay the connection—and they have legitimate arguments for doing so—the importance of the criminal world's relation to Bitcoin can't be discounted.

Bitcoin will help facilitate criminal transactions. There is no point in denying this, as it only takes a few minutes on a Deep Web marketplace offering drugs and other illegal goods and services to get a sense of Bitcoin's role in such things. (The Deep Web is the portion of the Internet that can't be indexed by traditional search engines.) It would be equally accurate, however, to say that cash facilitates criminal transactions. One would only have to spend some time on a certain street in the downtown district of any metropolitan area to understand that cash is still the primary method criminals use to buy and sell illegal goods and services.

I debated with myself endlessly on how to approach this chapter. The criminal element of the Internet was undoubtedly essential to Bitcoin's early price-setting and adoption, but I in no way want to imply that the crimes it helped facilitate wouldn't have happened without Bitcoin either online or on the street. Nor do I want to imply that all—or even a large portion of—Bitcoin users are involved in criminal activity on the Deep Web or elsewhere. Because of Bitcoin's relative anonymity, shady transactions on the Deep Web were one of its earliest uses, but the currency has since evolved into a legitimate payment method used by legitimate customers, freelancers, and employees.

Still, crime was instrumental in Bitcoin's early life and it will continue to be a factor in its future.

The Silk Road

What is called the "open web" makes up only a small part of the Internet. There is a sea of data underneath the open web that few will ever see. It is made up of banking transactions, corporate transactions, emails, IRC chatrooms, Usenet communities, academic and corporate intranets, and a variety of other things not indexed by Google and the other major search engines; it is called the Deep Web.

One of Bitcoin's earliest claims to fame was as the digital currency that allowed a bunch of criminals on an intentionally hidden sector of the Internet known as the Dark Web—a small part of the Deep Web—to sell drugs to America's youth. With the exception of a few publications, much early coverage focused on the panic-inducing claims that "drugs were being sold on the Internet" and "some strange Internet money was making that happen."

Well, the latter idea is false. The Internet has always been used to sell drugs and illegal items. Drugs were being sold via Internet even back in the Usenet days before web browsers existed. No matter how hard the feds worked at trying to prevent drug transactions in various systems, some drugs always made it through. Even today, drug sales are hardly limited to the Deep Web. It is impossible to get accurate numbers but an argument could be made that the open Internet—*i.e.*, what most think of when they hear the word "Internet"—is just as significant, if not more so, to the drug game. Although billions are (or were) being spent on online marketplaces such as the Silk Road, most drug dealers aren't tech-savvy enough to take advantage of them. They are, however, tech-savvy enough to use Facebook, Instagram, Craigslist, and a myriad other sites. In September 2014, *Venture*

Beat's Fletcher Babb began an article with the simple statement, "Instagram has ushered in a golden age for the drug trade."[1]

The same was said about the Silk Road and Bitcoin when those services first entered mainstream culture and awareness. It was hyperbole when Babb said it about Instagram and although it might be less hyperbolic to say the same about the Silk Road, it is also an exaggeration to blame these services for the rise of the Internet drug trade.

Instagram is used to sell drugs. It is used for a lot of other things: for humblebragging about a recently cooked meal or for offering legions of out-of-shape viewers the chance to ogle attractive workout gurus. It is also used to sell drugs, but hardly anyone calls for it to be shut down or banned, the way West Virginia Senator Joe Manchin called for a ban on Bitcoin in February 2014.[2]

Bitcoin and the Deep Web are also used for completely legitimate purposes. There are no concrete estimates on the size of the Deep Web, but everyone agrees it is orders of magnitude larger than the Internet we browse daily. Most of the data is useless to outside parties, but within this vast sea of information, people have started building networks and services hidden from the mainstream users of the Internet and law enforcement agencies. Many of these sites use the .onion domain extension and have a long string of seemingly random letters and numbers as their URL.

---

[1] Babb, Fletcher. "Instagram Has a Drug Problem." VentureBeat. September 19, 2014. Accessed June 22, 2015. http://venturebeat.com/2014/09/19/instagram-has-a-drug-problem/.

[2] Fung, Brian. "Sen. Joe Manchin Calls for a Bitcoin Ban as Regulators Seek 'Accelerated Push'." *Washington Post*. February 26, 2014. Accessed June 22, 2015. http://www.washingtonpost.com/blogs/the-switch/wp/2014/02/26/sen-joe-manchin-calls-for-a-bitcoin-ban-as-regulators-seek-accelerated-push/.

Although the number of those who are using the Deep Web for illegal activity undoubtedly increases as you move deeper into it, the Deep Web still serves legitimate purposes. Wikileaks started out as a Deep Web service, and the ability of journalists to communicate with sources and of whistleblowers to release information anonymously is an important tool for freedom that should be protected at all costs.

Of course, privacy is an important concern for others besides cypherpunks, Bitcoin enthusiasts, and criminals. The largest institutions in the world remind us that encryption is essential not only for specific groups but also for freedom itself. In May 2015, the United Nations released a special report on encryption that in no uncertain terms laid out the justification for privacy as a human right:

> Encryption and anonymity, and the security concepts behind them, provide the privacy and security necessary for the **exercise of the right to freedom of opinion and expression in the digital age.** Such security may be essential for the exercise of other rights, including economic rights, privacy, due process, freedom of peaceful assembly and association, and the right to life and bodily integrity. Because of their importance to the rights to freedom of opinion and expression, restrictions on encryption and anonymity must be strictly limited according to principles of legality, necessity, proportionality and legitimacy in objective. [my emphasis]

UN Special Rapporteur David Kayne has recently taken a thinly veiled shot at the policies promoted by the so-called "Five

Eyes" (the US, the UK, Australia, New Zealand, and Canada, who are all part of an agreement to share surveillance) and its attacks on encryption. Kayne argues:

> States should promote strong encryption and anonymity. National laws should recognize that individuals are free to protect the privacy of their digital communications by using encryption technology and tools that allow anonymity online. [. . .] States should avoid all measures that weaken the security that individuals may enjoy online, such as backdoors, weak encryption standards and key escrows.

We might expect to hear Internet advocates and computer geeks talk about how important encryption is to privacy and freedom, but the point is really driven home when it is echoed by such a conservative, mainstream, and international entity as the UN.[3]

What does this have to do with the topic of Bitcoin and the criminal element?

As it turns out, a lot, because the encryption techniques that are essential to Bitcoin have been the focus of a public debate since at least the early 1990s, and that debate ended up placing everything related to the topic of encryption under the umbrella of criminal activity. The association between Bitcoin and criminal elements was born directly from that.

---

[3] Kaye, David. Report of the Special Rapporteur on the Promotion and Protection of the Right to Freedom of Opinion and Expression. United Nations' Human Rights Council, May 22, 2015.

Back in 1995, author Steven Levy visited the offices of the now-defunct Cygnus Solutions, an early Internet cryptography company, and spoke about what the early Cypherpunks of the day were trying to accomplish:

> The people in this room hope for a world where an individual's informational footprints—everything from an opinion on abortion to the medical record of an actual abortion—can be traced only if the individual involved chooses to reveal them; a world where coherent messages shoot around the globe by network and microwave, but intruders and feds trying to pluck them out of the vapor find only gibberish; a world where the tools of prying are transformed into the instruments of privacy.
>
> There is only one way this vision will materialize, and that is by widespread use of cryptography. Is this technologically possible? Definitely. The obstacles are political—some of the most powerful forces in government are devoted to the control of these tools. In short, there is a war going on between those who would liberate crypto and those who would suppress it. The seemingly innocuous bunch strewn around this conference room represents the vanguard of the pro-crypto forces. Though the battleground seems remote, the stakes are not: the outcome of this struggle may determine the amount of freedom our society will grant us in the 21st century. To the Cypherpunks, freedom is an issue worth some risk.

"Arise," urges one of their number, "You have nothing to lose but your barbed-wire fences."[4]

Before the advent of the Internet, an average person didn't have much use for cryptography. Sure, phone calls could be intercepted and a cryptographically secure phone would have been nice, but few worried that targeted government surveillance would be turned on them.

For years, the National Security Agency had a monopoly on cryptography. It was primarily used by government agents who had a real reason to worry that their communications were being watched by other governments. Then, in 1975, with electronic communication on the rise, Whitfield Diffie invented the first "public key" system, potentially allowing anyone in the world to communicate securely with anyone else in the world, assuming they had access to a computer that could do the cryptography work.

This system eventually led to the emergence of companies and services such as Phil Zimmerman's PGP encryption program. It went head-to-head against the NSA's Clipper Chip, a hardware-based cryptography solution designed to give the government its own backdoors into every phone and computer sold by US companies.

PGP and the cypherpunks won the battle, as the Clipper Chip was shown to be insecure. The concept of government-endorsed backdoors faded from the cryptography community—although that didn't stop the NSA from covertly adding its own backdoors, as when it paid security firm RSA to preserve security flaws for its

---

⁴ Levy, Steven. "Crypto Rebels." Wired 1.02. May 1, 1993. Accessed June 22, 2015. http://archive.wired.com/wired/archive/1.02/crypto.rebels.html.

snooping operations.[5,6] Yet it could be argued they eventually lost the larger battle for the mind—if not the heart—of the general public. Even though the public had gained the ability to keep its communications private, the vast majority didn't feel like they needed to.

From the mid-1990s and until Edward Snowden's revelations of widespread and illegal government spying, the general public overwhelmingly used the Internet, email, and other forms of electronic communication completely unencrypted, mostly oblivious to the inherent risk. Meanwhile, the government designed surveillance programs and built backdoors into our technology.

Even today, after Snowden's revelations, the vast majority of users still send their emails unencrypted and browse the web using Firefox, Chrome, or Internet Explorer—rarely do they add extra security features. Browsers built with security in mind make up less than one percent of total Internet use.

The cypherpunks and cryptographers of the early '90s fought for our right to use privacy tools; the hackers and tinkers of today have extended this. To them, the fight has become not only about the right to use privacy tools but also the right to use any tool they can create with mathematics.

It should be pointed out that within the Bitcoin community itself there isn't anything approaching a unified vision. Despite the media's portrayal of the community as radical libertarians, there are plenty of users with other belief systems and affiliations.

---

[5] Higgins, Parker. "On the Clipper Chip's Birthday, Looking Back on Decades of Key Escrow Failures." Electronic Frontier Foundation. April 16, 2015. Accessed June 22, 2015. https://www.eff.org/deeplinks/2015/04/clipper-chips-birthday-looking-back-22-years-key-escrow-failures.

[6] Snyder, Brian. "Exclusive: NSA Infiltrated RSA Security More Deeply than Thought - Study." Reuters. March 31, 2014. Accessed November 12, 2015. http://www.reuters.com/article/us-usa-security-nsa-rsa-idUSBREA2U0TY20140331.

Likewise, the vast majority of libertarians aren't as radical as some in the cryptocurrency community. But there is also a sect of crypto-libertarian believers who do have a set of consistent and clear principles that generally pushes their software in a certain direction.

This group is often called libertarian but that title isn't quite accurate. Given recent developments, it might be meaningless to use such labels. In an October 2014 op-ed piece for CoinTelegraph, I explained why I thought the old arguments about capitalism versus communism were about to die out:

> As we move into the blockchain future, new governmental systems will arise that are far superior to both [capitalism and communism].
>
> [We could see a blockchain government] that provides both the individual freedom of the most laissez-faire economy while creating such an excess of wealth that basic needs are taken care of for every citizen.

And so I would call this particular group not libertarian but cryptotarian, more concerned with what math limits them to than what the government limits them to. Open-source software is proving to be a powerful tool in their quest.

The documentary *Deep Web*, directed by Alex Winter, opens with a quote from OpenBazaar developer Amir Taaki: "The fascists, they have resources, but we have imagination. We are making the tools to take back our sovereignty."[7]

The same sort of philosophy was behind the Silk Road. It also continues to motivate Brian Hoffman's OpenBazaar, Cody

---

[7] *Deep Web*. Directed by Alex Winter. Performed by Cindy Cohn, Andy Greenberg. Epix, 2015. VoD.

Wilson's 3D-printed gun, Darkwallet, and a dozen other tools that scare the shit out of people who have devoted their whole lives to upholding the status quo.

The Silk Road was an unregulated marketplace and a gathering place for like-minded individuals, many of whom were true believers in the philosophy described by Amir Taaki in the *Deep Web* documentary.

On October 2, 2013, FBI agents arrested Ross William Ulbricht and accused him of being the infamous Dread Pirate Roberts, the elusive administrator of the Internet's largest underground marketplace, the Silk Road. On February 4, 2015, he was found guilty of all seven charges filed against him, including conspiracy to distribute narcotics, money laundering, hacking, and "continuing a criminal enterprise"—better known as the "kingpin" provision and normally reserved for the leaders of criminal organizations such as drug cartels and the Mafia. Then, on May 29, he was sentenced to life in prison without the possibility of parole. Judge Katherine B. Forrest implied that she was making an example of the young man:

> There must be no doubt that lawlessness will not be tolerated. There must be no doubt that no one is above the law—no matter one's education or privileges. All stand equal before the law. There must be no doubt that you can't run a massive criminal enterprise and because it occurred over the Internet minimize the crime committed on that basis.[8]

---

[8] "Ross Ulbricht, aka Dread Pirate Roberts, Sentenced in Manhattan Federal Court to Life in Prison." FBI. May 29, 2015. Accessed June 22, 2015. https://www.fbi.gov/newyork/press-releases/2015/ross-ulbricht-aka-dread-pirate-roberts-sentenced-in-manhattan-federal-court-to-life-in-prison.

Some contend, however, that the case against Ulbricht was not so open-and-shut. Although it is hard to argue that Ulbricht wasn't involved with the Silk Road at all, there are questions regarding how the evidence was collected, who collected it, and what, exactly, it proved.

Before discussing Ulbricht's case, I'll offer a quick recap of the Silk Road marketplace. As I've already mentioned, the Silk Road was a service hidden in the Deep Web. Like most Deep Web services, it could only be accessed by using the web browser Tor, which was originally developed by either the US Navy or the CIA, depending on which source you believe. It was developed to provide a reliable way to communicate without sending messages over the regular Internet, where they could be easily intercepted.

It has since become open source and taken on a life of its own, enabling secure anonymous communication. Tor is currently used by journalists, privacy advocates, stalking victims, and people who just generally wish to stay anonymous.

The problem this presents to the government is that services such as Tor are undermining their law enforcement activities. This effect, according to *Deep Web* director Alex Winter, has led to the kind of conflict of interest only possible in massive bureaucracies. During a directors' chat on Epix after the movie's premiere, Winter alleged that certain segments of the government work to undermine Tor's encryption while other segments work to increase Tor's privacy features.

Winter isn't the only one to believe this. The Tor director, Roger Dingledine, has claimed that the Department of Homeland Security and the UK's Government Communications Headquarters were spreading software meant to undermine Tor.

Meanwhile, the US government increased its funding for the development of Tor to $1.8 million in 2013.[9]

Let's return to the Silk Road. It served as a marketplace hidden within the Deep Web and was only accessible by Tor. It allowed people to buy and sell virtually anything but was primarily used for the sale of illegal and gray-market drugs. Buyers and sellers communicated using PGP technology and completed transactions using Bitcoin. It was a bastion of Internet anonymity and initially the authorities were at a loss on what to do about it.

Action was spurred on by New York Senator Charles Schumer, who demanded that the federal government shut down the site and then went on to show every teenager watching just how easy it was to order drugs online.[10]

Law enforcement first infiltrated the Silk Road the same way they infiltrate any other criminal organization: by posing as members of that organization. They managed to track down a seller with the username Chronicpain; they seized his and other sellers' accounts but didn't arrest the owners of those accounts. From there, they managed to communicate with Dread Pirate Roberts and implicate him in a large number of crimes.

The crime that got the most media attention and was used to deny Ross Ulbricht bail was the alleged ordering of three murders. According to the government's accounts, Dread Pirate Roberts ordered three hits: one in retaliation for a theft, one on a former vendor turned witness, and one on a blackmailer.

---

[9] Kelion, Leo. "NSA and GCHQ Agents 'leak Tor Bugs', Alleges Developer - BBC News." BBC News. August 22, 2014. Accessed June 22, 2015. http://www.bbc.com/news/technology-28886462.

[10] "Schumer Pushes to Shut Down Online Drug Marketplace." NBC New York. Accessed February 6, 2016. http://www.nbcnewyork.com/news/local/Schumer-Calls-on-Feds-to-Shut-Down-Online-Drug-Marketplace-123187958.html.

The total murder-for-hire count was eventually raised to six, and Ulbricht was deemed a "threat to society" and denied bail. Soon after, the government dropped the murder-for-hire charges, but they still managed to keep Ulbricht from getting bail and publicly painted him as a heartless murderer.

Many suspect the reason the government dropped the charges is that they were unlikely to stick.

The actions of two government agents who were heavily involved in investigating the Silk Road case and had direct communications with Dread Pirate Roberts cast some doubt on the case. In March 2015, Secret Service Agent Shaun Bridges and DEA Agent Carl Mark Force IV were arrested and charged with money laundering and wire fraud. Force was additionally charged with theft of government property and conflict of interest. Bridges had allegedly stolen $800,000 worth of Bitcoin and transferred it into his personal account. Force also allegedly stole bitcoins and allegedly did much more, including taking payments from Dread Pirate Roberts, stealing from the Silk Road and trying to sell Dread Pirate Roberts/Ulbricht information about the investigation. He also allegedly tried to blackmail Dread Pirate Roberts while posing under a different identity. Additionally, Force was the agent Dread Pirate Roberts allegedly attempted to hire to carry out or act as a liaison for the hit.

You might see the problem here. Bridges allegedly stole money from the Silk Road and then Force allegedly took money from Dread Pirate Roberts to kill the person Force said stole the money—a Silk Road employee. Force also allegedly took money for the killing of the vendor-turned-witness and helped stage that death. He then allegedly blackmailed Dread Pirate Roberts and allegedly took money from him to kill the fictional black-mailer. Rather than passing this money onto his superiors, Force allegedly kept most of it for himself.

As noted in the affidavit against Force, he actually encouraged Dread Pirate Roberts to use PGP and didn't provide his superiors with the private key. It gets worse than that. Force was permitted to have one identity on the Silk Road: Nob. Investigators now believe he had multiple "sock puppet" accounts on the site and that he utilized them and his connections in law enforcement for personal gain.[11]

From the Department of Justice's press release:

> Force allegedly sold information about the government's investigation to the target of the investigation. The complaint also alleges that Force invested in and worked for a digital currency exchange company while still working for the DEA, and that he directed the company to freeze a customer's account with no legal basis to do so, then transferred the customer's funds to his personal account. Further, Force allegedly sent an unauthorized Justice Department subpoena to an online payment service directing that it unfreeze his personal account.

Essentially, Ross Ulbricht was denied bail and painted as a murderer in the media because the online persona Dread Pirate Roberts allegedly hired a fictional hitman to kill two people who

---

[11] Jeong, Sarah. "Criminal Charges Against Agents Reveal Staggering Corruption in the Silk Road Investigation." *Forbes*. March 31, 2015. Accessed June 22, 2015. http://www.forbes.com/sites/sarahjeong/2015/03/31/force-and-bridges/.

didn't exist in retaliation for acts that either never happened or were acts of government agents themselves. The two agents primarily responsible for his arrest were—by the government's own admission—completely corrupt and actively working to hide evidence in the case. The murder-for-hire charges were never proven in court but nonetheless affected the opinion of both the supposedly impartial judge and the public.

On the day that he was apprehended in October 2013, Ross Ulbricht was sitting in the San Francisco library with his laptop open. Authorities had figured out that if he were allowed to close it, it would encrypt the data and they would be unable to access it. (As Jacob Müller-Maguhn pointed out, "One must acknowledge with cryptography no amount of violence will ever solve a math problem."[12]) After distracting him, agents say they were able to separate Ulbricht from his laptop before he could close it. It was allegedly logged into an admin account for the Silk Road; Ulbricht appeared to have been caught red-handed.

But in a 2013 *Forbes* interview with Dread Pirate Roberts, the admin explained that the moniker—an homage to a character in the movie *The Princess Bride*—had been passed down to him from a previous administrator and that he would later pass it onto someone else.[13]

This is what Ulbricht's defense attempted to claim—that Ulbricht was at one time the head of the Silk Road but that he

---

[12] Assange, Julian, Jacob Appelbaum, Andy Müller-Maguhn and Jérémie Zimmermann. *Cypherpunks: Freedom and the Future of the Internet*. New York: OR Books, 2012.

[13] Greenberg, Andy. "An Interview With A Digital Drug Lord: The Silk Road's Dread Pirate Roberts (Q&A)." *Forbes*. August 14, 2013. Accessed June 22, 2015. http://www.forbes.com/sites/andygreenberg/2013/08/14/an-interview-with-a-digital-drug-lord-the-silk-roads-dread-pirate-roberts-qa/.

left it after it grew in popularity. The defense claimed he was then lured back in, in order to be set up as the fall man. The explanation is not as implausible as it might seem. Force was (allegedly) providing the real Dread Pirate Roberts with inside information. He was accused of and eventually admitted to hiding the specific contents of his conversations with Dread Pirate Roberts and how much he was specifically paid.

Is it possible that the real Dread Pirate Roberts, perhaps working in conjunction with Force, set up Ross Ulbricht by luring him back to the Silk Road and planting information on his computer? A detailed log of Ulbricht's alleged criminal activities was found on his computer, but how likely is it that someone of his education would leave such a log unencrypted? Ulbricht's defense made the argument that it might have been planted on the computer.

A jury of his peers found Ulbricht guilty on all counts but his defense was prevented from informing the jury about the two agents' alleged misconduct or the *Forbes* interview. The government's claim was that it located the Silk Road servers—and thus all subsequent evidence—through a "leaky captcha" on the Silk Road. (A captcha is a set of letters or numbers you have to fill in at a website to prove you aren't a bot; a leaky captcha is one that reveals identifying information about the site.) This claim has been soundly discredited by security experts around the web,[14] but the defense's witnesses who would have contradicted this explanation were not allowed to testify. Finally, the government's

---

[14] Cubrilovic, Nik. "Analyzing the FBI's Explanation of How They Located Silk Road." New Web Order. September 7, 2014. Accessed June 22, 2015. https://www.nik-cub.com/posts/analyzing-fbi-explanation-silk-road/.

own investigations show that many other people were suspected of being Dread Pirate Roberts at one time or another.

The Silk Road launched before Dread Pirate Roberts joined the site, and evidence from the trial suggests the "legend" of the pirate was hastily launched after a discussion among the site's leadership. This is speculation, but creating an anonymous and revolving "leader" is the perfect way to set up a fall man when the dominoes begin to fall.

My aim is not to cast guilt on or proclaim the innocence of Ross William Ulbricht. As is the case with so many other scandals in the Bitcoin space, an entire book could, should, and almost certainly will be devoted to this topic. At the time of this writing, Ulbricht's appeal process is underway. All I am saying is that it would be nice to see Ulbricht get to present a real defense.

In addition, Ulbricht was given the harshest penalty possible, harsher than what the prosecutors were seeking. Another Silk Road vendor who was charged with similar crimes was sentenced to a mere 17 months. That defendant pleaded guilty so it was reasonable to expect a shorter sentence; but the contrast is disproportionate. Ulbricht's sentence was an expensive price for him to pay for his attempt to exercise his constitutional right to a trial. The sentence surpasses that of murderers and child molesters and as his defense site points out, is matched only by the likes of Charles Manson.

Ulbricht's harsh sentence does not appear to be solely a result of his crimes. The Silk Road and the philosophy behind it use technology to usurp the government's power. The government says you can't have these kind of tools. The Silk Road was shut down but it was replaced with a dozen other sites, ranging from Silk Road 2, Sheep Marketplace, and Agora (all defunct) to

Valhalla, Alpha Bay, and Dream Market (currently operating). These are occasionally brought down as well but second-generation, open-source, and completely decentralized alternatives are right around the corner. Soon there won't be anyone to arrest except the individual vendors—and then what will the government do? Arresting individual dealers has been a strategy for the drug war on the streets for decades and only the most devoted drug warriors would try to claim it has been a success. There is a direct correlation with online piracy that we can look at. When Napster was taken down, it was a setback for the pirating community. Centralized systems acted as a weak point. Since decentralized torrenting went mainstream, there hasn't been much the government and other organizations have been able to do to prevent piracy. They have targeted individual uploaders, but that has done little to slow the growth of online piracy.

Other Tor Services and How to Use Them

The shutdown of the Silk Road and Ross Ulbricht's life sentence didn't deter people from using Tor and Bitcoin to continue criminal activity. Sites with similar layouts and the same rules still exist. At the time of this writing, Valhalla and AlphaBay are two of the most popular and reputable, but their status could change at any time. Deepdotweb.com and Reddit's subforums r/Darkmarkets and r/DarkmarketNoobs are great resources for individuals looking to order something from the Deep Web.

Ordering from these sites requires PGP and Bitcoin. Guides on how to use Bitcoin can be found in this book and countless places online. GnuPG (or GPG for short, often still referred to as PGP) is the open-source version of PGP, which was the world's most popular and arguably powerful personal encryption software until GPG was released. It was invented by Phil Zimmerman and owned by the PGP Corporation until 2010, when it was purchased by Symantec.[15]

Since Windows is extremely unsecure and Tor has been shown to be compromised, it has been suggested that users with particularly strong concerns about privacy and anonymity should take the extra steps of using TailsOS, which I mentioned earlier.

Even with all possible precautions taken, law enforcement will be attempting to do everything they can to unmask buyers and sellers on these markets. Although a certain level of confidence is gained by following some best practices, what is secure today might not be in the future.

In addition, most coin mixing services take place on the Deep Web. Coin Laundry has been around for a while but as is true of any centralized Tor service run by an anonymous person, this could change at any time.

There are other illegal services on the Deep Web much darker than the drugs, fake passports, and Netflix accounts normally found on the Silk Road's successors. Everything from child pornography to snuff films can be found there. These services have little to nothing to do with the Bitcoin community, and are near-universally condemned by its members. Their only connection to Bitcoin is that they sometimes use Bitcoin to perform transactions. In late 2014, the UK Internet Watch Foundation reported that it had found more than 200 sites promoting child

---

[15] Duncan, Geoff. "Symantec Buys PGP For $300 Million." Digital Trends. April 29, 2010. Accessed June 22, 2015. http://www.digitaltrends.com/computing/symantec-buys-pgp-for-300-million/.

porn that accept Bitcoin, 30 of which had Bitcoin as their only payment option.[16]

There are many more such sites that accept credit cards or PayPal. The problem for law enforcement is that it is easy enough to get MasterCard or PayPal to freeze the offenders' funds and halt payments. With Bitcoin, which lacks a central authority, that is impossible. Because of this feature of Bitcoin, despite the inherent potential problems in using the currency, you can expect more disreputable services to accept Bitcoin as payment in the future.

In the long run, the adoption of Bitcoin might end up working against the criminals. As blockchain analysis technology gets more advanced, there is no telling what could be gleaned from it in the future, and it only takes one mistake for a dedicated sleuth to build an entire tree of transactions. In other words, if you reveal your identity once with a single transaction—perhaps because you don't mix up your coins or you reveal your IP address or admit to making a wallet—a detective could follow transactions to dozens of other wallets and start making connections to continually track your transactions.

There are also sites that exist in a gray area—such as the Bitcoin mixing services and forums I mentioned earlier that are legal but questionable either politically, morally, or culturally.

But we should also remember what good Tor and the Deep Web have done for society. For all the unseemly and outright disgusting elements of its darkest corners, the Deep Web has become a bastion of privacy in a digital world that is devoid of it.

---

[16] Hern, Alex. "Paedophiles Sell Child Abuse Images for Bitcoin." *The Guardian.* April 14, 2015. http://www.theguardian.com/technology/2015/apr/14/paedophiles-sell-child-abuse-images-for-bitcoin.

Deep Web communities include revolutionary book clubs, mild sexual fetish blogs, anonymous chatrooms that remind one of the early chatrooms of the early to mid-'90s, anonymous social networks, bulk coupon sellers, and anonymous confessions sites (tamer than you might imagine). There is even a blog about the victimless crime of exploring Virginia Tech's steam tunnels.

These might seem like minor things but they are subsets of our culture that might otherwise not exist. Things can be legal and still be embarrassing—not everyone wants to go to Yahoo! Answers to ask about their hemorrhoids or express their deepest paranoia or unpopular political opinions.

The Deep Web has also helped oppressed people speak out against their government. When Turkey attempted to ban Twitter and YouTube, Tor was the best option for getting past the government's firewalls. Multiple mainstream journalism publications have set up Tor hidden service sites, allowing whistleblowers to leak information without revealing their identity.

The experience of trawling the Deep Web is somewhat akin to traveling the Internet before Google made it easy. The freedom that comes with true anonymity is powerful and results in both good and bad, and that isn't going away anytime soon.

Bitcoin's ties to criminal activity aren't limited to the Deep Web. Bitcoin is playing an increasingly large role in malware, ransomware, and gray-market services.

Online gambling was an early and obvious use for Bitcoin and that trend has continued unabated since the first dice sites hit the Internet. Today, nearly any event can be bet on using Bitcoin and nearly every casino game is available. There are even peer-to-peer betting sites that allow you to wager on the outcome of custom events—from the results of a presidential election to the next time a celebrity will be arrested to whether it is going to rain in Las Vegas tomorrow. As long as you can find someone to make that bet with you, it is possible to make a Bitcoin bet using a third-party escrow system.

Porn, of the legal variety, has much use for Bitcoin and this continues to be an area of growth. More porn sites are accepting Bitcoin, not because their contents are illegal, but because using Bitcoin will help customers avoid a potentially embarrassing credit card statement and eliminate the risk of being overcharged.

But the most common illegal Bitcoin activity on the Internet, by far, is simply scamming people out of their bitcoins. In many people's opinion, it is the largest threat to the Bitcoin ecosystem. Bitcoin is attracting new people all the time and their first taste of the cryptocommunity is often a negative one.

Bitcoin-focused malware is growing in popularity. The most common tactics include installing hidden mining software, and encrypting important files and then holding them for ransom.

The last example is by far the most frightful. The malware—this particular form is known as "ransomware"—cryptographically encrypts a victim's files, focusing on things it deems important, such as documents and photographs. It then demands payment in Bitcoin for the key to unlock the files. The software usually includes a timer counting down, with the threat that if it reaches zero, the price to unlock the files will increase.

According to security blogs, more often than not, victims who pay the ransom fail to get their files unlocked. There are some sites that use already-discovered passwords to attempt an unlock for free but the ransomware itself remains practically unbreakable.

Another scamming tactic is the distributed denial of service (DDOS) attack, where the attacker takes a site offline by sending too many requests for the site to handle. This is an old trick but we are seeing the attackers demand bitcoin payments more often. For instance, the infamous hacker/blackmail group DD4BC has attacked multiple sites, starting with gambling sites—including nitrogensports.eu, the first site to go public about its blackmailing— and has now moved on to Bitcoin media sites and other services.

Unsurprisingly, Bitcoin also has its fair share of Nigerian prince-like scams. These are usually easy to spot by their "too-good-to-be-true" offers. They will claim things like having found an exploit in the Bitcoin system that allows them to double the victim's coins. Of course, once the victim sends coins in, they never get them back.

More intelligent scams are harder to spot. A new Bitcoin user might be hard-pressed to tell what is legitimate and what is designed to separate them from their coins so caution is always recommended.

The criminal element helped Bitcoin set its price and find its first use. Its irreversible transactions, relative anonymity and global reach make it uniquely useful for certain crimes. But it is important to stress, again, that Bitcoin has grown past that use. Nevertheless, I expect that although legal Bitcoin use might grow at a faster rate than its illegal alternatives, more criminals will use Bitcoin as well. Every currency attracts criminals and Bitcoin has proven to be no different.

What makes Bitcoin stand out is its ability to help criminals and to thwart them. In addition to the public blockchain and its record of every transaction—including criminal ones—there are other ways Bitcoin can make things more difficult for criminals.

Credit card fraud and schemes can't take place in a Bitcoin ecosystem. One of its main advantages is that you don't have to hand over personal information. If you buy a product online with bitcoins and it turns out the seller is a scammer who simply decides to keep your bitcoins, you can't issue a recall on the order. At the same time, however, you don't have to worry about that person taking anything else from you. You don't have to cancel your credit card and you don't have to worry about the seller charging more than they say they will. You can't be double-charged. They get what you gave them and nothing more.

With proper escrow systems and wallet security, your online purchases can be completely secure. You don't have to trust the merchant, a bank or a credit card company. If the merchant loses hundreds of millions of customer records as Target did in 2013,[17] it won't affect Bitcoin users, who wouldn't have given Target information the hackers could use in the first place.

The downsides of Bitcoin security, like the cumbersome process of securing large amounts of Bitcoin, temper these advantages somewhat, but as more services are built, things will become easier.

In short, Bitcoin is exactly what it has been billed as: online cash. It can be a powerful tool for criminals as well as a powerful tool for those who don't want to trust their financial privacy to companies such as Target and Apple.

---

[17] Wallace, Gregory. "Target Credit Card Hack: What You Need to Know." CNNMoney. December 23, 2013. http://money.cnn.com/2013/12/22/news/companies/target-credit-card-hack/.

Chapter 8:

Mt. Gox: Bitcoin's Defining Moment?

Magic: The Gathering Online Exchange is a systemic risk to Bitcoin, a death trap for traders, and a business run by the clueless.

—Andreas Antonopoulos, BitcoinTalk forum, April 2013

Originally, I was going to dedicate this chapter to a number of high-profile Bitcoin scams but I quickly realized that glossing over the Mt. Gox fiasco would be a disservice to the reader. Mt. Gox was more than a simple theft; it was a pivotal moment in Bitcoin history. Arguably, it was the most important event so far, negative or positive, for the still-young currency. There is no doubt that it was the most publicly visible event in Bitcoin history, a factor that has an importance all of its own.

The most positive thing that can be said about the Mt. Gox fiasco—and it was exactly that, a fiasco—is that it did not kill Bitcoin. Despite the many pronouncements and predictions to the contrary, Bitcoin has gone on to further acceptance, legitimacy and funding, even though its price remains deflated compared to its peak before the collapse. This persistence shows not only the resilience of the currency but also the faith that a number of wealthy and powerful people are putting into Bitcoin.

The Tokyo-based Mt. Gox was the world's largest Bitcoin exchange until, after months of technical issues, the exchange admitted that it had lost the majority of its customers' bitcoins as well as a few hundred thousand of its own bitcoins. The total loss was 850,000 bitcoins, a number that at the time was worth around $480 million. Before and during its failure, the Mt. Gox exchange was run by Mark Karpelès, who had purchased it from Jeb McCaleb. Karpelès had a history of financial and tech crimes. He never hid those facts and even talked about them on his public blog but at the time his background remained largely unnoticed.

On February 28, 2014, looking more contrite than he had in his entire public life, the embattled CEO of the one-time largest Bitcoin exchange in the world sat in front of the Tokyo District court and tried to explain how he lost $480 million-worth of a currency most people in the world had never even heard of. Mark Karpelès's company was declaring bankruptcy and, knowingly or not, closing a chapter in Bitcoin's history.[1] Karpelès, who, evoking the genius tech gurus of the mid-2000s, had famously worn a t-shirt and jeans to nearly every public appearance, was finally wearing a suit. This change in appearance might seem like a small thing, but it personified the end not only of Mt. Gox but also of Karpelès's—and in many ways, the Bitcoin

---

[1] McMillan, Robert. "The Inside Story of Mt. Gox, Bitcoin's $460 Million Disaster." Wired.com. Conde Nast Digital, March 3, 2014. Accessed May 19, 2015. http://www.wired.com/2014/03/bitcoin-exchange/.

community's—arrogance. He would never again be able to present himself as a successful tech entrepreneur. Although Karpelès has attempted to lift his head from the sea of obscurity a few times since the fall of Mt. Gox, he is consistently shouted down by a chorus of hate.

It is a merciful end, to tell the truth, even if the case still lacks the satisfaction of justice and retribution. Since 2012, intermittent complaints had been popping up about slow withdrawals from Mt. Gox. They culminated in February 2014, when the site finally went down. Withdrawals officially halted on February 7,[2] but they had already dwindled to a trickle and virtually ceased as far back as mid-January. As it turned out, Mt. Gox was insolvent long before it officially halted withdrawals. It now appears that a slow theft took place over the course of a year and was made possible because of lax security practices that Mt. Gox was either unable or unwilling to fix.

Yet for all the problems that Mt. Gox caused Bitcoin by the end of its life, the exchange was essential to Bitcoin's early development. When Mt. Gox transitioned from a site designed to trade digital Magic: The Gathering cards to trading Bitcoin, it was instrumental in developing a market and price for Bitcoin. Previous to Mt. Gox, most Bitcoin trades took place off market. Two people would meet, usually online, and one of them would say something like, "I'll give you 500 bitcoins for two dollars," and the other participant would say that was either too high or too low—and they would negotiate from there. With a central exchange like Mt. Gox, an opportunity for real price discovery

---

[2] Southurst, Jon. "Mt. Gox Halts ALL Bitcoin Withdrawals, Price Drop Follows - CoinDesk." CoinDesk.com. February 7, 2014. Accessed May 18, 2015. http://www.coindesk.com/mt-gox-halts-bitcoin-withdrawals-price-drop/.

and liquid markets emerged. Rather than two people trying to figure out what a bitcoin was worth to them, they could simply see what other people were willing to pay for one and what had been paid for one in the past. This allowed bitcoins to obtain a real price point and a real value.

That said, the warning signs that something was wrong at Mt. Gox were everywhere. The biggest lesson one can learn from the incident is that warning signs should not be ignored.

Bitcoin is considered a volatile currency and compared to most fiat currencies, it is. But it is far more stable now than it was in 2011 when Bitcoin's price could jump from $1 to $30 in less than a week. At that time, it was transitioning from an obscure and mostly worthless currency to something covered by every media outlet with a technology department. It had arguably become the most successful new currency since the euro and was certainly the most visible. This increase in value and public attention should have corresponded with an increase in security at Mt. Gox but it did not. In June 2011, thousands of bitcoins went missing. A lot of blame was passed around and it was eventually discovered that the loss was the result of the former owner's account being hacked. The user controlling that account artificially created bitcoins in the Mt. Gox system and dumped them onto the market, driving the price to less than a dollar. He then bought back the now-cheap coins and withdrew them from the Mt. Gox system. The estimates on the number of lost bitcoins ultimately settled around 2,500. Although about 500,000 bitcoins had been "sold" on the exchange, Mt. Gox reversed the transactions so only a few thousand of the bitcoins were left unrecovered.

Mt. Gox was able to move on despite this hack. It was still the world's largest Bitcoin exchange with a strong position in an exploding market. Instead of turning things around and paying closer attention to security, Mt. Gox would go on to inadvertently burn thousands of bitcoins by accidentally sending them to Bitcoin addresses that didn't exist, essentially taking them out of the Bitcoin ecosystem forever.

Thanks to the security blog WizSec, we have since discovered that Mt. Gox was slowly leaking bitcoins throughout 2011 and 2012, and that by the end of 2012 it was virtually insolvent.

No one knows for sure who stole the Mt. Gox bitcoins. There are several theories, each of which seems to have a reasonably large stack of supporting evidence.

The explanation put forth by Mt. Gox and Mark Karpelès is a recurring one in the world of Bitcoin: a hacker got access to the Mt. Gox wallets and managed to steal hundreds of thousands of bitcoins over a long period of time. The Mt. Gox team had simply failed to notice the theft. This explanation actually makes a lot of sense, because it involves all the human dynamics needed for such a heist to be successful. There was a group of people resting on a large sum of money, confident in their place but incompetent in their task. That is a completely understandable situation if you assume Karpelès and company were caught off guard by the sudden increase in the value of and attention to Bitcoin. There are also the limitless skills and treachery of the shadowy and anonymous hacker, a caricature that has been a constant in nearly every media portrayal of Internet crime since the very concept of Internet crime entered the public imagination. This hacker is a cliché but one grounded in truth. There really are shadowy, anonymous hackers with near-limitless talents who make a career out of doing the kinds of things we end up reading about in the news. These people aren't unique to Bitcoin. Just ask Target.

The second theory is possibly the most popular, likely because Karpelès is so easy to hate. This theory is a simple one: Karpelès is scamming everyone. Proponents of this idea insist that Karpelès stole from his own company and is simply waiting for the legal process and public scrutiny to pass. Once this happens, he will take the hundreds of thousands of bitcoins that he has secret control over and cash out in some anonymous way. For this theory to be accurate, Karpelès has to be both extremely daring and extremely stupid. When you lose hundreds of millions of dollars in Bitcoin, public scrutiny isn't simply going to pass. Karpelès's life is in danger and the Internet has an infinite memory. Yet no one ever said that Karpelès isn't daring and stupid. The suspicious timing of the start of the Bitcoin leak, which started immediately after the completion of a proof-of-solvency test—an audit where a third party confirms a company has the funds they say they do—adds credence to the theory, as do the actions of the so-called Willy and Markus bots I will discuss in a few pages.

Another theory seems more plausible but lacks a concrete perpetrator. It is likely that other Mt. Gox employees had access to the inner security workings of the exchange and any of them could have siphoned the coins. Employee involvement would explain why Mt. Gox didn't notice anything for nearly a year. With no obvious suspects other than Karpelès himself, this explanation is ultimately unsatisfying. Finally, a lower-profile employee would certainly find it easier to sneak away unnoticed than Karpelès, the CEO.

The last theory is the latest to appear and involves the same two government officials we met in the previous chapter. As you'll recall, in 2015, DEA agent Carl Mark Force IV and Secret Service agent Shaun Bridges were involved in the Silk Road investigation before being arrested for allegedly committing several crimes as the investigation took place, including the theft of hundreds of thousands of bitcoins from the Deep Web marketplace.[3] According to prosecutors, Force had contact with Mark Karpelès during the investigation. According to emails found in court documents, Karpelès had reached out to authorities expressing his interest in helping them investigate bitcoins coming in to the exchange from illegal sources.

Instead, Force allegedly pressured the Mt. Gox CEO into doing business with him. After Karpelès refused, the government seemingly coincidentally seized two million of Mt. Gox's fiat reserves. Force allegedly sent Karpelès the message, "Told you should have partnered with me!" shortly after the seizure. Although there is currently no publicly available evidence that either Force or Bridges was directly involved with the Mt. Gox theft, the apparent corruption of the two officers has led to speculation that they were involved in some way. The two agents also allegedly revealed to members of the Dark Web marketplace that Karpelès was cooperating with them, lending credence to the theory that it was a hacker—possibly one working in conjunction with a Mt. Gox employee, since Karpelès was making some powerful enemies in the Internet underground.

Assigning blame in the Mt. Gox case is not something that can be done in this book. The case is nearing the JFK-assassination level of conspiracy and complexity. Several books could easily be written about what happened, what is alleged to have happened,

---

[3] Popper, Nathaniel. "Goldman and IDG Put $50 Million to Work in a Bitcoin Company." *The New York Times*. April 29, 2015. Accessed May 19, 2015. http://www.nytimes.com/2015/04/30/business/dealbook/goldman-and-idg-put-50-million-to-work-in-a-bitcoin-company.html?_r=0.

and what might have happened. When the trials are completed and investigators reveal everything they know, I suspect those books will appear. In the meantime, I will leave the determination of guilt to the investigators who are heavily involved in the case.

Some information, however, can be gleaned from the investigation of WizSec, an online security researcher. Bitcoin began leaking out of the Mt. Gox hot wallets in 2011; this process continued until 2012. Those coins were sent to temporary addresses before being sent to a larger gathering address and then to exchanges for either mixing or sale. Some of the coins were even deposited back into Mt. Gox itself.[4]

A different exchange, Kraken, was awarded arbiter status in the Mt. Gox case. That means it had control of the remaining funds and would be working with the authorities on how they should be distributed. Kraken has not been completely forthcoming with details and records for independent investigators, which is not unusual and might even be a legal requirement. It is also unclear how thorough the Mt. Gox records were. Nevertheless, through extensive blockchain analysis, information present in the Mt. Gox database leak and the proof-of-solvency completed by Mt. Gox in 2011, WizSec was able to track the likely holdings of Mt. Gox from that time until its failure in early 2014.

How, exactly, did someone drain some of the largest wallets of a completely traceable currency without anyone noticing? Reports indicate that Mt. Gox didn't continuously monitor its cold storage wallets (*i.e.*, Bitcoin wallets that aren't connected to

---

[4] Nilsson, Kim, Daniel Kelman, and J. Maurice. "WizSec: The Missing Mt. Gox Bitcoins." WizSec.jp. N.p., April 19, 2015. Accessed May 19, 2015. http://blog.wizsec.jp/2015/04/the-missing-Mt. Gox-bitcoins.html.

the Internet and are therefore theoretically safe from theft) but would use them to periodically refill its hot wallets when they ran low, due to normal variance in daily trading.

WizSec explained on his website how this situation could lead to a slow draining of wallets that could go unnoticed by Mt. Gox's internal security:

> One possibility is that without any monitoring of the storage or comparing incoming and outgoing amounts, Mt. Gox staff may have blindly kept pouring their cold storage into their leaking hot wallet, assuming that they were just dealing with frequent swings in deposits/withdrawals and that on average the cold storage was being refilled at roughly the same rate they were draining it.

In any case, Mt. Gox had less Bitcoin than its customers believed it held. By 2012, its reserves were depleted and things only got worse from there.

In 2013, a string of strange trades caused some to suspect there was an unusual amount of bot trading at Mt. Gox. Bots are scripts that buy and sell Bitcoin on the various exchanges. Although bot trading is common in Bitcoin trading today, the activity of these bots was curious. Trading bots normally act out the desires of their owners: buy if Bitcoin hits one price, sell if it hits another. It is actually a bit more complex than this, with bots able to make decisions within parameters in order to buy and sell continuously throughout the day. The point is bots don't act much differently than a rational day trader would if that day trader could stay awake for 24 hours a day. These bots weren't acting like rational day traders. They were instantly buying up groups of bitcoins at seemingly random prices. It is now suspected, though not confirmed, that this was done to ease the effects of operating with a fractional reserve, in which there is less money in the system than customers own. One bot's activity in particular was so bizarre it gained a nickname: the Willy bot.

The evidence of inside involvement in this unusual bot activity comes from transaction details that were leaked in late 2013. The accounts linked to suspicious bot behavior only acted one at a time. They would appear, purchase about $2.5 million worth of bitcoins, and then never act again. These accounts were responsible for $112 million in trades. The bots never sold any of the 270,000BTC they purchased.

This trading activity wasn't the bots' only suspicious characteristic. The first known Willy bot account had a user ID number that was higher than the current level of regular customer IDs, suggesting that it was created outside of the normal user account creation system. This led some to dig deeper, which brought about the discovery of a precursor bot—dubbed Markus by its discoverer—that also had a higher-than-normal user ID number and was behaving similarly.

The Markus bot had operated without paying any transaction fees to Mt. Gox. In addition to having Japan listed as its region, the bot had a Tokyo IP address like Mt. Gox, though the IP address could have easily been faked. Strangest of all, however, was that the bot seemed to have made large purchases at a static price rather than a variable price based on the current sale offers for Bitcoin. This detail led to fairly grounded speculation that the pre-Willy bots—and possibly the Willy bot itself—weren't actually buying any bitcoins at all.

The bot activity has nothing to do with the theft itself. WizSec has all but proven that the missing Mt. Gox coins were already missing by the time the bots came onto the scene. What it does seem to indicate, however, is that someone at Mt. Gox might have been trying to cover something up as early as 2012.

As I mentioned above, the Markus bot had an unusually high user ID number: 698630. In the 2014 leak, there were two versions of the April 2013 transaction log: a condensed but provably unmodified version with usernames taken out, and a regular version that included usernames and could have been modified. In the former version, Markus can still be identified by comparing its transactions to the transactions in the latter version that includes usernames. The bot's unusual purchase prices appeared modified to fall in line with what one would expect, and its high ID number was changed to 634. In the leak that occurred in 2011, there was a user with the customer ID 634. It belonged to "MagicalTux"—the same username that Mark Karpelès used on BitcoinTalk, his blog, and Twitter.

After the Markus bot had apparently ceased trading, the Willy bot continued, at times making up 90 percent of the total trading volume in an hour.[5] It should be noted, however, that no definitive link, other than patterns in trading behavior, was ever established between the Markus bot and the Willy bot.

Things soon went from bad to worse. Already seemingly covering up losses with bot trading activity, Mt. Gox had its Wells Fargo and Dwolla (a PayPal-like service) accounts seized by the US government, subtracting a few more million in fiat from its

---

[5] Nilsson, Kim. "WizSec: Mt. Gox Investigation Update and Preliminary Release." WizSec.jp. February 14, 2015. Accessed May 19, 2015. http://blog.wizsec.jp/2015/02/Mt.Gox-investigation-release.html.

reserves. This seizure led to the first instance of officially halted withdrawals. They would eventually resume, though with sporadic interruptions.

For a short time in late 2013 and 2014, Mt. Gox attempted to blame its issues on a known flaw in the Bitcoin protocol: the transaction malleability exploit. It works as follows. A malicious actor, playing the part of a miner or a full node, would submit false versions of other users' transactions with a different destination ID. The system should be able to prevent this by checking the transaction ID's hash and the sender's signature, but it neglected to do this in an older version of Bitcoin. If a malicious actor can change the user ID and get the modified version of the transaction confirmed on the blockchain before the legitimate one does, then that malicious actor has gained the ability to interrupt and redirect Bitcoin transactions.

Although the transaction malleability bug was a real issue, it was never exploited to the degree that it could account for even a fraction of the bitcoins lost during the Mt. Gox collapse. The numbers simply don't add up. A paper published on arXiv. org completely discredited the official excuse that the transaction malleability bug had caused Mt. Gox's financial woes.[6] The paper concluded that only 386 bitcoins in the entire Bitcoin ecosystem were involved in possibly successful transaction malleability exploit attempts before Mt. Gox prevented user withdrawals. There is no possible way that it could have contributed significantly to the failure of Mt. Gox.

---

[6] Decker, Christian, and Roger Wattenhofer. "Bitcoin Transaction Malleability and Mt. Gox." Computer Security - ESORICS 2014 Lecture Notes in Computer Science (2014): 313-26. ArXiv.org. March 26, 2014. Accessed May 18, 2015. http://arxiv.org/abs/1403.6676.

As accusations mounted and more customers expressed their dissatisfaction, Karpelès eventually stepped down from the Bitcoin Foundation,[7] much later than many felt he should have. The start of 2014 was turbulent with more users complaining about withdrawal issues on a daily basis. By February, most people assumed no more money, fiat or Bitcoin, was coming out of Mt. Gox. One American flew to Japan from Indiana to personally ask Karpelès for his money back. It was perhaps the first Bitcoin-related act of political theater that took place outside of the Internet.[8]

We can now return to the last day of February 2014 and to the defeated and dejected Karpelès sitting in that suit in front of the Japanese District Court and filing for bankruptcy. Mt. Gox would be shut down and there would be no redemption story for it or its CEO. The man who reportedly forced his employees to call him "the king" had lost his kingdom. The dream was over and Karpelès looked as if he knew it. If Karpelès were the perpetrator of the theft, he didn't look as if he expected to end up there.

Mt. Gox's final breath caused a huge ripple effect that broke into the mainstream consciousness and shaped many people's perceptions of Bitcoin. Those perceptions continue to color Bitcoin's reputation today.

The Weekly Standard published an article with the title "Bitcoin is Dead."[9] *Salon* wrote about how the Mt. Gox hack—along with

---

[7] Sidel, Robin. "Mt. Gox Resigns From Bitcoin Foundation." *The Wall Street Journal.* February 24, 2014. Accessed May 19, 2015. http://www.wsj.com/articles/SB10001424052702303426304579401883794330454.

[8] Southurst, Jon. "Watch This Man Confront CEO of Mt. Gox Over Missing Bitcoins." CoinDesk.com. February 14, 2014. Accessed May 19, 2015. http://www.coindesk.com/watch-man-confront-ceo-mt-gox-missing-bitcoins/.

[9] Last, Jonathan V. "Bitcoin Is Dead." *The Weekly Standard.* weeklystandard.com. March 5, 2014. Accessed May 19, 2015. http://www.weeklystandard.com/bitcoin-is-dead/article/784187.

the (likely bogus) "doxxing" (*i.e.*, exposure) of a California man as Satoshi Nakamoto—spelled the currency's doom.[10] Everyone from Reuters[11] to Yahoo[12] seemed to be anticipating Bitcoin's demise. A few saw a silver lining[13] but most thought it was the end. Senator Joe Manchin of West Virginia called for an outright ban on Bitcoin.[14] Even the long-time Bitcoin blogger, security researcher, and cryptocurrency evangelist twobitidiot (real name Ryan Selkis) lamented "Bitcoin's Apocalyptic moment" upon learning the news.[15]

The concerns, it should be said, were valid. One could be forgiven for expecting the 2014 Mt. Gox collapse to be the end of the currency. A total of 3.5 percent of all the bitcoins that can ever exist disappeared in the Mt. Gox theft. It wasn't hard to imagine this was Bitcoin's end.

---

[10] Leonard, Andrew. "Sorry, Libertarians: Your Dream of a Bitcoin Paradise Is Officially Dead and Gone." Salon.com. March 7, 2014. Accessed May 19, 2015. http://www.salon.com/2014/03/07/sorry_libertarians_your_dream_of_a_bitcoin_paradise_is_officially_dead_and_gone/.

[11] Hadas, Edward. "An Early Obituary for Bitcoin." Reuters.com. January 8, 2014. Accessed May 19, 2015. http://blogs.reuters.com/edward-hadas/2014/01/08/an-early-obituary-for-bitcoin/.

[12] Lyster, Lauren. "Mt. Gox on Verge of Collapse, Bitcoin Plunges: Is This the End for the Virtual Currency?" Yahoo Finance. Daily Ticker, February 25, 2014. Accessed May 19, 2015. http://finance.yahoo.com/blogs/daily-ticker/bitcoin-mt--gox-deleted-141110461.html.

[13] Carson, Biz. "This Week in Bitcoin: Mt. Gox's Meltdown May Prove Bitcoin Is a Real Currency." *Gigaom.com*. Gigaom, 28 Feb. 2014. Web. 19 May 2015. http://finance.yahoo.com/blogs/daily-ticker/bitcoin-mt--gox-deleted-141110461.html.

[14] Fung, Brian. "Sen. Joe Manchin Calls for a Bitcoin Ban as Regulators Seek 'accelerated Push'." *The Washington Post*. February 26, 2014. Accessed May 19, 2015. https://www.washingtonpost.com/news/the-switch/wp/2014/02/26/sen-joe-manchin-calls-for-a-bitcoin-ban-as-regulators-seek-accelerated-push/.

[15] Selkis, Ryan. "Bitcoin's Apocalyptic Moment: Mt. Gox May Have Lost 750,000 Bitcoins." *TBI's Daily Bit*. Tumblr, February 24, 2014. Accessed May 19, 2015. http://twobit-idiot.tumblr.com/post/77745633839/bitcoins-apocalyptic-moment-mt-gox-may-have.

In mid-March 2014, 200,000 of the bitcoins owned by Mt. Gox were discovered in a long-forgotten wallet.[16] That gave some hope to the people looking for restitution but there is no hope of reviving Mt. Gox.

The legal process that followed the collapse of the exchange has been painfully slow, which is sure to cut into that 200,000BTC stash as expenses mount. The claims process for former Mt. Gox customers started more than a year after the collapse. No one seems to know when that claims process is going to be completed. In the meantime, cash is flowing out of the remaining funds to large investors and to pay Mark Karpelès's legal expenses. It seems unlikely that, with so many drains on the funds, there will be much left for actual Mt. Gox customers.

And yet Bitcoin didn't die. One could argue it was permanently maimed but it has managed to carry on. The Mt. Gox collapse served as a warning to the rest of the community, helping shape future developments in the Bitcoin infrastructure.

Bitcoin is a decentralized currency. Centralizing where the community holds those coins eliminates some of Bitcoin's advantages. Mt. Gox essentially functioned as a bank by holding on to everyone's currency, eliminating the decentralized aspect. Banks and their malfeasance are often cited as a driving force behind people's interest in Bitcoin. Unfortunately, unlike banks, Mt. Gox was free from regulations and lacked insurance. It incorporated all the negative aspects of banks with none of the oversight that has been applied to them over the decades. With such a large

---

[16] Lyne, James. "$116 Million Bitcoins 'Found' At Mt. Gox And How To Protect Your Wallet." *Forbes Magazine*. March 21, 2014. Accessed May 19, 2015. http://www. forbes.com/sites/jameslyne/2014/03/21/116-million-bitcoins-found-at-Mt.   Gox-and-how-to-protect-your-wallet/ - 1501b9419695.

number of bitcoins in one place, Mt. Gox became a huge target for malicious actors and acted as a central point of failure. Still, a centralized marketplace where people can buy and sell bitcoins is essential to price discovery and ultimately the entire Bitcoin ecosystem.

This conundrum led to various projects attempting to create a decentralized exchange. A few have been completed: BitHalo, Nxt's marketplace, and Blocknet are scheduled to be released or receive major upgrades by the time this book goes to print. If anyone will use them—or if they are released at all—remains to be seen.

A decentralized exchange would allow users to trade bitcoins for fiat without depending on a third party. As opposed to over-the-counter trades, a decentralized exchange could have an order book and a price that changes based on market demand. Although the concept of a decentralized exchange had existed before the Mt. Gox collapse, it was this event that instantly moved the idea to the top of nearly everyone's to-do list. Sadly, most Bitcoin trading today is still performed using centralized servers. No decentralized service has hit that sweet spot of usability, security, and privacy. Once it does, the issue of integrating this decentralized exchange with traditional financial systems will still exist.

Even more important than the push toward decentralization was the realization that Bitcoin's short childhood was over. Real money was being put into the system, and with real money come real criminals. Bitcoin had become a target, not of governments or banks but of the very people it appealed to. It is the technically inclined who stand as Bitcoin's biggest asset and its biggest threat. Bitcoin's value exists because of its utility and that utility is completely wrapped up in how secure it is. Regardless of how strong the base protocol of Bitcoin itself is, third parties can hurt its reputation. It only takes one hacker to seize a stash of bitcoins and ruin years of built-up trust and good will.

That said, the smart money continued to bet on Bitcoin even after the Mt. Gox fiasco. While the price was in a steady decline for the remainder of 2014 and the first three quarters of 2015, venture capitalist money funneled in as never before. The year 2014 was a record-breaking one for cryptocurrency investments[17] and as of this writing, 2015 was already on track to beat that record. More recently, financial giants Goldman Sachs,[18] USAA,[19] and NASDAQ[20] all announced they were jumping on the Bitcoin bandwagon and were exploring technologies based on the blockchain. The list of merchants that accept Bitcoin has also continued to grow and now includes Microsoft, PayPal's Braintree, Dell, DishNetwork, Expedia, Overstock.com, The American Red Cross, RE/MAX London, Save The Children, Edward Snowden's legal defense fund, and

---

[17] DeMartino, Ian M. "Smart Money Bets On Bitcoin: Top Three Investments In Bitcoin History Occurred In 2015." Coin Journal. May 1, 2015. Accessed May 19, 2015. http://coinjournal.net/smart-money-bets-on-bitcoin-top-three-investments-in-bitcoin-history-occurred-in-2015-op-ed/.

[18] Popper, Nathaniel. "Goldman and IDG Put $50 Million to Work in a Bitcoin Company." *The New York Times*. April 29, 2015. Accessed May 19, 2015. http://www.nytimes.com/2015/04/30/business/dealbook/goldman-and-idg-put-50-million-to-work-in-a-bitcoin-company.html.

[19] Rocham, M. "Financial Services Giant USAA to Study Use of Bitcoin Technology." *International Business Times*. May 9, 2015. Accessed May 19, 2015. http://www.ibtimes.co.uk/financial-services-giant-usaa-study-use-bitcoin-technology-1500514.

[20] Casey, Michael J. "Nasdaq to Provide Trading Technology for Bitcoin Marketplace—Update." NASDAQ OMX, March 23, 2015. Accessed May 19, 2015. http://www.advfn.com/nyse/StockNews.asp?stocknews=JPM&article=66023268.

countless others.[21,22] One Bitcoin exchange, Circle, is registered and compliant with the New York Department of Financial Services. During the 2016 US presidential race, Rand Paul, a major candidate for the Republican nomination, was accepting Bitcoin donations.

I don't pretend to know what the future of Bitcoin looks like. However, Mt. Gox was arguably the worst thing that could have happened to Bitcoin and it didn't kill the currency. Bitcoin has moved on and looks stronger now than it did in late 2013. That counts for something.

---

[21] Franzen, Carl. "Newegg Now Accepts Bitcoin." The Verge. Vox Media. July 1, 2014. Accessed May 19, 2015. http://www.theverge.com/2014/7/1/5860556/newegg-now-accepts-bitcoin.

[22] Chansanchai, Athima. "Now You Can Exchange Bitcoins to Buy Apps, Games and More for Windows, Windows Phone and Xbox." Microsoft. December 11, 2014. Accessed May 19, 2015. https://blogs.microsoft.com/firehose/2014/12/11/now-you-can-exchange-bitcoins-to-buy-apps-games-and-more-for-windows-windows-phone-and-xbox/.

Chapter 9:

Other Bitcoin Scams and Common Tactics

> You will never find a more wretched hive of scum and villainy.
> We must be cautious.

> —Obi-Wan (Ben) Kenobi, *Star Wars Episode IV: A New Hope*

If you want to invest in Bitcoin safely, there is a simple way to do it. Purchase Bitcoin on an exchange or through someone you know who has it, withdraw it to a local wallet, and print it out onto a paper wallet. You can then use the QR code on that wallet to add funds when you want to increase your investment. Every time you want to withdraw any of your bitcoins, you will have to withdraw all of them, and the wallet will no longer be as safe as an untouched paper wallet.

It isn't the most convenient way to hold your Bitcoin if you plan to spend or invest it in other ventures, but it is the safest way to invest in Bitcoin itself without getting scammed.

If you want to go a step further and invest in new technologies or companies, you will have to start wading into the cryptocurrency community. Once you do that, at least at the time of this writing, you are almost guaranteed to come across the worst elements of that community. As with all cultural and economic phenomena, Bitcoin has attracted all kinds of people. Criminals are certainly included in this mix, perhaps disproportionately when compared to the general population. And these criminals like to prey on people new to the scene.

Many major cultural phenomena seem to have this downside. We might compare the history of Bitcoin's emergence with that of the hippie movement. In 1967, several mainstream media outlets covered the growing acid wave in the Haight-Ashbury district of San Francisco; popular music of the time—such as Scott McKenzie's *San Francisco (Be Sure to Wear Flowers in Your Hair)*—advertised the lifestyle that was developing there. This public attention caused streams of disenfranchised youth to descend on the city looking for free lodging, free food, free drugs, and free love. But the economics of thousands of people wanting stuff for free and increasingly fewer people willing to give it to them simply didn't work out in the long run. Eventually, some of the older, more experienced residents of Haight-Ashbury began to prey on tourists visiting the district as well as new arrivals.

There are many theories as to why the hippie movement originating in Haight-Ashbury didn't survive, and I am not in a position to judge. What was clear to just about everyone who wrote about the movement, however, was that the massive influx of people put a stress on the community. It is safe to say that by 1969, someone trying to find a hippie in Haight-Ashbury was at least as likely to find someone masquerading as one with the intention of profiting off the movement's reputation.

There are a lot of parallels to be drawn between Bitcoin and Haight-Ashbury. When the price of Bitcoin exploded in 2011 and again in late 2013–early 2014, the currency attracted the attention of mainstream media outlets and through them, hundreds of thousands of semi- and wannabe technonerds desperate to catch the next wave of digital wealth. But there already were thousands of people in the Bitcoin economy and they had years of experience in a realm where experience was exceedingly rare.

Unlike the hippie movement of the late 1960s, which was based on rejection of money and material goods, the Bitcoin movement is all about money. Bitcoin is a currency, after all. Although the behavior of the Haight-Ashbury scammers was in opposition to the hippies' philosophy, the Bitcoin "movement" revolves around money, so it shouldn't surprise anyone that it has attracted those whom Hunter S. Thompson would call "the Greedheads."

Many of us were attracted—some might say lured—to Bitcoin by the eloquent words of people such as Andreas Antonopoulos and Roger Ver, two well-spoken Bitcoin evangelists, each of whom was at one point or another labeled a "Bitcoin Jesus." They promised a new economic system, one that would be less dependent on greed and thievery.

Instead, what one is currently likely to find in the cryptocurrency community is a sea of schemes and coin types that are doomed to failure for a variety of reasons. In some cases, their developers don't have the skill to compete in an increasingly competitive market. In others, the schemes are scams from the get-go. And sometimes they simply lack the security required to survive the technological onslaught that hits every major crypto-currency company at one point or another.

This chapter will not properly prepare you for every scam you will find in Bitcoin. Instead, it will give you a general overview of the biggest scams to hit the cryptocurrency market, so you can get an idea of what has happened before and hopefully gain some skill in recognizing the scams that are still going on today.

You can run into two types of scams in the Bitcoin community but depending on how deep you go, you might only ever see one of them. The first is a straightforward type of scam: a service, usually a casino or exchange, closes while people have their bit-coins deposited and the customers never see their funds again. In some cases, the event is due to a hack; in others, it's the creator who ran away. As Bitcoin's economy solidifies, these scams are becoming easier to avoid. The "safe" exchanges that have insur-ance and oversight are able to provide a relatively secure position for those who want to save and spend bitcoins. Although nothing is guaranteed in Bitcoin, these Mt. Gox-like events are becoming more rare; although popular multi-cryptocurrency exchanges still have controversies and issues, the Bitcoin-only exchanges—Circle, Coinbase, etc.—are relatively safe for small-to-medium Bitcoin holdings. Long-term savings should still, and will always be, better off in an offline wallet, but the era of pure Bitcoin exchanges collapsing every few months seems to have passed. These scams/events are still a risk in gray-market services—Bitcoin launderers, porn sites, casinos—as well as black-market services, but the average user is relatively safe.

The second kind of scam is a bit more complex and tougher to recognize. The important principle to keep in mind is that if it smells like a Ponzi scheme, it likely is. Bitcoin doesn't change that.

Companies will offer a service, often using "cloud mining" (*i.e.*, they will mine for you and you will "rent" the hardware from them) as a front, and will pay out money to users—supposedly from the mining profits, though often they actually come from new investors. More recently, as cloud mining has become less popular due in large part to the number of scams in the space, new scams have been born. Some scammers pretend to be Bitcoin day traders or to be launching a brand new exchange that is *sure* to become the best around. One of the most tried-and-true scams is to create a new currency and claim that it is poised to challenge Bitcoin. What you have to remember is that there are tons of companies already doing these things.

Since there are established exchanges that the vast majority of the community uses, a new exchange has a long, uphill battle before it becomes profitable.

Mining is easily verifiable on the blockchain. If the service can't present an address with enough coinbase inputs—*i.e.*, inputs designating the creation of new coins through mining— to be consistent with the amount of hashing power it claims to have, then it shouldn't be trusted. In my personal opinion, it is best to avoid cloud mining altogether. If it is something that can't be verified on the blockchain, you'll have to use common sense. Remember, just because something is a "Bitcoin business" doesn't mean it has any inherent advantages over any other business. As with any other business, it should have some kind of good online reputation. That reputation isn't the be-all, end-all, but it should tell you something about whether a company is worth dealing with.

If a company is claiming that it sells enough novelty "physical bitcoins"—or anything else—to pay returns to investors, then look for customer reviews with pictures. Check out the site's Alexa rating at Alexa.com and see if its traffic is consistent with that amount of business. Whois.com will allow you to look up who owns a website's domain name. If, instead of a real name and address, there is a service such as "WhoisGuard" or something similar, this is a sure sign the owner of the business doesn't want its customers to know who they are. With a business such as an online casino, that might be reasonable; in 99 percent of other cases it is not and the company should be avoided.

The most important thing to remember is that if it sounds like a scam, it probably is. Be wary of anyone who promises you instant or unrealistic returns on your investment. The basics of Ponzi schemes work in cryptocurrency just as well as in any other business. If older investors are being paid with the capital from new investments, you are dealing with a Ponzi scheme. People will claim all sorts of things to make it seem as if revenue is coming from elsewhere, so you have to do your own research and dig deep into anything at which you are going to throw any money.

The offenders listed below hail from all over the Bitcoin spectrum. Many had been considered pillars of the community before they went down. Mt. Gox's Mark Karpelès, who isn't on this list only because his case necessitated a whole chapter, once sat on the Bitcoin Foundation's Board of Directors. The current respect of the community is not a guarantee that a figure is reputable or trustworthy. There was a time that GAW Miners, a company I will talk about later, was considered a giant of the mining industry. As mentioned before, things are solidifying and companies that can be trusted are becoming more apparent, but scams are still commonplace.

Before I get into the detailed list, here are a few other pointers to keep in mind:

- If another company or person holds your private key, they essentially hold your bitcoins. Much of the appeal of Bitcoin is that no bank can lock down your money but if you give someone your private key, you essentially give them the ability to use it as they please.
- Pump-and-dumps happen all the time in the altcoin space. Every announcement by a coin's development team or community has to be taken with a grain of salt. Their motives are not always clear, and as the coin's creator, they likely hold a large number of coins themselves, so it is in their interest to inflate the price. If they can get an increase of even a few cents as a result of an exciting announcement of a feature (that might or might not ever be released), they stand to make a huge amount of money when they sell the coins after the price increase.

  Beyond that, there are groups out there—independent of coin developers—that will find an altcoin with a small enough volume that their group's total wealth can move the market by itself, simply by buying up relatively small amounts over time. These individuals, largely seen as shady by the rest of the community, will move a coin's price up, only to dump it at a predetermined time. To complicate things further, the individuals in the group depend on their leader to refrain from dumping his coins before the rest of them. It is not unheard of for groups to be accused of having an inner circle among their membership that gets the "real inside information."
- Large groupings of Bitcoin and other monies attract scammers and hackers. Exchanges become targets for hackers and

even the most well-meaning companies can have a hard time recovering from a hack that cost them something in the six- or seven-figure range.

- Diversification is key. If you hold all of your coins on one exchange and it gets hacked, you will lose your entire holdings. If you keep them spread among several exchanges, you will not lose more than a portion. If there is a rallying cry behind the Bitcoin movement, it would be the idea of decentralization. There is no reason for your bitcoins to be centralized. The same goes for offline and paper wallets as well. Even if a wallet is secure, you shouldn't hold everything in it. If you insist on keeping everything in paper wallets, make sure you don't keep all of them in the same place. Physical robbery and potential damage are still a risk.

- Altcoins are a shitshow. That is not to say that they are all scams or that even a majority of them are. It is just that there are far too many for the market to support. At least 95 percent of even the good altcoins will fail. A few from the current crop will make it to the next stage of cryptocurrency history, but most will die on the vine. Being a developer for a dying coin is a scary reality, especially if you were a well-meaning developer with dreams of changing the world using your technology. Realizing after years of hard work and dedication that it was all for nothing might lead one to become desperate. And desperate people do desperate things, like compromise their ethics.

- There are a lot of scammers in the Bitcoin space and they are technically talented. Not everyone is the really good hacker they like to portray themselves as—more on this later—but enough of them are that it is safer to assume you are encountering them all the time. As a result, always be vigilant in your security practices. If you have any significant amount of money in an online wallet, then two-factor authentication (*i.e.*, authentication with a pair of elements such as a password and a special one-time use code) is a must.

- Scams that work on the Internet in general have been carried over to cryptocurrencies as well, sometimes with a bit more sophistication. Phishing scams are common and the thieves have proven capable of spoofing legitimate Bitcoin companies' email addresses. You can expect phishing attempts to continue. Use common sense, never follow links to accounts and then log in, and don't believe any "double your bitcoins here!" emails. There isn't a Nigerian prince on the other end and there isn't a pot of gold at the end of that rainbow.

Scams and hacks are different. A scam is a service that steals from its customers, either because that was the original plan or because the owner decided to do it subsequently to cover losses or for other reasons. Hacks are bitcoin thefts by an outside source that occurred due to a security lapse. Most scams claim that the loss was actually a hack, as was the case in two of the cases below.

MintPal

MintPal was a cryptocurrency exchange with a large number of supported currencies and a professional look. Unfortunately, looks can be deceiving.

The MintPal scandal is as convoluted as any other scam in cryptocurrency history, including the Mt. Gox failure. Almost tailor-made for the big screen, it involves fake identities, corporate takeovers, and a cliffhanger.

MintPal's problems began with what appears to have been a legitimate hack in July 2014. The hack primarily involved the loss of eight million VeriCoins. VeriCoin uses a proof-of-stake algorithm to confirm transactions. Proof-of-stake algorithms give weight to those who have significant holdings of the cryptocurrency, resulting in a somewhat stable interest rate—typically anywhere between one and five percent, depending on the coin. Unlike proof-of-work coins such as Bitcoin, which depend on hashing rates, proof-of-stake coins depend on accounts running a full node and confirming transactions in a process called staking.

If one actor gains 51 percent of the total coins staking at any one time, then they could overrule any other stakers and double-spend their coins. (Stakers are proof-of-stake coins' version of Bitcoin's miners. See the proof-of-stake definition in the keyword guide for a more detailed explanation.) The amount of VeriCoin stolen represented around 30 percent of the total VeriCoin supply and since most users don't bother to stake their coins, the stolen coins would, if staked, have easily overwhelmed the network.

This ultimately resulted in VeriCoin creating a hard fork and modifying the blockchain,[1] one of the most controversial and difficult things that can be done in the cryptocurrency community.

---

[1] Higgins, Stan. "8 Million VeriCoin Hack Prompts Hard Fork to Recover Funds." CoinDesk. July 14, 2014. Accessed June 22, 2015. http://www.coindesk.com/bitcoin-protected-VeriCoin-stolen-MintPal-wallet-breach/.

The blockchain is supposed to be infallible; it is revered like a religious text, since it is the indisputable account of the coin's history. Changing it, cryptocurrency advocates will often say, is impossible.

But it is possible, and VeriCoin proved that. It simply requires more than 50 percent of participants to agree to the change. If more people are mining the modified blockchain than the original blockchain, the new chain becomes the legitimate one. Everyone was aware of that, but many dismissed the possibility that a community could agree to it. The MintPal hack forced the VeriCoin community to make a difficult decision. They rewrote their coin's history because if they didn't, there would have been no future. Not only would a huge number of its users have lost their holdings, but also confidence in the coin would have vanished because one unknown scammer would have had complete, even if only theoretical, control over the network.

But the collateral damage done to VeriCoin in the MintPal hack is only a footnote in the prologue of the MintPal scam. After the hack, Alex Green, the CEO of a company called Moolah, appeared to come to the rescue of the suddenly troubled exchange. The company bought only 30 percent of MintPal and was given control of it. Green, whose real name was later revealed to be Ryan Kennedy, portrayed himself as a security expert and promised to overhaul the exchange and make it more secure.

When the site relaunched, it was plagued with problems and many users were unable to log in to access their funds. Eventually, the funds in the hot wallet were moved to an account allegedly controlled by Kennedy. Kennedy resigned from Moolah and revealed his true identity before disappearing.

He eventually resurfaced, having been arrested by UK authorities along with his partner Chelsea Hopkins. They were released on bail and the trial is still pending as of this writing.[2]

One significant lesson to learn from the MintPal failure is that appearances aren't indicative of legitimacy. Of the mainstream multi-cryptocurrency exchanges, MintPal had one of the prettier website layouts. I remember at one point commenting to a friend that MintPal had, in my opinion, the most "legitimate" look but those looks ended up being deceiving. The point is that you have to look deeper than just a website layout to judge the security capabilities of an exchange. Had people looked deeper into the identity of "Alex Green," a lot of people could have saved a lot of money.

The Sheep Marketplace

The Sheep Marketplace was built as a successor to the Silk Road after federal authorities shut that site down. The Silk Road 2 had also recently shut down, with its owners making off with the bitcoins held in that system.

Many suspected that the Sheep Marketplace would follow the same pattern and their fears turned out to be correct. Withdrawals at the Sheep Marketplace stopped working and the leader of the site fingered an individual user as the perpetrator of the scam. Evidence to the contrary surfaced and the site quickly shut down. Most blame the owner as the perpetrator of the scam.

---

[2] Riley, Duncan. "MintPal Scammer Ryan Kennedy Arrested in U.K. over Theft of 3,700 Bitcoins." SiliconANGLE. February 23, 2015. Accessed June 22, 2015. http://siliconangle.com/blog/2015/02/23/MintPal-scammer-ryan-kennedy-arrested-in-u-k-over-theft-of-3700-bitcoins/.

Reports eventually surfaced, by way of Czech news sites, that the alleged former owner of the Sheep Marketplace, Thomas Jiřikovský, had been arrested not on drug and organized crime charges as Silk Road administrator Ross Ulbricht was, but rather on money-laundering charges after buying a luxury home and putting the rest of the stolen bitcoins into his girlfriend's bank account by way of shell companies he set up.

Those reports were never confirmed and former users of the Sheep Marketplace have little-to-no hope of recovering their lost funds, considering the nature of their business on the site.[3] The lesson that can be learned here should be obvious: if you are doing something outside of the law with your bitcoins, then there is little recourse for you when things go wrong.

Paycoin/GAW

Paycoin is a cryptocurrency created by former mining company GAW Miners. GAW Miners and its sister company, ZEN Miners, were owned by a man named Homero Joshua Garza, who went by Josh Garza. Garza had gotten into cryptocurrency after running a broadband Internet company that was accused of ripping off its customers before abandoning them; it is currently under investigation.[4]

---

[3] "Breaking: Sheep Marketplace Owner Arrested." Deep Dot Web. March 27, 2015. Accessed June 22, 2015. https://www.deepdotweb.com/2015/03/27/breaking-sheep-marketplace-owner-arrested/.

[4] Mansfield, Erin. "SEC Investigates Vt. Broadband Company Founder." VTDigger. July 8, 2015. Accessed January 11, 2016. http://vtdigger.org/2015/07/08/sec-investigates-vermont-internet-service-company-founder/.

GAW Miners originally sold mining hardware. Initially, it was seemingly successful. Along with Butterfly Labs and KnCMiner, it was once considered part of the "Big Three" of the mining market. At some point, complaints about late shipments and accusations of used hardware began to surface, but that wasn't out of the norm for Bitcoin-mining companies at the time, with both KnCMiner and especially Butterfly Labs facing similar accusations and issues.[5,6]

GAW Miners eventually transitioned to a cloud-mining company with some features that were admittedly innovative at the time. Customers could buy hashing power and have it represented by an internal digital currency known at the time as hashpoints. Hashpoints, in addition to producing Bitcoin for its users—each hashpoint was supposed to represent mining power—could be bought and sold to other customers. If Bitcoin mining became more profitable, the hashes would as well. They represented an easy way for people to get into mining without the risk of long cloud-mining contracts. For a while, buying hashpoints on GAW's market was theoretically the cheapest way of buying mining power on the Bitcoin network. When the Securities and Exchange Commission (SEC) filed its complaint against GAW Miners and Garza, it alleged that GAW massively oversold its hashpoints and didn't have anything close to enough hardware

---

[5] Maina, John Weru. "FTC Shuts Down Butterfly Labs... Finally." CCN Financial Bitcoin News. September 23, 2014. Accessed June 22, 2015. https://www.cryptocoins-news.com/ftc-shuts-down-butterfly-labs-finally/.

[6] Gillis, Rick Mac. "Timeline of KncMiner's Struggle With the 20nm ASIC Bitcoin Miners." CCN Financial Bitcoin News. July 22, 2014. Accessed June 22, 2015. https://www.cryp-tocoinsnews.com/ccn-reveals-timeline-kncminers-struggle-20nm-asic-bitcoin-miners/.

to mine the bitcoins they were claiming to mine. The majority of mining payments, according to the SEC, were paid out with new investor money.[7]

Although many media outlets, particularly cryptocurrency-focused ones, did an adequate job reporting on GAW after the initial sale of Paycoin in December 2014, much of the initial investigation was done by users of BitcoinTalk, the most popular Bitcoin message board. The general thread, started by a user named suchmoon, will be cited, but the individual contributions can't be. It is simply too disorganized to be properly referenced, and some members would not welcome the attention. That said, their contributions were invaluable.[8]

Things weren't exactly how they appeared at GAW, and payments began to slow. It was eventually announced that hashpoints would stop mining and users would be able to turn them into a brand new cryptocurrency that, GAW promised, would be revolutionary. This has been a tactic commonly used by scammers for decades: once one scam starts to run its course, the next usually follows.

After running through a few candidates, the company and community eventually settled on the name Paycoin and the arguably largest altcoin-run scam to date was kicked off.

Although leaked emails obtained through an SEC investigation all but confirm the accusations below, for legal purposes it

---

[7] "SEC Charges Bitcoin Mining Companies." SEC.gov. Securities and Exchange Commission. December 1, 2015. Accessed January 11, 2016. http://www.sec.gov/news/pressrelease/2015-271.html

[8] Suchmoon, Miaviator, and More "GAW / Josh Garza Discussion Paycoin XPY Btc.com Bitcoinist. ALWAYS MAKE MONEY :)." Bitcointalk Post. November 14, 2014. GAW / Josh Garza Discussion Paycoin XPY CPIG BTCLend Xpyerr.ALWAYS MAKE MONEY :). Accessed June 22, 2015. https://bitcointalk.org/index.php?topic=857670.msg11401660%3Btopicseen#msg11401660.

should be pointed out that Homero Joshua Garza has not yet been convicted of a crime. But in light of the seemingly endless list of improprieties and lies, for the sake of readability, I want to get it out of the way now: the court of law hasn't confirmed the accusations below; although the evidence is overwhelming, it remains, from a legal perspective, alleged.

Paycoin's early site made a lot of promises. Paycoin supposedly had some very serious investors. It promised significant merchant support and included Amazon's, Target's, and other major merchants' logos, seeming to imply that these merchants would accept Paycoin for payment. Paycoin users, the site alleged, would be able to pay their bills using Paycoin.[9]

More important than all of that, at least for investors, was the promised $20 price floor. Paycoin's price, once launched, would never go below $20, stated GAW. To support this, a $100,000,000 "Community Action Fund" was supposedly created and it would be used to drive adoption, development, and pump the price whenever it fell below $20.

Paycoin was originally offered to "early adopters" at the price of four dollars a coin. As the December 2014 launch approached, this rose periodically, eventually reaching $12 a coin. $12 a coin is still significantly lower than $20, so investors who bought the story still believed there was significant and nearly risk-free money to be made. Early hashtalk.org posts about Paycoin included excited proclamations about how Josh Garza had saved their Christmas.

GAW launched a site called Paybase. It was meant to be the primary method of purchasing Paycoins and would be a site

[9] "Paycoin Is Here | Paycoin Digital Currency." Paycoin Is Here | GAWMiners, Republished by Archive.org. May 17, 2014. Accessed June 22, 2015. https://archive.is/0HEwd. http://paycoins.biz/paycoin/

customers could use to pay their bills and take advantage of
Paycoin's other alleged features. It was also where customers were supposed to be able to redeem their coins at $20
apiece. Although GAW had no control over the price of coins
at other exchanges such as Bittrex, it could promise to pay
$20 at Paybase. This, of course, was only tenable if the price
at exchanges such as Bittrex stayed at or above $20, or close
enough that the arbitrage opportunity was negligible (*e.g.*,
$19.95). Unless natural demand kept the price high enough,
GAW would have had to support the price on every exchange
that traded Paycoin. People could buy Paycoin on Bittrex and
then sell to GAW on Paybase, then use that money to buy more
Paycoin, completing a never-ending cycle until the price rose
to $20 or GAW ran out of money. This, ostensibly, is what the
$100,000,000 Community Action Fund was to be used for.
True believers thought that the price would stay above $20 nat-
urally, as feature after feature was released and merchant after
merchant got on board. It later became obvious that the fund
never existed, the features weren't coming, and the promised
merchants had no connection to Paycoin.

Giving Garza and GAW the benefit of the doubt and saying,
hypothetically for the moment, that they had every intention of
making this plan work and that it wasn't just a way to build
hype and fleece millions, there was an issue with the plan, even if
everything went off without a hitch.

GAW was heavily advertising Paycoin at $4, $8, and $12. It
placed an article in *The Wall Street Journal*'s MoneyBeat blog.[10]

---

[10] Casey, Michael J. "BitBeat: GAW Miners to Launch Bitcoin Challenger, Paycoin."
MoneyBeat RSS. November 25, 2014. Accessed June 22, 2015. http://blogs.wsj.com/
moneybeat/2014/11/25/bitbeat-gaw-miners-to-launch-bitcoin-challenger-paycoin/.

It had paid for advertising on every major cryptocurrency media outlet on the web and was sponsoring a major convention. Everyone who would have possibly had an interest in Paycoin early on had already heard about it and had an opportunity to buy Paycoin at those lower prices. Why would the typical Cryptsy or Bittrex user buy Paycoin at $20 when they could have purchased it at $12 or lower?

Paycoin needed a massively successful launch to justify that price tag, especially as GAW had already set the market lower by selling the coin at that price in its pre-sale and launch. There were very few people left in the cryptocurrency community who had not heard of Paycoin and would have missed out on the opportunity to buy in at the multiple prices lower than $20. Most of them didn't believe Paycoin was worth what Garza was selling it at and the ones who did had bought in already.

Instead of a successful launch, everything was bungled at every turn. First, Paybase was delayed until after Christmas. This led to a lot of complaints from investors who had invested what had originally been earmarked as Christmas gifts for their children. Paycoin had hyped a deal with Visa; when it never happened, Garza blamed Paycoin's detractors for scaring Visa off. Meanwhile, Amazon, Walmart, and Target all either denied connections with Garza or didn't respond to inquiries about Paycoin. Garza was unable to produce any proof of his claims that a deal was being worked on. Later, an email leak illuminated the issue, revealing that no communication between Paycoin/ GAW employees and the aforementioned companies ever took place or was even attempted. Furthermore, there was only a half-hearted and hastily made partnership with a company that didn't have permission to print Visa cards. Later, Garza would claim to be close on a deal to get a MasterCard-branded debit card, but MasterCard outright denied the claim.[11]

Essentially, every feature promised by Garza and GAW fell through. There was no merchant adoption worth talking about, no debit card, no bill pay, no PayFlash (a feature ostensibly allowing instant conversion of Paycoins to "usable funds at the largest merchants in the world"), and when Paycoin officially launched, it topped out at $13.50. Although GAW would later claim that it attempted to keep the $20 payfloor and stated that it did buy some Paycoins at $20, the open market price never even hit $14. If Paybase ever did pay $20 a Paycoin, it was only for the briefest of moments. Things held for a while as people still expected Garza to come through. Some even sounded giddy at the prospect of picking up more coins at this "reduced" price.

The floor was never supported and things began to fall apart quickly. An "Honors" program was announced in which users would deposit Paycoin into Paybase and GAW would honor the $20-a-coin promise but would only do this for a certain number of Paycoins a month. That was good enough to cause a temporary price recovery—which was quickly pushed down by a dump. However, it was soon pointed out by media outlets that the plan would take decades to repay the Paycoin purchased at launch; that the plan didn't make sense because users could still move Paycoin in a never-ending cycle of buying it on the open market and then selling it (even months later) at Paybase; and that even if it could work, it was most likely illegal.

---

[11] Johnson, Mike. "MasterCard Denies PayCoin Partnership." Coin Fire. February 25, 2015. Accessed June 22, 2015. http://coinfire.io/2015/02/25/mastercard-denies-paycoin-partnership/.

Even before everything fell apart, the community was angry enough that Garza had to cancel a speech at The North American Bitcoin Conference (TNABC) in Miami. The outrage had been bad enough that the leadership of the TNABC decided to let him speak as a way for the community to ask him the tough questions—and then Garza abandoned that plan and the organizers at the eleventh hour.[12]

Prime Controllers also became an issue at this time. Prime Controllers were a supposed feature of Paycoin. Like all proof-of-stake coins, Paycoin has its transactions confirmed by users keeping their wallets open and "staking" them. They then confirm transactions for the network and generate interest on their coins. In Paycoin, the interest rate was set to a relatively high five percent. But these Prime Controller accounts, which were supposedly auctioned off to the highest bidders, claimed a staking rate of 10 percent. It was originally unclear if these Prime Controllers were intended to do tasks somehow more difficult than regular staking, but it was later proven that they didn't do anything regular stakers didn't and were only a reward for paying more.

Regardless, things got far worse when it was revealed that many of the Prime Controllers, most of which were still controlled by GAW, were actually staking at rates much higher than 10 percent. Investigation of the blockchain revealed that certain Prime Controllers were staking at an absolutely insane 350 percent that was compounded multiple times a day to equal a total interest rate of 3,500 percent.

---

[12] DeMartino, Ian M. "Last Minute TNABC Changes: Garza Cancels, Robot Roger Ver and More." CoinTelegraph. January 16, 2015. Accessed June 22, 2015. http://cointelegraph.com/news/113314/last-minute-tnabc-changes-garza-cancels-robot-roger-ver-and-more.

If Paycoin had any credibility left in the cryptocurrency community, this scandal killed it. One of the most appealing features of cryptocurrencies is that they are decentralized and no single entity controls them. If Paycoin can simply be printed at will—and the Prime Controllers were undoubtedly digital money-printing machines—there isn't much that separates it from central bank-powered currencies. The only major difference is that instead of being backed by a powerful government, Paycoin was backed by the word of Homero Josh Garza and the company he founded, which was quickly proving itself to be very disreputable.

Soon after, the biggest news hit: an SEC investigation had been opened up on GAW Miners and Josh Garza. Garza initially denied the claim and stated that he was considering legal action against the website that reported it.

It was eventually confirmed—by other media outlets and then by actual SEC documents—that something was and continues to be going on with GAW, the SEC and other authorities.[13] That investigation is ongoing and as of this writing the SEC has had little to say publicly about the case. It was also revealed at that time that GAW had lawsuits filed against it, including for neglecting to pay an electric bill of more than $130,000. GAW did not show up for court.[14]

It all got uglier when Garza and many GAW employees had their emails leaked. Everything was seemingly out in the open

---

[13] Johnson, Mike. "Coin Fire+: GAW Miners Catches SEC, FTC, IRS, DHS Attention." Coin Fire. March 5, 2015. Accessed June 22, 2015. http://coinfire.io/2015/03/06/coin-fire-gaw-miners-catches-sec-ftc-irs-dhs-attention/.

[14] Higgins, Stan. "GAW Miners Absent in Ongoing Mississippi Court Case." CoinDesk. June 18, 2015. Accessed January 11, 2016. http://www.coindesk.com/gaw-miners-absent-court-case/

and nearly every suspicion about GAW and Paycoin appeared confirmed.

The emails showed Garza calling regular investors "muggles" after the name given to non-magical characters in the Harry Potter franchise. It also showed there were no conversations with Visa or MasterCard; that Garza had promised more than 100 percent of his company away; and that he had borrowed untold amounts of money from Stuart Fraser, a partner at Cantor Fitzgerald, a well-respected investment company.

Garza appeared to have allegedly stolen money from both Fraser and his own company, led employees on, fired an employee he was having an affair with after his wife got jealous, had an estate sale before disappearing, sold his three cars, lied to others about how he obtained those cars (he said the Tesla was a "gift from Elon [Musk]" even though a purchase receipt was found in his email), and had trouble paying his business partners, among countless other improprieties.

In most scenarios, this would be the end of a company. It would dissolve, everyone would go their separate ways and the customers would be left hoping the SEC investigation would get them some return on their investments. The problem was and remains that just because a coin was created by a disreputable person, and just because that coin has no redeeming qualities at all, doesn't make the coin go away.

Throughout the whole ordeal, Paycoin dropped in price. As of this writing, it is $0.05. This is a far cry from its promised $20 price floor but still sits above many legitimate and useful altcoins, which just shows that some people are willing to hold onto an investment—even one proven to be worthless—if they paid a lot for it. Few wanted to buy Paycoin at $20 a coin because, in part, they knew it had been sold for much cheaper; the inverse of that psychology has managed to keep the coin from dying completely. But it isn't going anywhere. Paycoin won't ever be the future or even a significant player in the cryptocurrency scene. It will toil in the depths of the altcoin world until everyone involved finally gives up or gets bored.

People paid a lot of money for Paycoin. So much so that selling at $5 or $1 would have been a major loss for them. They held further still as the coin dropped past the $0.50 and $0.25 milestones; then it got even worse. It is understandable that investors were hesitant to sell at those prices when they bought in at $12 but even the meager amount they could have received then would have been better than what they got by holding on.

If I sold you snake oil as a cure for the common cold for $12 and then you found out it didn't work as advertised or do much of anything else, would you be willing to sell it for a dollar? How about $0.50? What about $0.25 or $0.01?

The point is, you should be willing to part with ineffective snake oil at any price, because you know that it's worthless. But investors have a hard time seeing it this way. In their mind, they paid $12 for it and selling it for anything less than $12.01 is a failure.

It might be a failure, but selling at $10 is less of a failure than selling at $0.10—just as selling at $0.10 is less of a failure than selling at $0.01, and selling at $0.01 is still less a failure than selling at $0.0001 (which is possible in cryptocurrencies).

It is understandable that someone who has put so much money in would decide to wait and see what happens rather than drop coins when it is low. In general, selling while the price is low is never a good investment move—but Paycoin, despite its spectacular crash from its $14 heights, is extremely overvalued. Paycoin has more total coins than a currency such as Nxt and it has a worse and possibly malicious development team. It has Prime Controllers that could be turned on at any moment to ruin the currency. Few people who know what they are doing are still paying attention to what the "Paycoin Foundation" is doing. Paycoin's reputation has alienated the companies it once claimed to have partnerships with, the coin's creators are being investigated by the SEC, and, even discounting the Prime Controllers, it has an unusually high interest rate. Each NXT is worth about a penny and a half. As I mentioned earlier, at the time of this writing, a single Paycoin is worth about five cents. It'll probably be lower by the time you read this, but as long as a single Paycoin is worth more than a few hundred Satoshis (*i.e.*, a hundredth of a penny), Paycoin remains overvalued.

Many more promises were made and went unfulfilled. Coinstand was billed as a service where users could use their Paycoin to buy Amazon products while valuing each Paycoin at $20. That was eventually turned into five percent off, but it didn't matter for the vast majority of Paycoin holders because the system was only open to a small group of "beta testers" likely handpicked by Garza. (He had posted a message asking the community to nominate the most loyal members a week or two earlier.) A few people in that group did receive their orders but the products soon stopped coming, and today the site is gone and there is no talk of a revival.

As GAW fell apart, the leadership split and the newly formed Paycoin Foundation attempted to distance itself from Garza. Another developer, Phil Vadala, who had been in charge of Coinstand, split off from both groups and allegedly stole a few Prime Controllers from Garza, though it is unclear how Garza claimed ownership of Prime Controllers supposedly sold to private investors. Coinstand was later revealed to have been funded by Garza, despite his initial claims that he had nothing to do with the site.

This action led to Garza posting a Skype conversation with Vadala in which Garza claimed the Prime Controllers belonged to organized crime elements in Russia and a Middle Eastern investor who Garza said shouldn't be crossed.[15]

It never seemed to cross Garza's mind that admitting he had done deals with criminal organizations was a mistake. He also didn't think sending thinly veiled threats to one of his former developers and revealing that he was prioritizing supposed early investors—and criminal investors at that—over the community's interests might be concerning to the rest of the community.

I interviewed Garza about this event and he seemed baffled that I was more concerned with his comments than the theft allegedly perpetrated by Vadala.[16]

But as mentioned, Paycoin is still technically alive. It can still be bought and sold on various exchanges and there are a few people left in its community. The coin continues, albeit in a massively depressed state, despite Garza, GAW Miners, and ZEN Miners all being subjects to open SEC investigations.

---

[15] DeMartino, Ian M. "Josh Garza Breaks Down, Admits To Working With Mobsters, Going To Dubai In Bizarre Post." Mining Pool. May 6, 2015. Accessed June 22, 2015. http://coinjournal.net/josh-garza-breaks-down-admits-to-working-with-mobsters-going-to-dubai-in-bizarre-post/.

[16] DeMartino, Ian M. "The Josh Garza Interview." Mining Pool. May 11, 2015. Accessed June 22, 2015. http://coinjournal.net/the-josh-garza-interview-organized-crime-threats-and-is-he-in-america/

Paycoin will die when the last two members of the community leave and exchanges stop carrying it. Although its eventual death is considered a foregone conclusion by most, it does showcase how resilient real cryptocurrencies are. Paycoin broke nearly every principle the cryptocurrency holds dear (decentralized control, limited supply, transparency) and was run by a likely scammer who probably set out to create it with bad intentions, has vanished from public view, and has a pending court case with the authorities; and still the network continues to function. This bodes well for currencies with honest development teams and especially Bitcoin, which has its entire economy helping to support it.

The lesson that should be learned from Paycoin is this: just because a company gets coverage from mainstream media outlets doesn't mean it is reputable. Like all scammers, Bitcoin scammers tend to move from project to project; if a company is transitioning to a new venture, make sure it isn't just trying to bring fresh money into a quickly collapsing Ponzi scheme. If someone is promising you a 500 percent increase on your investment, they are lying. And just because "HODL" (yes, it's a humorous misspelling of "HOLD") is a good strategy when investing long-term in Bitcoin, holding the whole way down is not a viable strategy for altcoins that can lose nearly all their value quickly with no hope of recovery when controversy strikes.

Bitcoin is full of scams. That doesn't mean it is a scam or that it should be avoided. The Internet itself is likewise full of scams. But just as it took us a while to get used to the Nigerian prince scandal and the fake Bank of America phishing emails, it is taking us a while to get used to the scams that infect the cryptocurrency space in a similar fashion. Wherever money can be found, scammers are sure to follow. Bitcoin *is* money so it only makes sense that scammers would be attracted to it. All this means is: be cautious. Do your research and never invest more than you are willing to lose. It is almost a cliché at this point but Bitcoin really is the Wild West, only there is no sheriff to keep order.

Section II:
How to Invest in Bitcoin

Chapter 10:

How to Buy Bitcoin with a Bank Account, Cash, or PayPal

> Normally I would not recommend a book that tells you how to make money in the stock market. Most of these books are aimed at gullible folk, and they usually make much more money for their authors than they do for the investing public.
>
> —*Financial Times* writer Gavyn Davies

People have called Bitcoin a network, a distributed ledger, and various other things, and they aren't incorrect. But above all, Bitcoin is a currency, a way to track and transfer *value*. And when it comes to currency, people inevitably ask how they can get a lot of it.

I can't teach you how to get rich off Bitcoin. If I had a foolproof plan, I would be implementing it instead of writing this book. What I can do is give you a basic overview of the landscape, some fundamental techniques for working with Bitcoin, to hopefully set you off in the right direction.

Day trading, the practice of making daily trades in order to make a profit off of volatile securities, is undoubtedly lucrative for some. People make money every day buying and selling Bitcoin and other cryptocurrencies. I don't. Part of the reason is that I don't have the disposable income to risk and make the potential payoff worth the time and effort. But that isn't the only reason.

Cryptocurrency day trading is ruthless. Outside of Bitcoin and a few other major altcoins and projects, nearly every other cryptocurrency has a horrible long-term outlook with the only potential profit to be grabbed by riding usually manufactured speculative bubbles. The reason they have a bad long-term outlook is because most of them don't bring anything new to the table—or if they do, it isn't enough. Ethereum has gained acceptance with some mainstream companies, with large banks such as UBS and Barclays announcing experiments with the technology, but this is exceedingly rare.[1] Only a small fraction of altcoins bring anything new to the table, only a fraction of those have shown long-term viability and only a fraction of *those* have demonstrated any interest from outside the cryptocurrency community. That isn't to say the space isn't full of innovation and well-meaning developers; it is. But even as emergent technologies go, I can't call them a half-safe investment. Most of them only exist to pump-and-dump—more on that later—and bring nothing new to the table.

---

[1] Allison, Ian. "UBS and Barclays Are Front Runners with Bitcoin 2.0 Technology Ethereum." International Business Times RSS. IBTimes, August 5, 2015. Accessed October 29, 2015. http://www.ibtimes.co.uk/ubs-barclays-bnp-paribas-are-front-runners-bitcoin-2-0-technology-ethereum-1514138

At the time of this writing, the space is largely unregulated. Laws such as New York State's BitLicense are coming into effect, but authorities have so far focused on making sure exchanges are following anti-money laundering (AML) and know-your-customer (KYC) regulations. They don't seem to have much interest in preventing insider trading, market manipulation, or the other hijinks that are common with the more obscure altcoins and in any unregulated security market.

Much of the issue can be avoided by sticking strictly to Bitcoin and perhaps a few of the larger altcoins. The larger a market, the harder it is to manipulate, with or without regulators. The most common way to manipulate any market is to make small, incrementally higher buys to make the market appear to be going up. Once the market is high enough, the manipulator sells all of his or her cryptocurrency—or stock or other security—at the new price that they created. These are the basics of any pump-and-dump scheme. It is more difficult with larger markets because the manipulator will have to make more buys to influence the price.

My first direct experience with Bitcoin day traders was at the Bitcoin in the Beltway Conference in Washington, DC, in 2014. I met a few former Wall Street traders who had transitioned into Bitcoin consultants and day traders. After two days of nearly 12-hour-long conferences, I met up with them at an afterparty. As the party was winding down, one of them said something to me that made me realize that I don't have the dedication required to be a successful day trader. It was nearing 1:00 a.m., everyone was ready to pass out after two full days of conferencing and partying, and he asked if I wanted to hang out for a while longer because "the Japanese markets wake up in a few hours" and he was planning to make some profit on that action.

It dawned on me then that Bitcoin day traders are animals. You can't hope to compete with them unless you become equally obsessed. To get to that level, you will need more than this book. Making money without any actual work is an extremely competitive industry and requires, ironically, a lot of work. Unlike the stock market, the Bitcoin markets never close, and it is possible to wake up and find that all your hard work during the previous day was wiped out by a massive early morning price swing.

My recommendation is to bet on Bitcoin long-term. Purchase Bitcoin, put it in a safe place and then wait and hope that the price rises over the next five, 10 or 15 years. Buying Bitcoin is relatively straightforward; it simply requires finding someone willing to sell it to you. The first few chapters of this section explain how to obtain and store bitcoins with the intention of holding them long-term. If you are determined to get into day trading, this book gives you the basics but don't expect to make thousands of dollars without any work and without learning from someone more experienced. I recommend you search the Internet for guides not only on how to day-trade Bitcoin but also the fundamentals of trading traditional stocks. Many of the same principles transfer over to the Bitcoin world and unless you master them, you will always be a step behind the most advanced traders.

Buying Bitcoin with Cash

Buying bitcoins is possible in almost any country, although it is easier in some than in others. The most reliable and private way of buying bitcoins directly with cash is to use LocalBitcoins

(localbitcoins.com). To do so, log onto the site, select "cash" under "in person" in the payment method, type in your location, and see if anyone nearby wants to sell bitcoins for cash. You can either submit a buy order yourself and wait or find an existing sell order and purchase those bitcoins. If you wait, you might get a good deal from someone looking to offload their bitcoins quickly. If you buy bitcoins from someone who has already put in a sell order, you can expect to pay a small premium over the market price. You will then have to arrange to meet the seller in person, so make sure you read their reviews and pick a public place like a coffee shop.

To conduct the transaction, you will need a Bitcoin wallet. A web wallet with a mobile app is preferable to a paper wallet, because you want to be able to easily check that the transaction has gone through before you hand the cash to the seller. You can then transfer the bitcoins to an offline or paper wallet at your leisure.

The actual process is pretty simple but I'll go over it since it will likely be a new experience for you. First, you'll need a Bitcoin wallet, preferably one installed onto your smartphone. Armed with that and some cash, you can meet the seller anywhere you'd like that has an Internet connection. Each wallet app is different, but there should be a way to pull up a QR code, which is a black-and-white box like the one at the beginning of this book. The seller will scan that using his smartphone's camera and will then send over the agreed number of bitcoins. It shouldn't take long to show up in your app. If it isn't a large purchase, at that point you can hand over the cash and the transaction will be complete.

Theoretically, you should wait for three to six confirmations on the blockchain. I talk more about confirmations in the mining chapter but for now, just know that it indicates how many times the Bitcoin network has had a miner or full node check the transaction to make sure it is valid. Most wallet apps will give you an indicator of how far along a transaction is to being confirmed enough to be considered safe. This is really only necessary if the transaction is extremely large; for a smaller transaction, one confirmation is usually enough. A double-spend attack, where someone selling bitcoins tries to sell them twice before the network confirms the first transaction, is extremely difficult for reasons I talk about elsewhere in this book, but difficult doesn't mean impossible—so for large transactions it is best to wait until the transaction is confirmed.

It is possible to buy bitcoins with cash a few other ways on LocalBitcoins, including a cash deposit into someone's bank account or buying someone a gift card. You can also purchase bitcoins using any electronic payment method you can think of: Western Union, Walmart-2-Walmart, Skrill, and many more. LocalBitcoins offers third-party escrow to reduce fraud but sellers will often put high requirements on the buyer to prove their legitimacy. Ultimately, LocalBitcoins requires a lot of trust on the part of the buyer outside of local trades. In addition, US law enforcement is seemingly watching the site and has occasionally arrested sellers, accusing them of running unlicensed money-transmitting services. No buyers have been charged with any crimes, only sellers, but it is something to consider if you plan to buy and sell bitcoins regularly with the service.

The site Bitquick.co also offers bitcoins for cash deposits and uses an escrow system. You simply have to pick a user that has a bank in your area, take the information provided to that bank and deposit cash into that person's account. Three hours later, bitcoins should be delivered to the Bitcoin address you specified.

There is one other way to buy bitcoins anonymously with cash: Bitcoin ATMs. This method is highly dependent on your location, as Bitcoin ATMs are only starting to show up around the nation and the world. Some of them aren't anonymous and require phone numbers and government ID scanning before they can be used but others are pretty accessible. The fees for these machines vary from reasonable to outrageous, so do your research before driving a long way. There are some online tools available to help you find these ATMs. Coinmap.org, for instance, is an open-source solution to finding Bitcoin ATMs, as well as businesses that accept payment in bitcoins. Coinatmradar.com is another good service that provides information on fees and conversion types. Some Bitcoin ATMs only take fiat and put out bitcoins; others will allow transactions both ways, though they generally have higher fees.

Bitcoin is a digital currency, however, so it makes much more sense to purchase it online. Although there are only a few options for buying Bitcoin physically, there is a vast number of options for buying it digitally. Below are the most secure and reputable services. While there are countless others, many of which are perfectly safe, reliable, and reputable, it is impossible to list them all here.

The one bit of advice I can give is that if it sounds too good to be true, it probably is. Any site offering a significantly better price than other exchanges is probably running a scheme or a scam. A few cents off the price of Bitcoin is a reasonable spread but any massive difference between exchanges is quickly eliminated by traders looking to take advantage of arbitrage opportunities. If a site has a large spread, regardless of what it might claim, something funny is likely going on.

Buying Bitcoin with a Credit Card

Purchasing bitcoins with a credit card or a bank account is the quickest and probably cheapest way of obtaining bitcoins in the US, though it also creates an obvious link between your Bitcoin account and real-life identity. Most of the reputable services in the US follow the KYC (know your customer) and AML (anti-money laundering) laws and you will likely be forced to comply with them by providing information about your identity. Even if the particular jurisdiction does not have laws specific to Bitcoin, it will likely be subject to the local government's financial services laws. Moreover, most exchanges are attempting to get in front of any pending legislation by preemptively self-regulating.

As I have already mentioned, there are dozens of companies that will allow you to buy bitcoins using a credit card. The three giants of the industry, however, are Coinbase, Bitstamp, and Circle. Bitstamp suffered a hack earlier in 2015 and later had embarrassing details leak out in a court case with its insurance company but no consumer funds were lost. Coinbase and Circle both currently have spotless security records but you should always do a Google search for news on recent developments before handing over your credit card information.

The transaction fees are variable. Depending on the merchant, fees can range from zero percent for the first few thousand dollars per week to a flat one percent fee.

Most sites require identity verification so you will likely have to send a photocopy of your ID card as well as a bank statement or other proof of residence. Some sites might even require two forms of ID. Verification levels depend on how much you are purchasing. If your activity is deemed suspicious, you might be asked to provide further verification.

In addition, some of these sites—Coinbase in particular—have gained some notoriety for keeping an eye on their users' Bitcoin activity and taking (some would say) extreme actions against them. If, for example, they determine a user is using their bitcoins for illegal or quasilegal activities such as gambling, they might freeze that account. For this reason, anyone planning to gamble or even do a lot of business on LocalBitcoins should mix their coins using the methods described in Chapter 6. Or better yet, move the coins off the exchange and use a local PC wallet to perform transactions.

Buying Bitcoin with PayPal

Buying with PayPal comes with a certain amount of risk for the seller. No reputable exchanges accept PayPal directly, despite what some sites might claim when you run a Google search. A few sellers on LocalBitcoins will take PayPal but they will usually charge extra for the convenience and might only deal with accounts that already have a good reputation on the site.

The reason for these hassles is that PayPal transactions, unlike Bitcoin transactions, are reversible. This is technically true with credit cards as well but it hasn't been as much of an issue. The biggest issue is that PayPal accounts have been susceptible to hacking, mostly due to user error (weak passwords, etc.). If someone purchases bitcoins with a hacked PayPal account, PayPal will reverse the transaction, but the Bitcoin seller who legitimately sent the coins will have no way to recover the coins they already sent.

But that doesn't mean you can't buy bitcoins with PayPal. You just have to be a little creative. If you spend any time online, you might have heard about the online game and community Second Life. Second Life has its own built-in virtual currency called Linden Dollars. Linden Dollars is not a real digital currency, much less a cryptocurrency; it is simply an in-game currency that people are willing to buy with real currency.[2]

Linden Labs, the company behind Second Life, came up with the genius idea of creating a real economy existing in a virtual world and gave it its own currency. Linden Dollars allows users to buy and sell goods, services, and virtual real estate to and from each other, rather than buying everything directly from Linden Labs itself. Although Linden Dollars is completely centralized and Linden Labs can digitally "print" an unlimited number of Linden Dollars at any time, it has done a commendable job of keeping the right amount of scarcity while still giving new adopters a way into the economy. The virtual Second Life economy has grown to the point where there are authorized resellers of Linden Dollars. As with cryptocurrencies, Linden Dollars also fluctuate in value and some people even day-trade them. One authorized reseller is VirWoX and it has the option to cash out in bitcoins.

---

[2] "Linden Dollar Definition." Investopedia. August 28, 2011. Accessed June 22, 2015. http://www.investopedia.com/terms/l/linden-dollar.asp.

The PayPal → Linden Dollar → Bitcoin chain of transactions will end up costing you around a six percent fee, but it is probably the safest way to purchase bitcoins with PayPal.

Buying Bitcoin with Gift Cards

As mentioned above, buying gift cards and then selling them on LocalBitcoins is an option but there are others. Cardforcoin. com is a relatively new service. It started out allowing you to buy Starbucks gift cards with bitcoins and eventually evolved to allow users to buy and sell gift cards from a selection of stores, including Starbucks cards, with bitcoins. As always, do your own research, especially if you are reading this book years after it was first published.

The bottom line is that the most difficult aspect of the Bitcoin ecosystem remains getting into that ecosystem. Once inside, it is virtually effortless—other than making sure the companies you use are reputable—to take advantage of all the services offered within it.

If Bitcoin is going to enter into the mainstream, however, the community needs to make it easier for people to join. Services such as Circle go a long way toward making Bitcoin seem professional, but it is still too difficult for users to quickly buy bitcoins for their first time. Once set up, things are generally easy but getting over that initial hurdle remains difficult, as no one wants to upload personal documents or meet a stranger at a coffee shop to buy something they are only curious about. For Bitcoin to go mainstream, the community or a company needs to find a solution to the problem.

Purse.io

Purse.io is quickly becoming a staple of the industry. It gives Bitcoin users a five percent or more discount on Amazon goods when they buy with bitcoins. The flip side to that are people who want to turn their credit cards, Amazon gift cards, or PayPal accounts into Bitcoin. A Purse.io Bitcoin user places an order for the Amazon item he or she wishes to buy, and then someone who wants some bitcoin and doesn't mind paying the fee will purchase it for them and have it sent to the Bitcoin user's address. Purse holds the bitcoins in escrow until the items arrive at the Bitcoin user's residence. Currently, the service is one of the best ways for Bitcoin users to save money and for outsiders to quickly get into Bitcoin.

Chapter 11:
Working for Bitcoin

The Bitcoin ledger is a new kind of payment system. Anyone in the world can pay anyone else in the world any amount of value of Bitcoin by simply transferring ownership of the corresponding slot in the ledger. Put value in, transfer it, the recipient gets value out, no authorization required, and in many cases, no fees.

—Marc Andreessen

Getting paid in Bitcoin has been a breeze, except during the tax season, which can be complicated. I've done it for years now. I have also paid my rent and other bills using Bitcoin or dollars that I obtained by selling bitcoins.

It is a viable option for anyone with a marketable skill. Virtually anything that can be done online can be paid for in Bitcoin and the job market is quickly growing for in-person jobs as well. A total of $301 million in venture capital funds was invested into

Bitcoin in 2014, a number that jumped to more than $314 million in 2015,[1] and few will be surprised if that number increases again in 2016. That is a lot of start-ups looking to fill a lot of positions.

Working for a Bitcoin company is a sure way to get a steady supply of bitcoins, but doing quick and easy freelance work is also effective.

Where to Find a Job That Pays in Bitcoin

The first step to finding a job that pays in Bitcoin is knowing where to look. Coinality is the longest-running and likely most comprehensive Bitcoin job board on the Internet. It pulls jobs from individual companies' sites, freelance sites such as Elance and Reddit's subforum r/Jobs4Bitcoin to incorporate practically every Bitcoin job board on the web.

The most commonly available openings are, unsurprisingly, for coders. Bitcoin coders, web designers, mobile app developers—these skills are in high demand in the industry.

Writing is another good option. Most Bitcoin news sites accept news submissions. These news sites include CoinDesk, DeepDotWeb, Bitcoin Magazine, CryptoCoinsNews, and newsBTC. All pay their writers in bitcoins. Graphic design artists and copywriters are also likely to find a lot of work in the Bitcoin space.

For inexperienced or poor writers, shilling for a company by posting positive reviews is one way to earn some bitcoins, but this work is generally frowned upon by the community. Still, if one

---

[1] "Top Investor Tuesday - Bitcoin." PitchBook News. December 10, 2015. Accessed January 13, 2016. http://pitchbook.com/newsletter/top-investor-tuesday-bitcoin.

is desperate for bitcoins and doesn't mind angering some people and shilling for less-than-reputable services, it is one way to go, but keep in mind that working for a scam can be seen as being complicit in that scam, so I urge caution.

Bitcoin employment isn't limited to programmers and content creators, however. There is a growing demand in the industry for general business and marketing. As Nathan Wosnack, the COO of uBITquity and cofounder/CCO of Blockchain Factory, has pointed out:

> Technology smarts alone will not suffice; you need to be able to speak the language of the layman. I'd say the biggest needs are marketing and PR people. People who know how to talk to the general public, create marketing campaigns, and reach the general public are sorely needed within the crypto currency space.
>
> Bitcoin companies also need dedicated business development people with skills that span beyond crypto, and into general technology marketing. They need to have a grasp of the tech and the real life use cases. Because at the end of the day; if you can't sell your product or service to the customers, your idea is worthless.
>
> People in my experience have this foolish and often dangerous idea that with the advent of new technology (like Bitcoin and the blockchain) that the time-tested rules of business somehow don't apply at all. Sadly, they are mistaken.

Working for a business is one way to go. Another is to simply work for tips. It isn't the quickest way to turn a profit but putting out quality content and then asking for donations is certainly a way to pick up some bitcoins. Everyone from podcasters to musicians, bloggers, and artists has asked their audience to finance their projects. A few of them have managed to secure full-time gigs. I would suggest that anyone planning on going this route also accept other forms of currency, but Bitcoin can be a large and growing part of that income.

Selling Goods for Bitcoin

Selling goods, products, or services for bitcoins is another straightforward way to get into the Bitcoin ecosystem. Whether you have a business already and simply want to allow your customers to pay with Bitcoin or you want to resell goods you have lying around the house, there are numerous options available for accepting Bitcoin as a form of payment.

Currently, the biggest auction site where you can use Bitcoin is CryptoThrift. It has an eBay-like format and offers 30-day escrow on all sales (the seller is required to offer it and the buyer decides whether he or she wants to set it up). In 2014, CryptoThrift canceled its escrow service for a few months, citing security concerns. Those problems have since been ironed out and escrow is highly recommended for all buyers.[2] For sellers, this feature means that their funds could be held for up to 30 days, though

---

[2] DeMartino, Ian M. "CryptoThrift Suffers Security Breach, 15 BTC Stolen, Escrow Service Suspended." CoinTelegraph. October 7, 2014. Accessed June 22, 2015. http://cointelegraph.com/news/112691/cryptothrift-suffers-security-breach-15-btc-stolen-escrow-service-suspended.

in practice funds are typically released at the discretion of the buyers after they receive their items, assuming no conflicts arise.

Glyde is another peer-to-peer marketplace. Unlike CryptoThrift, it works with fixed prices, not unlike Amazon. The marketplace primarily sells cell phones, tablets, and video games. It provides insured shipping and packaging, and allows sellers to take payouts through a bank deposit, mailed check, or Bitcoin. Unfortunately, you can't directly use Bitcoin to purchase products.

There are also open markets such as r/Bitcoinmarket and the BitcoinTalk forums. These options can be extremely risky because there is no built-in escrow, but using a reputable member of the community as an escrow service—likely for a nominal fee—can remove some of the risk.

If you own a business, you can obtain bitcoins in a way that has little cost to you and benefits the entire Bitcoin ecosystem. Accepting Bitcoin is easy and can open up your business to an entire world of users eager to spend their money at a business that accepts their preferred method of payment.

The results might vary. Some companies have expressed that Bitcoin sales have not been impressive; others have been very happy with their numbers. Regardless of the particular outcome, it costs almost nothing to add Bitcoin to accepted methods of payment, and merchants can choose whether they want to dive headfirst into the deep end or simply dip their toes in the water.

There are two options for businesses accepting Bitcoin: they can either handle the Bitcoin transactions themselves or let someone else do it for them. PayPal's Braintree now allows merchants to accept Bitcoin for digital goods; Square allows merchants to accept Bitcoin and is working on a cash register that accepts both Bitcoin and Apple Pay; Shopify also allows its merchants to accept Bitcoin. These sites automatically sell the buyer's bitcoins for fiat, however, so they are not suitable options for merchants looking to acquire and hold their own bitcoins.

This service is provided by companies like Coinbase and Bitstamp. These companies allow merchants to decide how much they want to keep in Bitcoin and how much they convert to fiat. A merchant could, for example, try to set the amounts in a way that ensures the store will always break even in fiat and keep its margin of profit in Bitcoin.

Alternatively, a store could decide to simply accept Bitcoin itself. It could have a local wallet installed, display a QR code, and have a computer or tablet set up to watch the orders come in. An easier solution would be to use a web wallet and a smart device to accept transactions. In either case, the merchant would then get to decide how much, if any, Bitcoin he or she wants to turn into fiat and when to do so.

By accepting Bitcoin, companies don't just grab a small sub-section of technologically savvy geeks; they also open their business up to the world. A customer in China can purchase a product from a US-based company using Bitcoin without worrying about bank compatibility or exorbitant fees. The merchant will have the advantage of irreversible transactions and avoid the credit card fees that typically range from two to four percent. Many companies, retail companies in particular, operate with extremely small margins and a three percent fee might take up to half of their profits. Bitcoin, whose fees are typically below $0.02, represents a real game changer for them. For companies counting every penny, Bitcoin is unique in its utility.

Why Work for Bitcoin?

There are several reasons why one might choose to work for Bitcoin. It is an easy way to obtain bitcoins. For freelancers, accepting payment in bitcoins will expand their customer base and cut out unnecessary middlemen.

Sites like Freelancer and Elance take a percentage of payment for each job. This practice hurts both the customer and the freelancer but it is the price of getting connected to potential employers and being protected from being taken advantage of. Bitcoin doesn't just cut out the middleman; it can make doing business anonymously or near-anonymously much safer.

It also greatly increases the reach of your potential service. Anyone in the world can hire you if you accept Bitcoin. You won't have to worry about currency conversion fees or bank fees or if their country allows commerce with your country.

Despite these gains, there are some issues with working for Bitcoin that are still being ironed out.

Issues with Working for Bitcoin

Smart contracts—computer protocols that ensure a contract is followed—have been developed for Bitcoin and other cryptocurrencies and are getting more powerful all the time. Escrow is very useful because it gives the worker a third party to depend on to fulfill a contract if the employer decides not to do so. This situation isn't always ideal, and the balance of power between customer and client can swing wildly depending on a variety of factors.

The ultimate goal behind smart contracts is to eliminate the need for trust. They aren't quite there yet. And although escrow can be programmed, it still ultimately relies on the parties in the contract to act honestly. It is difficult, for example, for programming to determine if a website was designed to the client's specifications or not, since the quality of work is often subjective.

There are some criteria that could be programmed, however, and this holds great value. A search engine optimization (SEO) expert could promise a certain level of hits, for instance, and the contract could draw statistics from Alexa.com and make the payment only when the site hits those numbers.

Of course, people will always try to cheat the system. It seems to be part of human nature. In the example above, the SEO expert might buy cheap, artificial traffic that will immediately drop off as soon as he stops paying. Both the client and SEO expert might have had an understanding that the traffic was supposed to be legitimate, organic traffic, but without some way to code that agreement in, the client could easily be cheated.

Despite some of the current dangers and drawbacks, working for Bitcoin has a number of advantages. When I wrote for CoinTelegraph, I wrote for people who live in Russia and for a site that is based in the UK. It had writers from Vietnam, Mexico, and all over Europe and the US. CoinTelegraph didn't have the resources to work with the financial institutions in all those countries. It is unclear whether CoinTelegraph could have been launched at all had it depended on traditional financial institutions or PayPal. It was only through the global reach and permissionless nature of Bitcoin that CoinTelegraph was able to accomplish that.

Bitcoin has opened up the world for people working online. The Internet made communication with these people possible, but it wasn't until Bitcoin was invented that they could easily send you something representing value. The Internet made the world a global community. Bitcoin makes the world a true global economy.

Chapter 12:

Mining

We should have a gentleman's agreement to postpone the GPU arms race as long as we can for the good of the network. It's much easer [sic] to get new users up to speed if they don't have to worry about GPU drivers and compatibility. It's nice how anyone with just a CPU can compete fairly equally right now.

—Satoshi Nakamoto, December 12, 2010, the same day the
Nakamoto account posted its "final" message

Mining Bitcoin was once seen as the path to near-instant riches without any investment. By the time people realized it was something akin to that, it stopped being that. These days, mining is probably the least-effective way to obtain and invest in Bitcoin.

As I covered previously, mining is the process that confirms Bitcoin transactions. Participants in the network solve increasingly difficult mathematical equations to find what is called a "block" roughly every 10 minutes. Each block has a group of transactions as well as a condensed version of the previous block. If anything in the chain of blocks is changed, it will change the hash of the next block and therefore every block after it. So changing a previous transaction is not an easy task and would require recomputing the entire chain from that point. Therefore, participants can be assured that the longest chain is the correct one. This is how Bitcoin works and these miners are rewarded a small number of bitcoins every time they correctly solve a block, through a combination of transaction fees and new bitcoins being created (until the 21 million bitcoin limit is reached).

How complex the mathematical equations are is determined by the amount of total computing power—called hashing power—on the network. The difficulty of mining is adjusted every 2,016 blocks based on how quickly the last 2,016 blocks were solved. Once it became clear that there was something to this magical Internet money, people started jumping in and mining with ever-improving hardware. It quickly became an arms race with the first weapon coming in the form of gaming-focused video cards, then computers designed specifically to mine, and eventually chips specifically made for mining called ASICs (application-specific integrated circuits).

Bitcoin quickly went from a distributed digital currency that anyone could mine and that embodied Satoshi Nakamoto's directive that "one CPU equals one vote" (*i.e.*, that everyone with a computer could have an equal say in the validity of the blockchain and an equal chance at being rewarded bitcoins) to a fairly centralized and extremely competitive environment where only those who can afford to compete are able to.

I am not saying that Bitcoin has failed to embody Nakamoto's original vision, just that the specific aspect of mining hasn't lived up to the hopes of Bitcoin's creator. Even in 2010, Nakamoto and the rest of the community were aware of the coming arms race. We don't know what he would have thought of the ASIC farms that dominate the mining market today but it is clear that the current mining situation is far from his original hope of one-CPU-one-vote that was laid out in the original Bitcoin white paper.

Anyone can still mine, technically, but it is unlikely to bring in any rewards even if one uses a high-powered computer. What will happen instead is the miner will consume a lot of electricity and possibly damage the computer's CPU or GPU by overworking it. This warning does not stem from an overabundance of caution. I myself used my PC to CPU-mine some altcoins for a story and my computer's CPU has had overheating problems ever since. I'm not alone in that experience. Users can contribute by running a full node, which is basically just a Bitcoin wallet that has the entire Bitcoin blockchain downloaded and helps double-check transactions already confirmed by miners. They do not participate in the arms race and therefore do not reap any mining rewards but there has been some talk of adding a reward incentive for them.

Running a full node is recommended for someone looking to contribute to the Bitcoin network in a charitable way. It also comes with certain advantages for privacy-minded folk. If you run your own node, you can be sure that the node is not acting maliciously as you will be submitting your own transactions to the network, rather than depending on a third party.

As for mining, it is not for those light in the wallet. It takes a four- or five-figure investment to have any hope even of recouping your investment because of the arms race. Even if you manage to do so, the profits will still be razor-thin and any mishap in the form of hardware, power, or connectivity issues could make them thinner still. As the difficulty goes forever upward, the needed investment to turn a profit will only increase. Keep these warnings in mind.

If you are still determined to turn electricity into Bitcoin, you can do so and there are a few different ways of doing it.

First, if you don't have cheap electricity, don't bother with mining. It is difficult enough to turn a profit with cheap or even free electricity. Trying to do it somewhere with prohibitively expensive electricity is impossible. Mining is all about competing, and it is difficult to compete with people who have much lower expenses.

The avenues open to potential miners are getting more restricted every day. There are technically three options: solo mining, pool mining, and cloud mining. Cloud mining, which I touched on in Chapter 9 and will discuss in more detail later on, is really a fancy way of saying you are paying someone else to mine for you. Solo mining is only for hardcore masochists who would rather take the virtually impossible long shot of solving a block without the benefit of the massive hashing power obtained when joining a pool.

Most mining is done in pools. Pool mining is when a group of miners decides to group their hashing power together and share the rewards. This approach depends on some trust, since the individual miners have to trust that the pool operator will divvy out the rewards appropriately. Dishonesty would be noticed fairly quickly, however, and would do irreparable damage to the pool's reputation. The pool itself might even evaporate overnight and participants switch to another, more reputable pool.

Pool mining and solo mining both depend on some technically challenging software that runs in command-line on both

Windows and Linux. Some other software adds a pretty user interface, but the general idea is to run your miner with as little extra software taking up computational power as possible. CGMiner is the most popular version out there. It takes a little knowledge to get it running, but it isn't too daunting of a task.

The first step is to find a reliable and safe version of the software. Mining software can sometimes set off false positives for virus scanners. Because of this, mining software is often packaged with actual malware by third parties. This is why it is extremely important to download your mining software only from official and trusted sites.

Before setting up a miner at home, you should read an online guide from the pool you choose in order to make sure everything is set up to match their specifications. I include a quick guide here for the curious. One thing to keep in mind is that while mining is relatively simple, it isn't designed for the computer-illiterate. There seems to be a perception in the community that mining shouldn't be made easier for mainstream users, since more people will mean more competition and more difficulty, and that will decrease the profits that miners can get with their current hardware.

Mining isn't really that difficult, though. Practically anyone can do it by following a few simple steps. Just don't expect a pretty user interface that makes things simple. Most proof-of-work coin mining will work based on very similar methods but always make sure to consult your pool's guide.

Step one is to download mining software: CGMiner or BFGMiner. For the purposes of this guide, I will focus on CGMiner but the BFGMiner process is virtually identical. I will cover the process for Windows first.

After downloading the software, join a pool, create a "worker," and give it a name on the pool's website. Find the site's mining IP address—it should be readily visible on the pool's website. If you can't find it, check the site's FAQ page. It should be a TCP address.

Next, open up a text document in Notepad or similar program and type the following:

cgminer -o stratum+tcp://[enter pool URL here]:[enter port number here] -u [pool username].[pool worker name] -p [Enter your pool account password here]

Click "Save As" and change the file extension from .txt to "All files." Name it "StartMining.bat" and save it in the same folder as your CGMiner. You can now click that file and your miner should start mining automatically.

You should see a continuously updated log file of your progress and a summary of your hash rate. From this screen, you can also update your mining details and manage what pools you are mining into.

If you would prefer to solo mine rather than mine into a pool, that process is simple as well (minus the hardware requirement). First, you will need to download Bitcoin Core, or Bitcoin-Qt. This requires downloading the entire blockchain, which will not be a quick process. The blockchain has been experiencing rapid growth and sits at more than 52GB at the moment. By the time this book is published, the blockchain will be even larger.[1] The process is peer-to-peer, but you likely won't see speeds matching those of well-seeded torrents by downloading through the network. You can speed things up by downloading the first 20GB

---

[1] "Blockchain Size." Chart. Blockchain.info. Accessed June 22, 2015. https://blockchain.info/charts/blocks-size.

or so from a server, but plan for the download to take a day or even two.

Once you download the blockchain, you will have to make a small adjustment to the Bitcoin software to get mining started.

You can technically mine with just your CPU and a wallet but that is a quick way to burn out your CPU (with GPU-focused coins such as Bitcoin, anyway). For those who are interested in the process (or for those who want to solo mine a CPU-focused altcoin), however, here is how it is done:

Open or create a file called "Bitcoin.conf" in Notepad. You can find it in the programs folder \APPDATA\Roaming\Bitcoin. Add these eight lines:

```
server=1
listen=1
daemon=1
rpcuser=[Any name you want]
rpcpassword=[Any password you want]
rpcallowip=localhost
rpcport=127.0.0.1
port=[The port you want to use to talk to the Bitcoin
network; 8332 should work]
```

Now, with your wallet fully synced and the Bitcoin.config file correctly edited, open the wallet software and click Help, then Debug Window, and then Console.

With the console command line open, type in *setgenerate true -1* and the mining should start. To check whether it is running properly, type *getmininginfo* and information about current coin difficulty, current block, and your hashrate should be displayed.

There is also another option for the less technically inclined. GUIMiner is a piece of software that makes mining slightly more user-friendly. The blockchain still has to be downloaded but after the download, users simply have to download GUIMiner, run the program, and follow the simple steps the program will lay out. Use the information from the CGMiner guide and check the Devices section to make sure the program recognizes the GPU you want to use for mining.

If you want to get serious about mining—either solo mining or pool mining—you will have to invest a few thousand dollars in hardware. This is still no guarantee of easy profits and unless you have free or extremely cheap electricity, your money is almost assuredly better spent differently.

If you do have cheap electricity, you will have to buy some hardware. KnCMiner and Spondoolies are the two remaining enthusiast-level Bitcoin-mining companies, since both ButterFly Labs and GAW Miners have been taken down following a flurry of controversies. There have also been complaints about these two remaining companies, however. As is my general advice in all matters related to cryptocurrency, do your research before investing significant amounts of money.

Before buying any hardware, it's essential to check a Bitcoin-mining difficulty calculator to figure out your likelihood of reaching profitability. These are websites and apps that ask you to put in your electricity costs, expected hashing power, and expected difficulty, and will calculate your expected profits. Simply Googling "Bitcoin mining calculator" should provide several suitable options.

I do not recommend buying used hardware. Mining is extremely tough on hardware and it is impossible to figure out how much damage has been done to the CPU and GPU of devices by looking at a picture on a seller's website. Hardware with a shorter-than-expected shelf life can ruin an investment.

Cloud Mining

There is one method of Bitcoin mining that allows you skip all that hassle—but it comes with its own risks and, like every other method of mining, isn't recommended. Few cryptocurrency advocates would call it mining at all. This method, which I introduced earlier, is cloud mining.

Cloud mining is a scheme that is rapidly gaining both popularity and notoriety. Proponents of cloud mining, who mostly consist of companies trying to sell you on the idea, will say it allows investors to mine Bitcoin without having to worry about the headaches that come with mining on their own. The companies will be the ones dealing with things such as electricity costs, machine upkeep, and technical problems.

Cloud mining works like this: mining companies build giant warehouse-sized mining farms, sell or lease little pieces of those farms to customers, and in theory—after taking their own fee—pay customers based on the hashing percentage they own.

What you are essentially doing is paying someone else to mine for you. At this point you are no longer mining yourself. Instead, cloud-mining customers are investing into someone else's mining operations and have to hope that the operation will be more profitable than the fees paid and that the mining owner won't skim money off the top.

Of course, you can't even be sure that the company is mining at all. It is possible for cloud-mining companies to use the blockchain to prove they are actually mining and paying those profits to customers, but some don't. If the company does not prove it has the hashing power it says it has, don't go anywhere near it. Without that evidence, it is impossible to know whether what you are investing in is an actual mining operation and not a Ponzi scheme. Cloud-mining companies have been caught paying off older investors with new customers' purchases, which is the very definition of a Ponzi scheme.[2]

Some people contend that cloud mining doesn't make sense. If mining is more profitable than the fees gathered from customers, the reasonable question to ask is, why wouldn't the companies instead mine with that hardware themselves rather than pass those profits on to customers? Cloud-mining companies often say they use the money as start-up capital, but few, if any, have ever shown evidence to support this claim. Typically, cloud-mining companies already own the hardware before they begin taking orders. And if that is the case, why not just mine with the already available hardware? If the company believes in Bitcoin mining and its long-term profitability—and says so in sales pitches—it simply doesn't make sense from a business perspective to send those profits elsewhere.

However, I don't want to suggest that all cloud-mining companies are scammers. I am only saying their business model is a little questionable and a lot of them are, in fact, scammers. So why do it? Well, there aren't many other options. Solo mining is

[2] Madore, Paul H. "Scam Alert: Bitcoin Cloud Services." CCN Financial Bitcoin News. June 11, 2015. Accessed June 22, 2015. https://www.cryptocoinsnews.com/scam-alert-bitcoin-cloud-services/.

out of the question and even pool mining requires hardware that can hardly be called consumer grade. Again, I recommend that new users stay away from mining. It is too competitive to turn a profit and the difficulty is on a steady march upward.

Bitcoin mining is so difficult, even some mining companies stopped for a while. In January 2015, when the price dropped below $200 for the first time since 2013, mining difficulty did not match up with the price and the already thin profits for most miners disappeared. Many cloud-mining companies turned their users' accounts off, stating that the maintenance fees charged to customers were set to outpace the likely reward.[3] As the price rebounded, so did mining profitability, and things have seemingly settled down since then. Still, this episode made it very clear that Bitcoin mining is not for the faint of heart. It should only be tackled by those who have the resources and gumption to deal with the unstable market. Eventually, had the price remained depressed, the difficulty would have dropped, but the price soon rebounded.

I don't mean to say that mining itself is out of reach for the average user, just that *Bitcoin* mining is no longer feasible. One way to turn electricity into Bitcoin is to mine an alternative currency with a lower difficulty level and then trade that currency for Bitcoin. This approach still isn't a path to quick riches, but the potential for profit is much higher than it is in Bitcoin mining. Early Bitcoin miners profited from the increase in Bitcoin's price

---

[3] DeMartino, Ian M. "Interview with CEX.io's Jeffrey Smith on Why They Paused Mining and the Future of the Industry." CoinTelegraph. January 14, 2015. Accessed June 22, 2015. http://cointelegraph.com/news/113302/interview-with-cexios-jeffrey-smith-on-why-they-paused-mining-and-the-future-of-the-industry.

more than the increase in hashing power; the same concept can be applied to altcoins.

Like Bitcoin, most altcoins are secured through a proof-of-work method. There are three main algorithms that coins run, and hardware designed to work for one coin can be repurposed for any coin with the same algorithm. The three most popular algorithms are SHA-256, Scrypt, and X11. SHA-256 is Bitcoin's algorithm and can be seen as the "basic" algorithm of crypto-currencies—although it is anything but simple. Scrypt was the community's first attempt at heading off GPU mining rigs (*i.e.*, mining rigs with multiple, powerful graphics processing units) and ASICs, and it is used by Litecoin and dozens of other currencies. Despite its best attempts, Scrypt ASICs have still managed to hit the market. X11, along with its offshoots X5, X6, X12, etc., is a CPU/GPU hybrid that is again designed to slow the growth of ASIC miners; its most popular coin is Dash (formerly Darkcoin).

There are a lot of people with expensive but obsolete hardware out there and many of them are looking to point that hashing power at something. That is one reason why the altcoin-mining space is getting more competitive. SHA-256 ASICs that are no longer effective at mining Bitcoin can be pointed toward currencies with a smaller network and lower difficulty. The problem is that although that machine may be underpowered for the Bitcoin network, it can be extremely overpowered for smaller altcoins. This can and has led to the usually temporary centralization of mining operations for various coins. That has spread fears of a 51% attack occurring on these far less secure networks but no major accounts of such attacks have been reported so far.

Another reason for the increase in altcoin-mining difficulty has been the rise of multipools. These mining pools will focus on all the coins of a certain algorithm (SHA-256, Scrypt, etc.) and then mine the one that has the best combination of price and difficulty. The pool will switch automatically when another coin becomes more profitable. Generally, these pools will then dump those coins for Bitcoin or another digital currency of the user's choice.

This kind of action isn't always welcomed by the developers and communities of these smaller coins, which sometimes have their difficulty levels thrown out of whack thanks to the temporary and massive spike in mining power on the blockchain. These complaints have for the most part subsided as software was created to help ease the burden put on smaller coins. Meanwhile, coin developers realized that discouraging people from mining their coin was not only ineffective in getting them to stop but also ran counter to the political ideologies of much of the cryptocurrency community.

When picking a coin to mine, there are a few things to consider. First, is the coin pre-mined and if so, is it a reasonable pre-mine? A pre-mine is exactly what it sounds like. Before a coin launches, the developer creates a lot of that particular coin and puts it under his or her personal control. There are several uses for this fund, including paying developers or growing the community.

There is nothing wrong with setting aside some coins before the genesis block—the first block in a coin's blockchain—if those funds are actually going to be used to fund coin development and it is a reasonable amount. If the pre-mine is larger than a few percentage points, then it is likely that the developer is running a pump-and-dump scheme. A typical suspicious pre-mine will consist of a large percentage of the coin's total distribution, ensuring that even low prices will result in a significant profit for the creator.

The pre-mine "trick" isn't used that often anymore, because most of the community has gotten wise to it. The blockchain doesn't lie and will reveal any major holders of the coin and how much they hold. Some developers have tried to hide the pre-mine in the genesis block and then just ensure they get to mine *that block*, but even this tactic is an old one and is quickly noticed by members of the BitcoinTalk forums these days.

After you determine that a coin doesn't have a pre-mine or that its pre-mine was transparent and reasonable—pure proof-of-stake coins need some pre-mine in order to kick off the currency—then the next thing to look at is how likely the coin is to get on an exchange. Most altcoins see their biggest jump in value when they get on a major exchange and the public's interest is at its highest. Typically, early miners sell their coins at this stage and it is rare that an altcoin reaches those initial heights ever again. Therefore, when looking for a coin to mine, a good tactic is to mine a coin without exchange support and then sell it for Bitcoin once it gets on a major market.

Coins are more likely to be accepted to exchanges if they have an active development team and dedicated community that isn't shy about promoting the coin by Tweeting at exchange owners and asking them to put their coin on the site. Although harassing exchange owners is not recommended, following social media is a good way to guess what coins will be added next.

If you are an early miner of a coin that becomes successful enough to get on the major exchanges, it is possible to make a profit after trading it into Bitcoin.

When Bitcoin was in its infancy, confirming transactions by mining was one of the easiest and cheapest ways to obtain Bitcoin. Today, it is arguably the most difficult and expensive way. Mining, regardless of whether you are mining Bitcoin or an altcoin, takes time, electricity, and technical knowledge. Purchasing coins is far more effective than trying to create bitcoins out of electricity. Unless you have free electricity, a huge bank account, or a lot of trust in a cloud-mining service, mining probably isn't for you.

This might not be what Satoshi Nakamoto intended, but it is what we have.

Chapter 13:

HODL!

so i've had some whiskey
actually on the bottle it's spelled whisky
w/e
sue me
(but only if it's payable in BTC)

—BitcoinTalk member and unintentional creator of
Bitcoin "HODL" slogan, GameKyuubi, December 2013

Most people get into Bitcoin with the intention of investing. Having read stories about early Bitcoin adopters making a huge profit, potential investors have flocked to the currency in droves and they all want to know one thing: "How can I hit it big in Bitcoin?"

I am not someone you should turn to for serious financial advice. I do, however, have extensive experience with Bitcoin, and there is one solid piece of advice I feel I can offer to potential

Bitcoin investors: Hold your coins when the price is going down and hold your coins when the price is going up. Just hold your coins and wait.

I can't guarantee that Bitcoin will take off but if it does, all the current worry about Bitcoin's price and day-to-day stability will become irrelevant. There will only ever be 21 million bitcoins. If a substantial portion of international trade began using Bitcoin, the price of the currency would become astronomical. Add in the potential of stock trading, real estate deeds, and all the other possible uses for Bitcoin that seem just around the corner, and it becomes clear that its current price is extremely low, if you believe Bitcoin has a place in the future of finance.[1]

This is why the one piece of advice I give to any would-be Bitcoin investor is to simply buy and wait. This tactic of holding on to your Bitcoin, commonly referred to as "HODL" (a humorous misspelling of "HOLD") in the community, is one of the main doctrines of the Bitcoin faithful. As much as I detest adherence to the almost-religious dogma in the Bitcoin community, I will readily admit this particular tenet exists because there is some truth to it.

Bitcoin has seen at least three major spikes in price and they all followed the same pattern. First, the coin price drops slightly; then it jumps quickly to unprecedented heights. Then it falls a significant amount—to half its value or less—but always above the previous jump's top value. Later, it again jumps to heights that dwarf the previous jump.

---

[1] Hong, Euny. "Could One Bitcoin Come To Be Worth $1 Million? Q&A." Investopedia. May 14, 2014. Accessed June 22, 2015. http://www.investopedia.com/articles/investing/051414/could-one-bitcoin-come-be-worth-1-billion-qa.asp.

This pattern repeated itself from 2009 until 2014, when one of the "rules" of Bitcoin's price was finally broken. In early 2015, the price of Bitcoin dropped below $200, a lower value than its price before its previous late 2013–early 2014 price spike.[2]

This exception doesn't mean the pattern of massive spikes has come to an end, however. By the time you read this, it could have happened again. Or maybe not. The only thing that the drop of January 2015 proved is that things are unpredictable in this new market and any pattern used to predict the price is likely to be broken as soon as it becomes useful.

Savvy people have been looking for patterns in the stock market for decades without any success, and the stock market is filled with people who are (supposedly) intelligent investors. It also operates during certain times of the day and is mostly contained within the nation it operates in. Bitcoin trade goes on 24/7, has millions of unpredictable amateur investors all over the world, and is relatively unregulated. Predicting the price of something this chaotic would take Nostradamus-like talents.

That said, there is plenty of reason to expect that as long as Bitcoin plays a growing role in the Internet economy it will—eventually and over the long haul—increase in price. This "if" is a fairly big one—although blockchain technology will certainly continue to be used more and more, there is no guarantee that Bitcoin will be used as the currency of choice.

As I discussed in Chapter 5, there are a lot of things that give Bitcoin its value. One of the most important factors, after demand and utility, is how difficult it is to create a bitcoin. When

---

[2] Samman, George. "Bitcoin Price Drops Below $200: Have We Reached the Bottom?" CoinTelegraph. January 14, 2015. Accessed June 22, 2015. http://cointelegraph.com/news/113299/bitcoin-price-drops-200-how-we-reached-the-bottom.

Bitcoin got its first exchange rate in October 2009, it was calculated based on how much electricity was consumed by mining operations when a bitcoin was created.

Although there are other factors that go into Bitcoin's price, the cost of creation does create something of a floor for Bitcoin's true value. If it cost two dollars to create a single bitcoin (it costs far more, but to keep things simple, let's assume it's two dollars), then it is safe to assume that someone selling a bitcoin would want at least two dollars for it.

That doesn't mean the value will never drop below two dollars, because speculative trading and increased merchant adoption—without a corresponding increase in merchant holding—can cause the price to temporarily drop lower than what the miners would want to sell their Bitcoin for. Bitcoin is distributed enough that miners aren't the only group that has an effect on its exchange rate.

But the rate does ultimately come from them. If a bitcoin costs two dollars to make today and 10 dollars tomorrow, but adoption, utility, and demand all remain the same, then it is a fairly sure bet the price will go up. This is good news for long-term Bitcoin investors, because Bitcoin is consistently becoming more difficult to create; and roughly every six years, new bitcoins become twice as rare.

Bitcoin is rewarded to miners based on who solves a block. Each block used to be worth 50BTC but this went down to 25BTC a few years ago. The next block-halving—when the reward for solving a block is cut in half—is expected in 2016, likely in June, and will see the reward drop to 12.5 bitcoins per block. Therefore, in addition to the regular difficulty increase, it is about to become significantly more difficult to create a bitcoin.

The block-halving will not coincide directly with a jump in the price of Bitcoin. Speculative traders attempt to factor in sure bets like block-halving when deciding on a price they are willing to pay for Bitcoin. However, as I've mentioned, speculative traders aren't the only group that has an influence on the price of Bitcoin. They are constantly at odds with miners who only care about the cost of creating a bitcoin compared to the price of Bitcoin. They deal with the current reality, rather than price predictions. If a bitcoin cost 10 dollars to produce but the price had dropped to nine dollars, at least some miners would wait for the price to rise rather than sell at a loss. Speculative traders might be bearish or bullish—the terms used in financial markets to describe a downward or upward trend or prediction, respectively—on the price of Bitcoin and deal based on that prediction. In contrast, miners are only worried about their electricity bill.

I am not trying to disparage speculative traders. Their job is to imagine what the world will be like in the future—be it 20 minutes or 20 years—and make decisions based on that prediction. Miners don't have that luxury and have to make cold, calculated decisions based on what is going on now, not what might be in the future.

So speculative traders might think they are accounting for the reward-halving, and in many ways they are. Everyone knows it is coming and everyone is building it into their expectations, but things will change when their predicted future meets with present-minded miners. The question of when, exactly, this development will cause an increase in the price of Bitcoin is up in the air. The jump could come shortly before or months after the reward halves. It may never come because some unforeseen problem tanks or inflates the price of Bitcoin beforehand. What is for sure, however, is that Bitcoin will become more difficult to produce, which will cause miners to hold on to their bitcoins until they are valuable enough to at least break even.

There are countless strategies when it comes to investing in Bitcoin. Everyone has their own system and there certainly is a lot that can be gained by riding the volatile swings in Bitcoin's price. Ultimately, the safest advice is simply this: buy some Bitcoin, put it in a safe place (like a paper wallet), and then leave it alone. Come back in five years and reevaluate.

Responding to the assertion that 2014 was Bitcoin's worst year, the Bitcoin evangelist Andreas Antonopoulos once told would-be investors to give Bitcoin some time. After pointing to the $500 million in venture capital investment into Bitcoin companies, he insisted:

> Give us two years. Now what happens when you throw 500 companies and 10,000 developers at the problem? Give [it] two years and you will see some pretty amazing things in bitcoin.[3]

I disagree with the two-year timeline put forth by Antonopoulos but not with the general sentiment behind his statement. Two years is not realistic; although that amount of time might seem like an eternity within the cryptocurrency ecosystem, the general public—and especially the financial markets—don't move at the same speed.

---

[3] Bundrick, Hal M. "Andreas Antonopoulos: 'Give Bitcoin Two Years.'" Inside Bitcoins. February 8, 2015. Accessed June 22, 2015. http://insidebitcoins.com/news/andreas-antonopoulos-give-bitcoin-two-years/29708.

But Bitcoin is growing; this is undeniable. It also seems likely that in two years' time it will have grown more, and more traditional finance companies will be on board and more borderline users will have fallen over to the Bitcoin side of the fence. As that happens, there will be a lot of companies looking to acquire Bitcoin, if for no other reason than as fuel for their own blockchain-based services.

I don't disagree with Antonopoulos's quasi-prediction in general, however. The block-halving of 2016 and the continued increase in acceptance and investment indicate he is likely correct. But I would be careful about claiming that 2017 represents some kind of deadline (which some might surmise from Antonopoulos's comment). Bitcoin has been nothing if not unpredictable.

There has only been one constant in the Bitcoin world so far: Bitcoin is consistently becoming more difficult to create. As long as the currency continues to be used and adopted, the price will have to follow.

In short, buy some Bitcoin, drink some whiskey (or whisky, as the case may be), and HODL.

Chapter 14:
Day Trading

Are you sure you don't want to stay up with us? The Japanese markets wake up in a few hours, there will be some action then.

—A day trader whose name is lost to my memory,
said shortly after 1 a.m. at a Bitcoin convention afterparty

Day trading Bitcoin is not for the weak-willed or the halfhearted. I do not particularly recommend it. I don't do very much of it myself. For every person who can beat the system, there are more who can't. During a gold rush, the best thing you can do is sell shovels. During a war, the smart money goes into "defense" contracting. When there is an extremely volatile commodity, some day traders do get rich, some lose their shirts, and the exchange rakes in the fees either way.

There is also something that makes the day trader almost diametrically opposed to the philosophy and motivations of the rest of the Bitcoin community. Day traders love volatility. No other member of the community desires volatility. Miners, merchants, payment processors, long-term investors, people who work for Bitcoin—every one of these groups desires stability, not volatility.

At the same time, the community needs day trading. It makes up a significant part of the currency's legitimate use and volume. It is also one reason why the price climbed so high, so quickly. Those jumps brought a lot of real value into the Bitcoin ecosystem, both in fiat money and by making Bitcoin more valuable. Many of the early adopters who saw a return of 9,000 percent or more on their investment reinvested at least some of that money into Bitcoin-related businesses.

The thing about high-volume trading of any commodity is that it gets kind of "meta" after a while. Ostensibly, everyone is betting on what they think Bitcoin is going to be worth, only they aren't really betting on that. What they are really betting on is what they think the public, primarily other day traders, think the price will be in an hour, or half an hour, or 10 minutes.

Certain strategies can be followed that attempt to predict what the public will think next, not based on the theoretical value of Bitcoin but on the theoretical ineptitude of the average day trader.

I do not recommend you read this chapter and then jump into the world of near-unregulated Bitcoin day trading armed only with this book, your life savings, and a head full of dreams. I have not done that. In all honesty, I am not an experienced day trader and will not masquerade as one. This chapter will explain some basic tips and theories, as well as offer resources for more information. This is not meant as a comprehensive guide. I do not mean this disclaimer in a "cover my ass legally, but really, you are ready, wink wink, nudge nudge" kind of way. I am, at best, a toddler in the day trading world. So take the knowledge I have to offer, but then go learn from a master before you invest even what you think you are willing to lose.

You will be competing against real animals. Many of them, the most successful ones, are veterans of the stock market. Even they are concerned about the effects that a 24/7 global market can have on the junkies that previously lived on stock quotes. The quote at the beginning this chapter was said to me directly. Although I have forgotten the trader's name, I will never forget the enthusiasm with which he said it. *He was dead serious.* He wasn't giving me a tough time, either; he really thought that staying up until 3 a.m. to work the Bitcoin market as the Japanese started waking up was something I would be interested in doing, even though I had just covered the convention for the last 17 hours.

You should know, going into Bitcoin day trading, that guy is your competition. You don't necessarily have to beat the likes of this man, but if you are serious about making a profit, you will have to match his level of dedication. On the other hand, Bitcoin is very volatile compared to nearly every other commodity—stocks, precious metals, currencies—so there is a lot of money to be made if you can ride the waves.

Of course, if you are interested in day trading at all, you have by now heard the "buy low, sell high" principle that is and always will be the golden rule of investing, regardless of whether you are playing the long or the short game. Everyone knows this strategy, but day trading only works because most people don't adhere to it.

They want to adhere to it, they probably even think they adhere to it, but they don't. The problem is FOMO—the fear of missing out. The average day trader will see a quick rise in price and think, "Oh, this is the jump we have been waiting for, I'm going to miss it!" But, of course, in most cases, the day trader had already missed it and is buying in at the peak or close to it. Then when the price tanks, rather than hold out for it to rise again, the average day trader overreacts, thinks that this could be the next big drop, and sells. Of course, all professional traders and whales—the term for big Bitcoin holders—bought in when the price was low and sold when it was high.

The key is to stay calm, using certain indicators to gain some insight into the reality of the market as opposed to the current price of the coin. First, you need to know where to get information. The most popular resource and absolutely required reading if you plan to trade Bitcoin in any serious fashion is BitcoinWisdom.com. The website gives information on Bitcoin and all the major altcoins on all the major exchanges. In addition to order books, it also includes some basic tools useful for identifying trading opportunities.

There are other sites, such as Coinigy, that allow you to trade on multiple sites at once and give you a suite of tools that resemble those used by professional stock traders. It currently offers a free trial, after which it charges a fairly hefty fee. Depending on the kind of volume you want to put behind your day-trading activities, you might or might not find it worth the price.

The other principles of stock or currency day trading apply here as well: use market indicators to identify possible trading points and then capitalize on them. Day trading is a bit like surfing—you will fall and you will make mistakes, and you will be wrong a lot of the time. Just as in surfing, you will fall off your board a lot; it is a part of the sport. The key is to stick with it until you are right more often than you are wrong and to use small amounts until you get a feel for the market. Bitcoin is helpful in this because you can "practice" with insignificant amounts—five dollars or even less—and then move to larger bets when you are ready.

The main thing you are looking for is variance between where your indicators say the price should be and where the market price actually is. Generally, the market should rebound closer toward where it was previously. There are general trends down or up, but they generally happen in "stairs" rather than "elevator" jumps as the price tests new bottoms or highs.

The first concept that you should know is that of the double bottom. When a bear (down) market is about to transition to a bull (up) market, it will first test things with a double bottom. What this means is that when the price hits a new low, soon after there will be a quick but small rise in price, followed by another drop, typically equal to or smaller than the previous drop.

This is an indicator that some people are buying at the new lower price and a rebound is imminent. Keep in mind this pattern is not the only factor that should be considered when making a trade, because double drops can sometimes instead be temporary pit stops on the way down even further.

There are other fundamental indicators that every trader needs to know about. They are the moving average (MA), the moving average convergence difference (MACD), the relative strength index (RSI), and the on-balance volume (OBV). I will also cover Fibonacci retracements, which are less of an indicator and more of a helpful visualizer.

Coinigy and Brian Beamish—a.k.a. The Rational Investor— put together a great series of videos on day trading Bitcoin using their tools. I highly recommended watching these videos. They can be found on Coinigy's YouTube channel.

Beamish's system works like this: when the indicators draw an "M" it is a sign of a bearish market. Conversely, when they show a "W" you are likely to see a bullish market. Beamish recommends that you identify at least three independent indicators before considering it a trading opportunity.

Moving Average (MA)

The MA is the average price over a set amount of time. It helps reduce noise by smoothing out price swings. The two common types of MA are simple moving average (SMA) and exponential moving average (EMA). SMA is just the average of all the segments of time accounted for; the EMA gives weight to more recent indicators.

Moving Average Convergence Difference (MACD)

The MACD measures the relative strength of price swings by comparing more recent EMA prices to past EMA prices. The typical MACD setup takes the 12-day EMA average and subtracts the 26-day EMA from it.[1]

---

[1] "Moving Average (MA) Definition." Investopedia. November 24, 2003. Accessed June 22, 2015. http://www.investopedia.com/terms/m/movingaverage.asp.

Relative Strength Index (RSI)

The RSI compares recent losses and gains to judge the over-bought and oversold conditions relative to the average price.[2]

On-Balance Volume

The OBV tracks the current volume in a market compared to previous volumes. In theory, increased volume without a corresponding price increase means there should—again, in theory—be a price increase coming shortly.[3]

Fibonacci Retracements

The Fibonacci retracements are not an indicator but they are still a useful tool. These are graphs that illustrate likely bounce-back levels and ceilings using ratios and can be a useful guide for making the decision to get in and out of a coin investment. The ratios usually used are 23.6 percent, 38.2 percent, 50 percent, 61.8 percent, and 100 percent. Trace the Fibonacci retracement from the coin's highest price to its lowest price (for the timeframe you want to judge) and do not buy in at any box other than the 23.6 percent, or 38.2 percent boxes. Always sell in the 61.8 percent and 100 percent boxes. Rather than something that actually

[2] Bitcoin RSI Tutorial. Directed by Brian Beamish. Performed by Brian Beamish. Youtube.com/coinigy. April 25, 2015. https://www.youtube.com/watch?v=Vq2EC7OinQQ.

[3] "On-Balance Volume (OBV) Definition." Investopedia. November 24, 2003. Accessed June 22, 2015. http://www.investopedia.com/terms/o/onbalancevolume.asp.

predicts moves, it is more useful as a tool that helps you stick to the basic "sell high, buy low" principle and seeing it laid out in front of you can be helpful.[4]

Again, and I can't stress this enough, I am far from an expert on this subject. Do your own research and consider taking a class. At the very least, read and watch everything that is available for free.

Eventually, with some practice and dedication, you might find that you can turn a profit on Bitcoin volatility. Your success might tempt you into other markets. Day trading is just as exciting as gambling on anything else, and addiction can become a real problem, especially considering the hundreds of altcoin markets that are also available for 24-hour trading.

Bitcoin doesn't just allow users to invest in Bitcoin itself, altcoins and related services; it opens up an entire world of investment to anyone with an Internet connection.

Financial services go beyond simple bank accounts. Financial services are about increasing your wealth or at least making sure some of it will be around after you stop working. That means more than just saving; it means investing. Investment services are generally available to people in America but you usually either have to go through a middleman or be wealthy enough to afford the minimum account levels of services like E*TRADE. If you don't want to get into investing but you have a hunch gold is going up (or down), Bitcoin enables you to profit either way.

Bitcoin lowers these barriers not only for first world citizens but also for everyone else. The Bitcoin blockchain is designed

---

[4] Bitcoin Fib Tutorial - Fibonacci Retracements. Directed by Brian Beamish. Performed by Brian Beamish. Youtube.com/coinigy. April 25, 2015. https://www.youtube.com/watch?v=9Wj9ITc0444.

to transfer value and there is no reason that value has to be in Bitcoin. In theory, it can transfer anything of value. In the future, it is reasonable to expect that stocks and bonds will be traded on the blockchain as well. It seems almost inevitable. But we are not quite there yet.

In the meantime, there is Bitcoin day trading. It arguably has a negative effect on Bitcoin, because the instability it causes might harm the currency by making it less useful as a store of value. However, speculative trading remains one of the largest uses for Bitcoin and that volume would be missed if it disappeared overnight. The promise of quick riches, fool's gold though it might be, has also been successful in bringing more people to the currency. Speculative trading and Bitcoin will likely be bedfellows for a few more years. This association is hardly unique to Bitcoin.

Chapter 15:

Altcoin Trading and Pump-and-Dumps

Shame on you guys. You can't advocate for Bitcoin and the transformative changes it enables while also pumping some ridiculous alt-coin.

—Blogger Matt Branton, The Branton Bits, April 7, 2014

The same strategies that apply to Bitcoin can be applied to altcoins; the principles are the same. However, altcoins—especially once you get past the top few in market-cap size—are more susceptible to pump-and-dump tactics.

Pump-and-dumps are not unique to cryptocurrency. They have existed in the stock market and especially in off-market penny stocks that have low liquidity. The same pattern applies to altcoins. The lower the liquidity of the market (*i.e.*, how many people are buying and selling), the easier pump-and-dump schemes are to pull off and the more effective they can be.

The tactic is an old one. The basic idea is the same as what happens in investing: buy when the price is low and sell when it is high. The difference—and what gives the tactic its shady reputation—is that the people running the pump-and-dump are the reason for the price increase. When the "dump" happens, which is part of the plan, unsuspecting investors are left holding the bag.

This process can sometimes be harmful to a coin's long-term health. The artificial infusion of perceived value can be a roller coaster ride that those interested in the long-term prospects of a coin find distasteful. At the same time, for the coins that can handle them, pump-and-dumps are mostly harmless, except when it comes to the investors who find themselves on the wrong side of the pump.

Traditionally, pump-and-dumps follow the same general pattern. First, a group of investors will quietly buy an altcoin without much liquidity while the price is low. Sometimes simply buying the coin in large amounts is enough to get the pump going, but in more complex schemes, they will start spreading rumors. On the community site BitcoinTalk, people will start hyping the coin and how great its development team is or how great the community is or something along those lines. They might even get an article or two in a cryptocurrency news site. Then the investors, along with anyone else they convinced to join the scheme at this relatively late stage, will put in big buy orders all at once. With every big buy, the price goes up, and as I've discussed earlier, so does the fear of missing out that helps drive the ebbs and flows of the market. When they see the coin's price going up, perhaps encouraged by the news stories and positive posts they saw in the past few weeks, buyers will jump on the coin thinking that it is legitimately rising in value.

Then the so-called investors sell their now more valuable coin, the price plummets and the investors who were late to the game are left holding a commodity that is now far less valuable than it was before they entered the market. Some of the investors, even those who were a part of the FOMO group, will make some modest profit, but a lot more will be left holding a virtual bag of a worthless coin.

Again, such tactics affect all commodities with a low enough liquidity. It just so happens that there are many cryptocurrencies that have low liquidity compared to more traditional commodities. And since the space is virtually unregulated, pump-and-dumps have become commonplace.

The groups that run the schemes are fairly brazen in their tactics. The most infamous of them is the BobSurplus group. It has been behind some of the largest pump-and-dump schemes in the cryptocurrency world and is open about its efforts.

The man behind the group charges "investors" 2BTC to join his group. According to his marketing materials, he will tell these lucky investors the next coin he will be pumping. The "investors" then buy this coin, raising the price. Afterward, the coin gets dumped on those who bought into the hype.

There are numerous accusations that SurplusBob doesn't actually pump the price himself, instead simply pocketing the membership fees and using the hype to grow the coin. There have also been a few instances of former members of the group complaining that their profits were not as high as promised.[1]

---

[1] Fury, The Sound And. "The Story of Bob Surplus." Bitcoin Talk. December 17, 2014. Accessed June 22, 2015. https://bitcointalk.org/index.php?topic=896480.0.

There are too many sayings that apply to pick just one. Something about lying down with snakes seems appropriate.

The pump-and-dump scheme has seen many iterations during the short history of cryptocurrency. The most damaging instances, however, are the coins that were designed to be a pump-and-dump from the very beginning.

A popular way to launch a coin these days is through an initial coin offering (ICO). Any ICO should be considered suspicious, because it has the potential to funnel a huge amount of money to the coin's issuer. This is because for a coin to be issued in this manner, it has to be pre-mined. There is no "offering" unless there are coins to offer. In a completely fair distribution where initial coins go to the initial securers of the network, there is no reason for a proof-of-work coin to have an initial pre-mine, other than to benefit the creators of that coin.

Proof-of-stake coins, however, do need a small initial coin distribution. Unlike proof-of-work coins, which are rewarded to miners based on the hashing power they bring to the network, proof-of-stake coins reward miners based on how many coins they currently hold—generally a one- to five-percent interest rate. If there isn't anyone holding any coins, there is no one to give that interest to. So there has to be a small number pre-mined in order to get the coin going.

A lot of coins will start out as proof-of-work and then transition to proof-of-stake after a set number of blocks have been processed. Assuming there isn't also a pre-mine, this is the most surefire way to ensure the coin you are investing in has a fair initial distribution. Of course, you still can't be sure there won't be pump-and-dump elements once it starts trading on the open market. There most certainly will be and the coin's launch is a particularly good time to start a pump-and-dump.

But there are fair ways to distribute pure proof-of-stake coins. Potential investors simply have to investigate deeper. There are some things to consider. Coins are released in an "initial distribution," which is exactly what it sounds like: how the first group of coins that can be used to stake are distributed to people. Remember, proof-of-stake coins still use a worldwide network of computers run by its users to confirm transactions. The difference is that proof-of-stake doesn't care how much computational power you bring to the network and instead rewards based on how many coins you hold. The idea is that you are rewarded based on how invested you are in the network and how willing you are to hold onto your coins. But if no coins exist yet, the first group of them have to be created and distributed in order for there be any coins that are staked. Some coins do this with a short proof-of-work phase, which is arguably the most fair way to distribute the initial coins needed to launch a proof-of-stake coin.

An initial distribution shouldn't be more than a few percentage points; preferably just one percent of the coin will be released at launch. That way, there is time for the coin to grow while it gets distributed. Remember, this is supposed to be the birth of the coin, not a later stage in its life cycle. A high initial distribution means that the currency is almost certainly going to remain centralized in the hands of the few. By holding a large amount of the initial distribution, they will be able to run pump-and-dump schemes repeatedly before their reserves are exhausted. Additionally, if one entity holds too many coins and are staking them, it could theoretically alter the blockchain.

How the percentage is split up is also important. There are no hard-set rules but an initial distribution should include significant amounts earmarked for the general public. Having a small amount set aside for developers is not unreasonable, but remember: since they haven't released a coin yet, they haven't proven themselves either.

Ideally, the initial distribution of coins should be free. People should be able to send an email or something similar and get their portion of the coins. Although if a company is large, well known, and has technology it has been able to demonstrate publicly, then charging something isn't necessarily a deal breaker. But when developers start talking about initial "public" prices—as Josh Garza did with Paycoin—implying that private investors are getting a different price, it is a sure red flag.

Remember, prices should be based what a coin can do. If a coin hasn't done anything yet, it shouldn't have a price. When Paycoin launched, it had already sold rights to the coin to investors and former customers of GAW's mining operations at several price points before it launched with a "public price" of $20.[2] Paycoin never reached that price on the open market. But people who had received the coin for free or for cheap made a killing as hopeful investors bought the coin as it quickly fell through every floor put in front of it.

Even then, the initial distribution is virtually never the right time to buy a coin. The price almost always goes down at a certain point in time, even in legitimate coins. The best strategy is to wait and see what a coin does after launch. It took Bitcoin

---

[2] "Paycoin Is Here | Paycoin Digital Currency." May 17, 2014. Accessed June 22, 2015. https://archive.is/0HEwd. http://paycoins.biz/paycoin/

nearly eight years to get where it is today and it hasn't hit its peak yet. No one is going to "miss out" on being an early adopter for the next big altcoin because they didn't buy it when it launched; there is plenty of time to invest.

But a coin doesn't necessarily need the name recognition and media attention that Paycoin received before it launched, although that helps. Pump-and-dumps have been successful just because of the hype within the cryptocommunity.

If you want to avoid falling victim to a pump-and-dump scheme, the simple rule is to bet only on things that are provably real. Only bet on coins that have a real commitment to code— ones whose developers consistently work on the code and it is open source. Even if you can't program yourself, you can get some idea of how active a developer is by looking at how active their GitHub page is.

It is not foolproof to look simply at the number of git commits (*i.e.*, suggested changes)—a developer could make little git-pulls (*i.e.*, implemented changes) that have no effect on the code to make it seem as if they are active. But with a little digging you should be able to tell if the changes are significant. Code might look incomprehensible to you, but before dropping a significant amount of money into a coin, you should compare its code to the coin it is forked from. (Forking a coin means copying the code over to a new Git with the intention of making changes.) You can do that by going to GitHub and comparing the two projects. Some developers might try to disguise where the coin came from.

Very few coins are built entirely from the ground up, so there should always be references to something. If there aren't, then the developers are likely trying to hide their lack of work. If comparing two coins is beyond your capabilities, then depending on an expert to audit the code is one way to go, but be sure to research the auditor as well—there are sites that have given "proof-of-developer" certification to coins that had little actual work done to them. Often, the proof-of-developer certification pertains to how public the developer is with their real-life identity and not how much work they have put into the code.

If you find the code's source and there are few or no changes other than the name, there hasn't been much work done. That doesn't mean you should write the coin off completely, but you should wait to invest until there has been some provable progress. If a coin is not open source, then no investment should even be considered until it is.

Remember, the vast majority of coins are dumped as soon as they get on a popular exchange. It might not even be part of a pump-and-dump scheme. Miners and early adopters are getting their first access to open markets, so they are naturally going to cash in on their investment when they can. Regardless of whether it is malicious or not, there is rarely a reason to invest before that inevitable first dump unless you are one of the miners.

I don't particularly recommend chasing new altcoins looking for that next big payday. Either you will become a victim of a scam or you will invest in a well-meaning coin that has very little chance of becoming something sustainable. It's a good idea to research some of the more established altcoins, decide which ones you feel have a chance to survive long-term, and then invest small amounts in those coins with an eye on the future—realizing that investment might be gone in a few years.

Chasing profits through new coins is a fool's errand. If you have the hardware to effectively mine some of these coins, there's nothing wrong with mining them and then dumping when they get onto their first exchange, but it isn't worth buying new hardware to do this. At best, it is a way to squeeze a few more rounds of profitability out of Bitcoin-mining hardware you already own.

Chapter 16:
Peer-to-Peer Lending

> If you go out into the real world, you cannot miss seeing that
> the poor are poor not because they are untrained or illiterate
> but because they can't retain the returns of their labor. They
> have no control over capital, and it is the ability to control
> capital that gives people the power to rise out of poverty.
>
> —Muhammad Yunus, *Banker to the Poor:*
> *Micro-Lending and the Battle Against World Poverty*

Microloans have been the focus of Internet economists and third
world advocates for years. The idea is an old one: although charity is nice, a leg up is even better. Teach a man to fish and all that.

Microloan and microfinance sites have existed for years. The
most popular ones include Kiva, Opportunity Fund, and Accion.
They fill different niches and serve different functions but ultimately they all boil down to one thing: individuals giving loans
to other individuals, either as a charitable act or a financial

investment. The hope is to create avenues where excess money can make the most change. Twenty bucks given by me or invested by me into an individual might not do much, but pair it with 20 bucks from a hundred other users and suddenly it doesn't seem like such an insignificant amount—especially since the borrower is often in a third world country with a much lower cost of living.

Bitcoin has a lot of potential in this market due to two factors. First, its virtually nonexistent transaction fees make it particularly suitable for microloans. Although most microloans and microfinancing sites target the middle class and up as its lenders, Bitcoin-powered microlending sites allow even the poor to have an avenue to increase their meager savings via investments in other individuals. Fifty dollars, five dollars, even 50 cents can be invested with a reasonable expectation that the money will be paid back with interest. Investing such small amounts using traditional fiat systems would create a huge pain in the ass for lenders when it came time to pay the loan back. Either they or the middleman would have to send back dozens of small transactions every month using the slow and ineffective legacy system. Paying back investors with Bitcoin can be done instantly, simply and inexpensively. Internet-enabled but fiat-based peer-to-peer lending programs have created systems that are quicker and simpler than it would be without them, but they still ultimately go through the legacy system and are hit with significant fees because of it. Even with sites such as Kiva, a microloan site with a charity bent that takes no fees of its own and depends on separate donations to cover operating costs, not all the money gets into the hands of borrowers—because their "field partners," who help get money into the hands of borrowers, sometimes take a profit.

Although I am not a power investor, I have experience investing through BTCJam, by far the largest microloan/microfinance site powered by Bitcoin. The experience has been mostly pleasant. As with so much in the Bitcoin world, this kind of investing has its fair share of scammers. But don't let that scare you off. BTCJam does a good job of illustrating the risk, and the vast majority of borrowers are sincere in their desire to repay their loans. BTCJam also does its best to verify the identities of the borrowers, asking for photo ID, linked social media accounts, proof of income, bank accounts, and even eBay and PayPal accounts. It then gives each lender a grade based on the information they have provided.

High-grade loans pay off the vast majority of the time. Lower-grade loans offer higher interest rates but carry more risk. There are a few tricks to keep in mind. Most scammers follow one of a few set patterns. Be especially careful if you see that your loan would be the first to this particular borrower. Although everyone has to start somewhere, you might want to let other investors take that initial risk. Even though defaulting on a loan on BTCJam is not without its consequences, more than a few people are willing to burn that bridge for a quick payday. Investing in someone who has proven the ability to pay back loans is much safer than investing in someone who hasn't.

Likewise, pay close attention to the borrower's history. Most scammers know that lenders are hesitant to fund large debts and will attempt to build up trust by taking out and paying back a number of small loans. Afterwards, they will follow up with a large loan that they never intend to pay back. Be suspicious of lenders who have successfully paid back a few small loans and are now asking for five or six bitcoins.

The two tips above can be considered the "hard rules" of lending that should only be broken in the rarest of circumstances. Here's another that is simply something to keep in mind when picking borrowers to invest in: the further the person is from you, the more difficult it will be to track him or her down after a default. Although BTCJam will send all information to an outside arbiter who will give lenders an arbitration award that can be used in court, tracking down someone in (for example) India and bringing them to an Indian court over a $200 loan might not be feasible or worthwhile.

I don't want to suggest that lenders should not invest in borrowers from other countries, because providing opportunities to entrepreneurs in third world countries is one of the biggest societal benefits to come out of microloans and microfunding. Rather, I simply urge caution when investing in borrowers who are not within the same legal jurisdiction as you, especially if they break the hard rules I mentioned.

When you are considering making a loan, you should pay attention to BTCJam's rating system, the comments by more experienced lenders, and the feasibility of the borrower's plan for repayment. If you want to ignore any or all of my tips, feel free to do so. It might even pay off. The most important strategy to keep in mind is diversification—be sure to lend to a number of different borrowers. With enough diversification, BTCJam loans should pay out overall—assuming you aren't only investing in risky loans.

Most loans on BTCJam are pegged either to US dollars or the fiat currency of the borrower. This is to protect the borrower and lender from Bitcoin's sometimes massive price swings. Although loans are made and paid back using Bitcoin, the amount of

Bitcoin required for the loan and the repayment will generally be based on the exchange rate of the fiat currency the borrower chose. This system allows the lender to maintain a somewhat reliable revenue stream—assuming proper research is conducted—and hedge against the fluctuations in Bitcoin price while keeping money "active."

Some loans aren't tied to fiat price, but these are only recommended for borrowers who make their money in Bitcoin. They can be useful for those who are bullish or favorable on the Bitcoin price but still want to do something other than let it sit in a wallet somewhere. The selection of Bitcoin loans is more limited than that of fiat-based loans, however.

From a borrower's perspective, BTCJam—and in the future, services like it—provide the opportunity to receive a loan at a reasonable rate without needing to pander to a bank. Business models that might not offer high enough returns for a bank or a venture capitalist are suddenly viable. Borrowers can also use BTCJam to get out from under the thumb of traditional lenders by using a loan to pay off their debts and consolidating them into one low-interest loan gathered from the crowd. To be fair, however, there does appear to be more risk involved here than in traditional peer-to-peer sites such as Kiva, because the Bitcoin connection seems to make borrowers feel as if they can get away with not paying back their loan. Still, the vast majority of loans are paid back, especially the high-ranked ones.

Providing loans has been one of the most profitable activities for bankers since the invention of banking. Just as the Internet has reduced the influence of traditional record labels, Bitcoin has the potential to lessen the power of the traditional banking industry. Although banks and bankers will likely evolve and survive the introduction and evolution of Bitcoin, their monopoly on loans is quickly coming to an end. When the people become the bank, there is less need for a traditional banking system.

Microloans and microfinancing are among the most prominent areas where Bitcoin—and the Internet in general—can have a huge impact. As is true of many other functions of Bitcoin, microfunding and microlending can be accomplished with fiat currencies. But what makes Bitcoin significant is that it can do it better. Microloans and microfinancing are about individuals helping out other individuals in a way that benefits both parties. In this peer-to-peer transaction, there is no reason to use the traditional financial middlemen. Instead of using a bank to send money to Kiva or another service, which then has to send that money to another bank that will then transfer it to the borrower—as fees accumulate along the way—lenders can send funds directly to borrowers. In the worst-case scenario, they have to go through one intermediary such as BTCJam, which takes a fee of only one to four percent.

Although some might claim the music industry is in trouble because of the Internet, the truth is that the Internet has been great for the vast majority of artists. The only artists who lost out are the ones who sat at the top of the charts and were used to selling millions of records based on one hit song. But for less-visible artists and bands, the Internet has been a way to gain exposure across the world, and this exposure has helped them escape the obscurity of bars and garage shows. The only group in the music industry that was truly hurt by the Internet was the record companies that made billions of dollars from the creative endeavors of true artists. As soon as distribution—which used to be under the companies' control—moved to the Internet, many artists no longer needed them.

Bitcoin and microloans are doing the same with the banks. Banks have overhead: employees, electricity, advertising and everything else that comes with running a business. All of that is factored into the cost of the loan. Crowdfunded loans, particularly crowdfunded loans that use Bitcoin, don't have to cover any of these expenses and can offer a better rate than the banks. The greatly reduced overhead costs benefit both lender and borrower.

The only group they don't benefit is the group that held a monopoly on lending. "Held" being the key word in that last sentence.

Chapter 17:

Investing in Other Commodities Using Bitcoin

The beauty of diversification is it's about as close as you can get to a free lunch in investing.

—Financial writer Barry Ritholtz

Bitcoin doesn't just allow users to invest in Bitcoin itself, altcoins and related services. It also opens up an entire world of investments to anyone with an Internet connection.

Something I said toward the end of Chapter 14 bears repeating: financial services go beyond simple bank accounts. As I noted, financial services are about increasing your wealth or at least making sure some of it will be around after your working years. This means more than just saving; it means investing. Investment services are available to people in America but one generally has to go through a middleman or be wealthy enough to afford minimum account levels with services such as E*TRADE.

Bitcoin lowers these barriers. The Bitcoin blockchain is designed to transfer value, and that value does not have to be in the form of Bitcoin. In theory, the blockchain can transfer anything. Deeds, birth certificates, marriage certificates and passports can all be committed and saved onto the blockchain in a cryptographically secure way. It is reasonable to expect that in the future, stocks and bonds will also be traded on the blockchain.

But the time when anything can be traded on the blockchain is not here yet. The altcoin Ripple has made the most headway in accomplishing this goal. It uses "trusted gateways" to allow users to buy commodities such as gold, as well as various currencies—both cryptocurrencies and fiat currencies. Trusted gateways are entities, like precious metal investment companies, that can be trusted to honor assets they put on the Ripple network. The gateway issues a promissory note for the commodity. This can then be transferred to any Ripple user, who can sell it to someone else or return it to the gateway for Ripple for the current value of that commodity at any time. Let's say a precious metal company puts out a "silver coin" and backs it with 10,000 ounces of silver. It releases 100,000 silver coins, making each coin worth one-tenth of one silver ounce. Investor A buys 10 silver coins at market price and the price of silver goes up 10 percent. Investor A could then return it to the precious metal company and get a 10 percent return—minus any fees the company may charge—or sell it to investor B, who thinks silver will rise even higher. Investor B could buy the silver coins from investor A without any fees and then hold on to them until silver goes even higher. He then would be able to turn that back to the precious metal company for a higher price than he paid investor A for it. Of course, the inverse is also true: if the price of silver goes down, so will the value of the silver coins.

The issue much of the cryptocommunity has with this system is that the trusted gateways need to be trusted. People are simply trading one middleman for another. It has run into some issues with trusted gateways not living up to the "trusted" part of its name, but it is still an interesting system.

Stocks and similar securities have not been added to the Ripple network yet. The chief reason for their absence is regulation. There are laws against encouraging "non-credited" investors from investing into securities and stocks in the US and that has slowed this potential market, for good or ill.

Although the Ripple network might currently be too slow for high-volume stock day trading, it could be done, with some concessions. In theory, anything can be transferred on the Ripple network, assuming you trust the gateway. But Ripple has always been careful not to step on any regulation toes. More centralized than other cryptocurrencies, Ripple Labs could feasibly be held responsible for additions to the Ripple network. In fact, it ran afoul of regulations once already, though it settled out of court.[1]

There have also been cases of stocks offered for Bitcoin on Dark Web marketplaces, although their validity is questionable. Buying "stocks" on the Dark Web simply means you are buying a promissory note from a Dark Web dealer, not something I would recommend. Considering their occupation usually also consists of selling drugs and hacked accounts, their promissory notes probably don't account for much. I would highly recommend against buying any kind of "stock" in any dark market

---

[1] Todd, Sarah, and Ian McKendry. "What Ripple's Fincen Fine Means for the Digital Currency Industry." American Banker. May 6, 2015. Accessed January 14, 2016. http://www.americanbanker.com/news/bank-technology/what-ripples-fincen-fine-means-for-the-digital-currency-industry-1074195-1.html.

just as I would warn against buying one from an individual in a chatroom or message board.

The point is, if the regulation were not in the way, it would be possible to trade stocks using the blockchain. It probably will happen someday soon, either via Ripple or another altcoin, or Bitcoin itself. Non–Wall Street markets are becoming more popular every year. Eventually, cryptocurrencies could create a fully peer-to-peer stock market without any kind of middleman outside of code and cryptography. In that kind of system, people would cryptographically sign their ownership of stock away to investors who want to buy that stock, and investors would be able to trade with each other, without fees, from all over the world. The company Serica is working on a peer-to-peer marketplace that would theoretically allow the purchase of pretty much any commodity, including stocks and land titles, but these features are currently in private beta (*i.e.*, being privately tested) and can't yet be accessed by the public. Furthermore, no one really seems to know how it will work.

In addition, Overstock.com CEO Patrick Byrne, a longtime Bitcoin advocate, is currently working on a marketplace that will challenge Wall Street. Unlike many other cryptocurrency "stock market" projects, Overstock is actually going through the proper channels to stay on the right side of regulation. At first, Overstock will only offer its own company's stock, but the hope is that other companies will soon follow suit.[2]

This chapter is not about the future, however. It is about how Bitcoin can help diversify your investments today. I will mention

---

[2] Leising, Matthew. "Discount Retailer Overstock Has New Target: Upending Wall Street." Bloomberg.com. January 14, 2016. Accessed January 14, 2016. http://www.bloomberg.com/news/articles/2016-01-14/discount-retailer-overstock-has-new-target-upending-wall-street.

some services that are for-profit businesses that are subject to failure at any time. As is the case with all Bitcoin businesses, I can't guarantee they will be around in a year or even six months. None of them paid me to be included in this book; I simply picked the ones I believe are the most reliable. That said, when you are giving money to a company, you should always check them out first. Reliable information often changes quickly, so always check to make sure things haven't changed since this book was published.

Trust has been a problem for gold bugs for decades. Since the Gold Reserve Act in 1933, there have been strict controls on who can hold and sell gold. This regulation requires investors to trust a third party to physically hold their gold for them. This can be risky, because without transparency it can be impossible to know if the company has overextended itself. Sure, it might hold 20 gold bars in a vault but what if it owes 200 gold bars to its customers? What happens if customers all ask for their gold back at once? Over time, regulations have reduced this risk, but bank failure remains a concern for anyone who doesn't have their gold locked up in a safe in their house.

Just as in fiat investing, most Bitcoin gold investing won't result in you holding an actual bar of gold. You can find sites that will sell that to you, especially if you live outside of the US, but most sites operate by owning gold at a certified gold-and-bullion services company.

Moving into the realm of cryptocurrency increases the risk. It is not that Bitcoin itself adds any risk; rather, the company that converts Bitcoin to gold (or silver or other commodity) is another potential point of failure. You now depend not only on the holder of the actual gold to survive and remain honest but also the company that takes your Bitcoin and buys that gold for you.

The leader in this space is Uphold. This service enables investments into a variety of fiat currencies and commodities. You simply deposit (or send) your bitcoins into your Uphold account and then transfer them to various "cards" inside your account, each representing a different currency or commodity. If the price of that currency or commodity rises compared to the price of Bitcoin, then you'll have more bitcoins in your account.

Uphold is meant to be more than a simple investment tool, however. It is also meant to bring the benefits of cryptocurrency to those who can't afford to have their savings wiped out by a swing in the price of Bitcoin. Users can hold their Bitcoin in a variety of commodities and currencies. Transferring in and out of the physical commodities costs a small fee, generally between 0.5 and 2 percent. However, users who have had their identity verified can exchange various currencies and Bitcoin for free.

Another useful feature of Uphold is that users can use their balance, denominated in whatever currency or commodity, to pay for products anywhere Bitcoin is accepted. On Uphold's back end, it will send the appropriate amount of Bitcoin based on the price of Bitcoin versus that commodity or currency, and then sell the corresponding amount of the commodity or currency, and then repurchase the Bitcoin to refill its reserves.

Currently, Uphold allows users to hold their Bitcoin in the US dollar, the euro, the Japanese yen, the Swiss franc, the Chinese yuan, the Indian rupee, and the Mexican peso as well as gold, silver, platinum, and palladium. Oil is slated to be added to Uphold's list of supported commodities.[3]

---

[3] DeMartino, Ian M. "Bitreserve Wants You To Hold - and Spend - Oil." CoinTelegraph. December 12, 2014. Accessed June 22, 2015. http://cointelegraph.com/news/113085/bitreserve-wants-you-to-hold-and-spend-oil.

In addition to having a wide array of commodities and currencies, Uphold is unique in its transparency. It runs an extension of the blockchain named the "reserve chain," which shows every asset Uphold currently holds as well as information about every transaction it makes—how much Bitcoin is sold for, how much each commodity is sold or bought for, etc. This level of transparency is unheard of in the financial world and Uphold has good reason to offer it.

Uphold was started by CNET founder Halsey Minor. Minor was once a billionaire, having made CNET into the first non-pornographic media company on the Internet to turn a profit. He went on to cofound the widely successful Salesforce.com and Grand Central Communications, the latter of which was subsequently bought by Google and rebranded as Google Voice.

After a few bad commercial real estate investments, a fine art addiction, the financial crisis of 2008, and various lawsuits filed by and against him, by the late 2000s Minor was broke. In 2013, Minor—one of the first success stories of the Internet era—filed for Chapter 7 bankruptcy. Uphold is Minor's comeback attempt. In addition to assuring people that it's a safer bet than other cryptocurrency-based businesses, Uphold's transparency assures users that their funds won't be used to feed Minor's creditors or his art addiction.[4]

That might sound like a low blow, and apologies to Halsey Minor if he feels that way, but it is true. People are hesitant to hand their money to someone who burned through billions, regardless if it was entirely his fault or not. The reserve chain proves

---

[4] Stone, Brad. "Halsey Minor Returns, Bearing Bitcoins, via Bitreserve." Bloomberg. com. May 15, 2014. Accessed June 22, 2015. http://www.bloomberg.com/bw/ articles/2014-05-15/halsey-minor-returns-bearing-bitcoins-via-bitreserve.

that their money is being held responsibly. According to Minor, Uphold's motto is, "What our members do with their money is their business, but what we do with their money is everyone's business." The reserve chain is the technological embodiment of that. This kind of transparency, Minor believes, will open a whole new industry of business-to-business services that enable transparency not only for Uphold but also for companies that want to use Uphold to hold their own commodities in a way their customers can check in on. When I interviewed Minor in November 2014, he spoke about the growing opportunity:

> One company [that approached Uphold stated that] their business partners wanted to know (A) the money they are putting in is safe and (B) they want transparency. [. . .] Investors are using the albatross of the non-bitcoin system, [they can't see what is going on but] everyone wants to see what is going on, and we actually provide that. No bank does that. There is no bank system for transparency. As it turns out, there are all kinds of businesses that actually want to have transparency as part of their business model.
>
> This verifiable transparency will enable different kinds of business models than [exist] today.[5]

Verifiable transparency is important for regular investors too. Any company can claim to sell you gold and it might even peg

[5] DeMartino, Ian M. "Halsey Minor's Bitreserve Is Designed To Fix Bitcoin Volatility, But It Is Doing Much More." CoinTelegraph. November 21, 2014. Accessed June 22, 2015. http://cointelegraph.com/news/112966/halsey-minors-bitreserve-is-designed-to-fix-bitcoin-volatility-but-it-is-doing-much-more.

your Bitcoin to the price of gold. But without real reserves backed up by a reputable gold provider, you are actually investing into the company's promise to pay you based on the price of gold, rather than betting on the price itself.

This might ultimately be true with Uphold as well; if it suddenly shuts down without warning, any money held in it would be lost. Regardless, it is probably the safest bet for gold in the Bitcoin ecosystem. It holds its gold at Gold Bullion International, one of the most respected gold dealers in the world. This, I'm told, is a more secure way to hold your gold than an electronic transfer fund (ETF). Combining that with the reserve chain, users can be fairly confident that the assets they hold at Uphold are real and relatively safe.

BitGold—not to be confused with Nick Szabo's pre-Bitcoin "bit gold" proposal—also sells digital versions of gold that are backed up by and exchangeable at physical Brinks-secured locations. As with Uphold, the process is fairly straightforward after signing up on the BitGold website. Explaining the individual steps isn't necessary because it is easy enough and the website design is bound to change over time. One notable addition is that BitGold offers a MasterCard-powered debit card that can be funded with the gold held on BitGold's system.

Several other options exist. BitGild, for instance, will send physical coins or bars of gold, silver and platinum to you via snail mail. VeldtGold will do the same with gold and is based in the US. These are just a few of several reputable services.

Purchasing commodities and diversifying savings into other currencies are financial tools that were previously only available to those who could afford them. Now, thanks to Bitcoin, an entire world of financial security is opening up to those who want it.

Bitcoin itself can offer a hedge against one's home currency—not a bad idea if you are living in, say, Ukraine—but it is subject to its own volatility.

When the Russian ruble dropped in price, many Bitcoin enthusiasts claimed that Bitcoin could be used by Russians to preserve their accumulated wealth. Unfortunately, as badly as the ruble performed during those months, Bitcoin performed worse, and Russians would have had little to gain by storing their wealth in Bitcoin. Still, it was a solid concept and if Bitcoin had not been in the midst of its worst recession in its short history, it would have worked. The point is, Bitcoin could have been a store of value not as vulnerable to the Russian government's actions on the world stage. Furthermore, Bitcoin could have been used to facilitate the transfer of value from Russian ruble to Bitcoin to gold or another stable store of wealth.

In June 2015, Greece, which was in the middle of a financial crisis, instituted measures to stop its citizens from moving their euros out of the country. Bitcoin was being mentioned in the media as capable of foiling such measures.[6] At this time it could be argued that Bitcoin is too volatile to be a reliable way to store one's savings. It could, however, be used as an intermediate step and allow people to store their savings in the dollar, gold, or silver, or in a number of other commodities that can be bought using Bitcoin. And this could be accomplished without having to reach the minimum purchase levels, which are typically extremely high, or, as was the case in Greece, be beholden to laws limiting what you can do with the money.

---

[6] Kelly, Jemima. "Fearing Return to Drachma, Some Greeks Use Bitcoin to Dodge Capital Controls." Reuters. July 3, 2015. Accessed January 14, 2016. http://www.reuters.com/article/us-eurozone-greece-bitcoin-idUSKCN0PD1B420150703.

It wasn't simply that the Greek government was unconcerned about what Bitcoin would do to their capital controls; it was also that it couldn't do much if it wanted to. With bitcoins easily transferable on cell phones, it would have taken a physical and digital embargo to prevent tech-friendly Greeks from moving their euros outside of the country in the form of bitcoins.

As recently as a few years ago, precious metal investment was overwhelmingly limited to the wealthy and connected. With Bitcoin, nearly anyone can store their wealth in nearly any form they want. Borders, politics, and regulations be damned.

Section III:

What Can Bitcoin Do for Me?

Chapter 18:
Remittance

More than 215 million people around the world live outside of the countries they call home. But most families that rely on remittances operate outside of the world's financial system as well. Despite the global prevalence of electronic money transfers, most migrant workers are excluded from the convenience of modern banking services, dependent on costly cash transfers that often require rural recipients to travel significant distances.

—Kanayo F. Nwanze, president of the International
Fund for Agricultural Development

The number one use for Bitcoin has been and remains speculative investment. For good or ill, the buying and selling of Bitcoin remains the most common reason behind Bitcoin transactions. As I've discussed, the wild swings in price make the digital currency extremely attractive to day traders.

When the Silk Road marketplace came along, it gave Bitcoin another use: buying things you didn't want the credit card companies or the authorities to know about. Eventually, the currency was also adopted by more mainstream merchants and became relatively more widely used as a legitimate way to pay salaries, buy goods and services, and so on. Every one of these things can be, and more often are, done with fiat currencies. But cash and other forms of currency also have countless uses. You can use fiat money to pay rent or for education or groceries. You can use it to invest and save and do a million other things. Initially, cryptocurrencies were limited to a few uses and many of them, like the Silk Road, were less than attractive to the average person.

What makes Bitcoin and blockchain technologies inherently attractive are the things they can do better than other currencies: Bitcoin and other digital currencies are perfectly designed for remittance, *i.e.*, sending money from one person to another, usually overseas. When we set aside the current difficulties people can have exchanging Bitcoin for a fiat currency, Bitcoin is undoubtedly better for remittance than any other service out there.

As I covered in the first section of this book, this blockchain is not controlled by any central authority and exists as a distributed network, not unlike the Internet. Using the distributed system, it is nearly frictionless—meaning there is hardly anything that hinders a transaction, like fees or delays—involving sending any amount of Bitcoin to anyone else on the network (*i.e.*, any other Bitcoin address). People can send money to each other using the legacy system, but going through them is often both slow and expensive. Western Union and other money transmitters are quicker, but they take a significant chunk of each transaction and collect billions in profits worldwide doing it.[1]

Bitcoin only requires a small transaction fee that goes to the miners. This fee is typically a fraction of a cent to a few cents. The amount has nothing to do with the size of the transaction but is instead determined by the current value of Bitcoin and how active the network is. Users have moved tens of millions of dollars on the blockchain, and each time it cost a few cents or less.

Remittance is big business. The World Bank predicts that global remittance will reach $681 billion this year (2016)[2] with most of that going to developing countries. Bitcoin allows users to cut out the middleman, as email did with telecommunications companies and the Postal Service. Now I can send value to another person on the other side of the planet and it is virtually free to do so.

Chris Horlacher, the CPA and CA of Equibit, has pointed out how Bitcoin adoption could improve the lives of people around the world:

The World Bank has stated that cutting remittance prices by 5 percentage points could save up to $16 billion per year. How about 100 percent? How would that affect the lives of the world's neediest? Total

---

[1] Anderson, Marc. "Global Remittance Industry Choking Billions out of Developing World." *The Guardian*. April 18, 2014. Accessed June 22, 2015. http://www.theguardian.com/global-development/2014/aug/18/global-remittance-industry-choking-billions-developing-world.

[2] "Remittances to Developing Countries to Stay Robust This Year, despite Increased Deportations of Migrant Workers, Says WB." April 4, 2011. Accessed June 22, 2015. http://www.worldbank.org/en/news/press-release/2014/04/11/remittances-developing-countries-deportations-migrant-workers-wb.

annual remittances already dwarf government aid and
go directly to the pockets of the poor, with no political
strings attached. Freeing up these resources will have a
profound affect on the quality of their lives and ability
to finally and permanently escape grinding poverty.

Things aren't quite at that phase just yet. For Bitcoin to have
this kind of impact on a global scale, the receiver needs a quick
way to convert it into the fiat currency of his or her home country. The Bitcoin network extends just about everywhere but
physical manifestations of it—places where you can get fiat for
Bitcoin—are lacking. In many areas, especially rural areas in third
world countries—the very places where people need remittances
most—it is often difficult to find a way to make the exchange at
a reasonable rate.

As of 2013, remittance fees take US$4 billion from the $60
billion African remittance market every year, according to the
World Bank. That is a lot of money not in the pockets of migrant
workers and their families. This has a hugely negative effect on
developing economies that could otherwise benefit greatly by
having emigrants send money back to their families who could
then contribute to the local economy. As a 2014 *Guardian*
article explains:

> There are five "corridors"—a country to country trans-
> fer—with an average fee higher than 20 percent, all of
> them in Africa. Migrant workers in South Africa, for
> example, paid an average of just over 23 percent in fees
> on the money they sent to Botswana in 2012, making
> it the most expensive remittance channel in the world.

Sending money from South Africa to Mozambique was the second most costly channel, with an average 22 percent fee imposed on transfers. [. . .] Experts say the price of sending money is inflated by two companies—Western Union and MoneyGram—which hold a duopoly over the global industry.[3]

This duopoly has led to a culture of arrogance from the two money-transmitting companies. The more-than-20-percent fees required from some African nations are the worst example of the effects of this duopoly, but even relatively inexpensive remittance fees are astronomical compared to Bitcoin's mining fee. Western Union remittance fees start at $4.99; this might change by the time this book is published. There might also be additional fees that depend on the amount transferred and the countries involved. Customers don't even get to see the fee until just before making the transaction.

Bitcoin users, on the other hand, can expect a miner fee (denominated in Bitcoin) roughly equivalent to two cents, although it changes and can often be free. In November 2013, a total of 194,993 bitcoins were moved on the Bitcoin network without any fees attached to the transaction. Paying a miner fee is not strictly required but is recommended to increase the likelihood that a miner will broadcast the transaction quickly. The fiat value

---

[3] Anderson, Mark. "Global Remittance Industry Choking Billions Out of Developing World." *The Guardian*. August 18, 2014. Accessed February 13, 2016. http://www.theguardian.com/global-development/2014/aug/18/global-remittance-industry-choking-billions-developing-world.

of this transaction was estimated to be $147 million.[4,5] No one knows who sent it or why but in practical terms it doesn't matter. The point is that someone sent $147 million without paying a cent. The money could have been destined for someone on the other side of the world or someone in the next room, or even just a different wallet controlled by the sender. The destination did not have any effect on the cost of the transaction.

The logistics of sending $147 million overseas using traditional means are complicated. Using services such as Western Union wouldn't even be an option, and IRS fees and taxes would likely take a significant chunk out of the total.

Those who want to transfer any amount—large, medium, or small—have a lot to gain by using Bitcoin rather than traditional services. At the moment, however, there are two major roadblocks standing in the way of Bitcoin becoming a major player in the remittance market: customer knowledge and infrastructure.

Despite Bitcoin's growing popularity, particularly in China and the US, the vast majority of people around the world still have no idea what Bitcoin is. If Bitcoin remittance companies want to start claiming some of the $681 billion global remittance market for themselves, they need to work on educating the public in places where information distribution is difficult. Alternatively, they need to develop a way for customers to use Bitcoin for remittance automatically, without customers even

---

    [4] "[Transaction 1c12443203a48f42cdf7b1acee5b4b1c1fedc144cb909a3bf5edbffafb0cd204." Blockchain, November 11, 2013. https://blockchain.info/tx/1c12443203a48f42cdf7b1acee5b4b1c1fedc144cb909a3bf5edbffafb0cd204.

    [5] Southurst, Jon. "194,993 BTC Transaction worth $147 Million Sparks Mystery and Speculation." CoinDesk. November 22, 2013. Accessed June 22, 2015. http://www.coindesk.com/194993-btc-transaction-147m-mystery-and-speculation/.

needing to be aware that their service uses Bitcoin to perform the underlying transaction.

A Bitcoin remittance company could set up shop in two countries and allow people to transfer money between them without having to educate their customers about the underlying Bitcoin technology facilitating the transaction. With Bitcoin's virtually nonexistent fee, the company would be able charge only what their overhead required. This is where Bitcoin ATMs are helpful, since it is much cheaper to maintain a small machine than an entire building with employees and everything else. Since educating the public about Bitcoin has proven difficult even in countries such as the US, where the average household has 2.43 televisions and more than 86 percent of households have Internet access, ATMs could serve as a popular way to stimulate interest. Access to information is much more limited in countries such as Ethiopia, where fewer than two percent of households have Internet access.[6] The problem is that even with ATMs, overhead is significant and it can be difficult to keep fees low enough to make inroads into the remittance economy. Ideally, both sender and recipient would have an accessible and inexpensive way of exchanging Bitcoin into the fiat currency of their choice and vice versa.

In order for Bitcoin to compete with Western Union and MoneyGram on a wide scale in various countries, the infrastructure needs to be in place for what is called the "last mile" of remittance. It is straightforward enough for someone to send Bitcoin to an individual in Ethiopia or Niger or wherever.

---

[6] "Internet Users by Country (2014)." Chart. Internet Live Stats. Accessed June 22, 2015. http://www.Internetlivestats.com/Internet-users-by-country/.

The problems arise when the recipient wants to exchange that Bitcoin for their local currency. Physical Bitcoin exchanges are not exactly common, and online exchanges, if they exist at all, require access to a bank account that can be difficult to obtain in third world nations.

There are two possible solutions to this problem. One is to build this infrastructure slowly over time; the other is to piggyback on existing services in order to finish this last step. Building this kind of infrastructure from the ground up is not something most Bitcoin start-ups are capable of. It requires fitting into the regulatory framework of every nation and in many cases, every region the company hopes to do business with. In the US, for example, companies need to obtain regulatory permission from each of the 50 states if they want a nationwide reach.[7]

Even after the regulatory mess of opening up a financial service in a foreign country is dealt with, there is still the matter of building a presence in this country while keeping overhead low enough that fees can remain significantly smaller than those of the traditional services.

This tactic has been pursued by a few companies, particularly Bitcoin ATM companies that can install their machines with relatively low overhead costs. Although these ATMs might be suitable for remittance, however, their relatively high fees have eliminated much of the advantage of using Bitcoin in the first place.[8]

---

[7] DeMartino, Ian M. "Igot Founder Rick Day: Regulation Has 'Absolutely' Hindered Bitcoin In The US." Mining Pool. April 22, 2015. Accessed June 22, 2015. http://coinjournal.net/interview-with-igot-founder-rick-day-regulation-has-absolutely-hindered-bitcoin-in-the-us.

[8] Wile, Rob. "Think Fees On Normal ATMs Are Expensive? Check Out What It Costs To Use A Bitcoin ATM." Business Insider. March 10, 2014. Accessed June 22, 2015. http://www.businessinsider.com/using-a-bitcoin-atm-is-actually-pretty-expensive-2014-3.

Rebit.ph is a Bitcoin remittance company taking the second approach. Hyperfocusing on one market, Rebit.ph is attempting to make Bitcoin remittance to the Philippines a viable option for Filipinos living overseas.[9] Rebit.ph cofounder Luis Buenaventura explains the strategy behind the service:

> These services accept bitcoin from overseas, convert it into pesos, dinars, or shillings, then deliver those funds to the final beneficiary via a variety of domestic transfer methods. The beneficiary doesn't need to know that those funds were ever transmitted via bitcoin, they only know that the sender had to spend a little less money while doing so. There's no volatility risk as the recipient never touches bitcoin; all risk is managed by the service.
>
> By specializing on just the last mile, there's an invitation for other bitcoin entrepreneurs from other countries to form informal corridors. A customer in Hong Kong needs to convert their HKD into BTC before sending it to the last-mile service, and one could make a reasonably profitable business out of performing that service for them.[10]

Bitcoin remittance requires regulatory compliance within the receiving country. Although any service looking to establish a

---

[9] Balea, Judith. "Bitcoin Remittance Service Rebit Rolls out Zero Transaction Fees, KYC Policy." Tech in Asia. January 15, 2015. Accessed June 22, 2015. https://www.techinasia.com/bitcoin-rebit-philippines-zero-fees-remittances-kyc/.

[10] Buenaventura, Luis. "The Bootstrapper's Guide To Bitcoin Remittances." TechCrunch. January 30, 2015. Accessed June 22, 2015. http://techcrunch.com/2015/01/30/the-bootstrappers-guide-to-bitcoin-remittances/.

physical presence or a digital presence that interacts with local banks will have to engage regulators in that country, these companies let senders worry about finding Bitcoin. Then the company can focus on making it easy for the receiver to turn that Bitcoin into their local currency cheaply, without them even needing to know that the sender used Bitcoin. There would be some overhead here but at least would only be on one side of the transaction—and by skipping the fees and delays inherent in legacy systems, it could still be significantly cheaper.

When a customer sends money using Western Union, the receiver has to pick it up at a Western Union office. There is a bit more synergy when using different banks as opposed to two competing money transmitting services. Again, however, this depends on both participants having bank accounts and even then it only works if the banks are on the same network (SWIFT, SEPA, etc.).

The Bitcoin network doesn't care what country the sender and receiver live in or what Bitcoin wallet each participant is using. Just as there is no difficulty sending an email from a Gmail account to a Microsoft Outlook account, there is no difficulty sending Bitcoin from one Bitcoin service to another—regardless of how little contact these companies have had, how much distance separates them, or how many borders sit between them politically.

As you might expect, this is one of the opportunities people talk about when they discuss Bitcoin's future price. If Bitcoin can grab some of that remittance market, the thinking goes, then surely its price will increase dramatically. There is undoubtedly some truth behind this but it isn't as simple as looking at the $60 billion African remittance market and thinking that if Bitcoin grabs 10 percent of it, Bitcoin's market cap will increase by $6 billion.

The assumption behind remittance, of course, is that receivers will dump their bitcoins as soon as they get them. This is logical; the transaction is designed to get money, not bitcoins, into the hands of the receiver. There won't be anything close to a one-to-one jump for every remittance transaction. The receiver is almost certain to dump most if not all of the bitcoins they get, potentially nullifying any effect that the corresponding purchase might have had on total Bitcoin market cap.

This will certainly temper any gain for investors, so I would suggest caution if you are reading this chapter salivating over a potential price increase if Bitcoin makes any headway into the massive remittance market. Bitcoin remittance transactions totaling $1 billion wouldn't increase Bitcoin's market size by $1 billion. It isn't a one-to-one correlation, especially in remittance, where the money is going out almost as much as it is coming in.

It would, however, cause a huge rise in the number of Bitcoin transactions. This rise would, in turn, increase the demand for Bitcoin, because a global remittance market that runs 24/7 would potentially always have value being exchanged. This means less Bitcoin will be available on the markets and there should be a corresponding price increase.

Furthermore, exposure to Bitcoin as a remittance tool will likely increase interest in Bitcoin. It can be hard for residents of the US or other first world countries to remember, but there are huge populations without basic access to banking services. As many as 2.5 billion people, or about half of the world's adult population, are unbanked with even more classified as underbanked.

Bitcoin can provide these services for the unbanked—and with third-party tools, can already offer a lot to the underbanked.[11]

When people start receiving money from their emigrant family members without a double-digit fee, it stands to reason that some of them will become interested in Bitcoin. As they become more knowledgeable about Bitcoin, they might see its utility for storing value rather than simply as a mechanism for transferring value.

Day by day, Bitcoin is becoming more accessible to people all over the world. As I write this, LocalBitcoins.com has extended to 244 countries and more than 8,000 cities.[12] Although there isn't enough liquidity—people buying and selling—in all those markets to make it an effective remittance tool for everyone, the tools exist to handle that liquidity where it exists.

Although Bitcoin's current volatility makes savings impractical, services such as Uphold allow users to hold dozens of different currencies on the periphery of the Bitcoin ecosystem. Uphold backs all its commodities and currencies with the actual commodity or currency itself, but every transaction is done through Bitcoin. Although it isn't open to the entire globe just yet, Uphold and services like it are rapidly growing and would allow even those in the third world to set aside some of their savings, no matter how small, without the need for a bank account.

---

[11] "Box 0.1." Global Financial Development Report 2014. N.p.: World Bank, n.d. 3. Print. ISBN: 978-0-8213-9990-3

[12] Localbitcoins.com Statistics. Program documentation. Accessed June 22, 2015. https://localbitcoins.com/statistics.

This lack of need for a bank account is a major advantage, since 75 percent of people making less than $2 a day remain unbanked as of 2012.[13] The main reason is poverty. When you make so little, it is difficult to save and meet minimum account requirements. Bitcoin solves this problem because a single Bitcoin can be split down to eight decimal points (*i.e.*, tallied in increments of 0.00000001BTC, 0.00000002BTC, etc.) and the system can accommodate transactions of any size, no matter how small. Moreover, Bitcoin accounts (wallets) have no minimum amounts.

Another reason is that rural residents often have to travel a long distance to reach a bank. Bitcoin is limited only by cell and Internet signals, and the areas they reach are expanding all the time. Not having to travel to perform banking services has proven to be very effective in turning the unbanked into the banked. M-Pesa is a mobile banking solution that was built by Safaricom, Kenya's largest cell phone operator. It has been essential for remittance within Kenya (from urban immigrants to their rural hometowns) and basic banking services for Kenya's lower classes.

M-Pesa is nothing like a cryptocurrency; it is centralized and keeps track of fiat balances rather than acting as its own currency. It's a bit as if PayPal were created by AT&T and existed solely on cell phones, and there were money-exchange stores all over the nation where you could withdraw cash from your account or pay bills directly.

---

[13] Renzenbrink, Anne. "World Bank: 75 Percent of Poor Don't Have Bank Accounts." CNN. April 19, 2011. Accessed June 22, 2015. http://www.cnn.com/2012/04/19/business/poor-bank-accounts/index.html.

This penetration has led to attempts by Bitcoin remittance companies to piggyback off the success of M-Pesa's success and use it for the last mile of Bitcoin remittance in Kenya. Both igot and BitPesa integrate with M-Pesa and expand the advantages it offers for domestic remittance internationally. People can send Bitcoin to their families in these countries using their cell phones; the recipients can use their own phones to exchange that money into M-Pesa money that can then be turned into fiat as it normally is.[14,15]

Bitcoin needs use cases beyond speculative trading and the purchase of black-market and gray-market goods. Its use cases also have to involve something Bitcoin can do better than current fiat options. Remittance is an obvious candidate. It can do what fiat currencies can more cheaply and quickly. It can also accomplish tasks impossible for customers using traditional services, such as sending small or extremely large amounts of money or providing advanced investment services for the previously unbanked.

It is also something that has the potential to change the world. The remittance economy has become a far more vital lifeline for developing nations than aid from richer nations. A handful of companies are pocketing untold millions, taking money out of the economy of both developed and underdeveloped nations. Removing these companies from the process will help the economies of all countries involved, though it will be particularly

---

[14] Torpey, Kyle. "Bitcoin Exchange Igot Launches in Kenya via M-Pesa Integration." Inside Bitcoins. February 25, 2015. Accessed June 22, 2015. http://insidebitcoins.com/news/bitcoin-exchange-igot-launches-in-kenya-via-m-pesa-integration/30194.

[15] Vigna, Paul. "Kenya's BitPesa Launches Beta Test of Remittance Service." MoneyBeat RSS. May 23, 2014. Accessed June 22, 2015. http://blogs.wsj.com/moneybeat/2014/05/23/kenyas-bitpesa-launches-beta-test-of-remittance-service/.

useful to the economies of developing nations that depend heavily on remittance from emigrants.

Can Bitcoin change the world? Well, it has the potential to change the lives of people who depend on money from remittance, and once you start changing people's lives, you start changing the world.

Chapter 19:

Microtransactions

When the Internet first came into public use, it was hailed as a liberation from conformity, a floating world ruled by passion, creativity, innovation and freedom of information. When it was hijacked first by advertising and then by commerce, it seemed like it had been fully co-opted and brought into line with human greed and ambition.

—Neil Strauss, author and journalist

Microtransactions are transactions ranging from a few cents to about five dollars. They were once heralded as the savior of the Internet economy, the logical replacement for advertising schemes that failed to generate sustainable revenue during the dotcom bubble. The idea was—and continues to be—that site visitors will fund the sites they visit by paying small amounts each time or for subscriptions. Microtransactions, it was thought, would provide a way for people to pay for online content directly, forcing advertisers to retreat to the world of television, radio, and billboards.

Not everyone believed this, of course, and advertising on the Internet eventually rebounded into a model that is, if not sustainable, at least workable in our current world.

Even though microtransactions have not yet replaced advertising, they have already become a major part of the Internet economy. They are currently used primarily by video game companies to sell items inside video games to users. Bitcoin, however, has the potential to make microtransactions smoother and more effective by eliminating the fees associated with transactions that go through the legacy system. Microtransactions performed by the legacy system are often ineffective, because they are cut in half or worse by middlemen and their fees. Even in unique situations where companies have deals in place to cut down those fees significantly, they are dependent on the buyer's (or sender's) bank not taking their cut.

Microtransactions have great potential. In traditional commerce, where one person buys one thing from another, the only dependent factors are how much the buyer is willing to pay for the item and how much the seller is willing to part with that item at a given price. Things became more complicated as economies grew and millions of people wanted similar items. In a large economy, the price of something—like a musical recording— isn't dependent solely on what the buyer wants to pay and at what price the seller is willing to sell; it is also dependent on distributors, marketing and legal fees, shipping costs, and other things that add to the price. An artist might be willing to sell their record for five dollars but if they actually *want* five dollars, they are going to have to charge a lot more.

The Internet broke down a lot of these walls. We don't need Tower Records to keep an inventory of every album anyone could ever want to buy. We don't need Sony to pay for CDs to be pressed or for marketing. All we need today is for an artist to offer his or her album on the Internet and people can pay them almost directly. The music labels and the record stores have been cut from the equation. And the result is more music and, not insignificantly, more affordable music than ever before. This is the significance of microtransactions: they enable sellers to list their products at the prices at which they really want to sell them. In the digital world, where items can be copied effortlessly and the seller doesn't have to "part" with an item to sell it, that price can be extremely small.

Today, if an artist puts his or her music on their website and I buy it for $5, the only middlemen left who take a cut of that $5 are the credit card companies or the banks when they take their cut. That could be 30 cents or it could be a dollar. The point is that it is friction—and more could be produced and consumed if we eliminated it.

Bitcoin is uniquely designed to meet this challenge. It is global, fast, and has low enough transaction fees that sending only a few cents or even a fraction of a cent is not a problem. No other service, including PayPal and Apple Pay, can claim these three things. For a microtransaction economy to thrive, all three characteristics are necessary.

Bitcoin microtransactions started out as—and can remain—a completely peer-to-peer service. As I've mentioned multiple times, anyone can send anyone any amount of Bitcoin. I can send two cents' worth of Bitcoin to someone across the world and they can send me 20 yen worth of Bitcoin in return. There is no need for a centralized service to group microtransactions together in order to lower transaction fees, which is often the case in services that use legacy systems. The transaction fees when using Bitcoin are already low enough.

Not all microtransactions are used to sell items such as music albums. Often they are used just to show appreciation. This is referred to as the tipping economy. On social networks such as Reddit and Twitter, people have started tipping each other Bitcoin as a reward for posts they like or whatever other reason they dream up.

It would be difficult to group these transactions together because they are often going to and coming from different people, and doing so intermittently. Given the different combinations of banks and credit card companies they could be using, and given that people often want access to their tips immediately, grouping them together would be near impossible. If someone wants to tip a content creator $0.20 because they like a meme that person created but they know the bank is going to take $0.19 of it or even $0.15 of it, it stands to reason that person will be less eager to give that money away.

With Bitcoin, the amount you send is the amount the person receives on the other end. Using their Bitcoin wallets, people can simply tip users and services the same way they would pay for anything else. A few services have been created that make this process easier.

ChangeTip was one of the first workable services and remains one of the most popular. ChangeTip integrates with a growing list of social media and content creation sites, including Twitter, Reddit, Facebook, GitHub, YouTube, and about a dozen more. With ChangeTip, users can send money denominated in fiat or

Bitcoin to anyone else on a supported site for free. ChangeTip will inform the receiver that he or she has been given a tip. The receiver will then have to sign up to claim the tip. Once the tip is claimed, it can be held in ChangeTip or withdrawn to the user's Bitcoin wallet or to a gift card.

ChangeTip is an easy and convenient service, though some have expressed privacy concerns, fearing that the company might sell information gathered from social media websites. The current CEO, Nick Sullivan, had pledged never to do that,[1] but ChangeTip's critics are still concerned about what might happen if the company is sold. As a few commentators have pointed out, without selling data, ChangeTip's potential for profit is fairly small[2]—although since that time it has implemented new sources of revenue such as the gift card option.

Despite misgivings from some Bitcoin users, ChangeTip has been instrumental in increasing Bitcoin adoption. Giving someone Bitcoin through ChangeTip doesn't require them to know anything about Bitcoin. It is only when they want to move that Bitcoin out of their ChangeTip account and turn it into fiat that they have to start learning about wallets, private keys, and various other aspects of the Bitcoin ecosystem.

ChangeTip isn't the only service enabling users to contribute to their favorite content creators. Another service, ProTip, was created by Christopher Ellis and crowdfunded through Kickstarter.

---

[1] Rizzo, Pete. "ChangeTip CEO Nick Sullivan: We Won't Sell User Data." CoinDesk. December 18, 2014. Accessed June 22, 2015. http://www.coindesk.com/changetip-ceo-nick-sullivan-wont-sell-user-data/.

[2] Sirer, Emin Gün. "Tips for ChangeTip." Tips for ChangeTip. December 29, 2014. Accessed June 22, 2015. http://hackingdistributed.com/2014/12/29/tips-for-changetip/?v=01.

It intends to make accepting Bitcoin donations as simple as putting a Bitcoin address anywhere on a website.

This goal is worthwhile, because one of ChangeTip's problems is that it isn't easy for content creators to integrate. ChangeTip is best used in environments like Reddit or Twitter where everything is set up for the user. But for websites or YouTube channels, things become more difficult. Website creators have to enter a bit of code. It isn't much, but it is a hurdle many website owners aren't willing to tackle.

The process currently isn't as easy as it could be and takes some effort by the content creator. ProTip doesn't require any special implementation by the website creator. If there is a Bitcoin address on a site, ProTip will find it and keep track of it (more on this in a second). Website creators can put in a ProTip script (and in future versions ProTip will enable features such as subscriptions and paywalls), but they also don't need to use ProTip at all.

In order for donors to be able to use the service, ProTip will install an extension in the user's browser. ProTip automatically scans websites for Bitcoin addresses and saves them for a week. The top five most-visited sites (or however many the user sets) during that week that have Bitcoin addresses on them will receive a portion of Bitcoin set aside by the user at the beginning of the week. If there are more than three addresses on a single page, ProTip will pick the first three it finds. Users can also "blacklist" websites and individual addresses—so that random addresses posted on Twitter or addresses in people's signatures on message boards are ignored, if this is what the user wants to do.

A budget is set up for each week; the user can choose if they want the donation to dole out automatically or after they review the recipients. It aims to be a no-hassle, fund-it-and-leave-it kind of program.

Content creators can simply put Bitcoin addresses anywhere on their site and ProTip will identify and remember them.

This donation model has had mixed success on the Internet so far, prior to the advent of Bitcoin. The more popular podcasts and YouTube channels with dedicated fanbases have been able to survive and even thrive off the kindness of their audience, but few, if any, have successfully cast aside the advertising model completely.

But there are also a lot of obstacles standing in the way of potential donors. First, they have to go out of their way to make the donation, a process that might involve signing up for PayPal or a similar service but almost certainly requires clicking through multiple webpages. Second, donations for small amounts simply aren't feasible with fiat currencies. Making dozens of small donations on the level of $0.25 or less isn't practical. You might be able to do it through PayPal, assuming you and the recipient reside in the same country and you tell PayPal the person is a friend, but otherwise PayPal's cut will be too large to make the donation worth making.

ProTip and Bitcoin, combined, remove these obstacles by making donations automatic and allowing for true microdonations, even those less than a cent.

We don't know how the public will react to workable microtransactions. It has been a proposed solution to funding content creation on the Internet for years but it has yet to take off. Advertising has too much money to throw at content creators, and content consumers are used to getting that content for free. The excessive reliance on advertising, which can often be perceived as dishonest, was the primary motivation for Chris Ellis to create ProTip to try to enable direct funding of content:

> I took the time out of making content, so that I could make an app to help people like me make money, so I could go back to making videos again.
>
> I want honesty to pay, because that is what Satoshi laid out in his original white paper. I wanted to work on a project that was keeping in scope of the original vision of bitcoin.
>
> What if we could build a tool that made honesty pay more than fraud? Giving artists, writers, videographers, the tools they needed to connect with their audience in a way that is more meaningful than Like buttons.
>
> Take a look at Taylor Swifts @replies [on Twitter]. It's mostly her fans saying "OMG follow me back." People want connection, they want experiences and the surprise of something new. Taylor has talent but she also got lucky and this is not the norm for many artists.
>
> The ones that don't sell out lead a tormented life where they question whether they are doing the right thing, [or] if they are good enough.
>
> The ones that do sell out go in to marketing and PR. Which is an industry designed to manipulate the way people make decisions.[3]

---

[3] DeMartino, Ian M. "Interview With ProTip's Chris Ellis On Saving Media." CoinTelegraph. March 19, 2015. Accessed June 22, 2015. http://cointelegraph.com/news/113741/interview-with-protips-chris-ellis-on-saving-media.

By transitioning away from advertising, we can promote independent media. Advertising convinces media outlets to ignore important stories, convinces us that we are inadequate without their products and corrupts art into commercial propaganda. There was a time when people hoped the Internet would avoid this fate; it has not. There has only ever been one somewhat reasonable alternative suggested: microtransactions fueling a tipping economy.

Nothing can guarantee that a donation-based economy is feasible, but Bitcoin gives it its best chance at success.

Chapter 20:

Start-up Funding

If you've got an idea, start today. There's no better time than now to get going. That doesn't mean quit your job and jump into your idea 100 percent from day one, but there's always small progress that can be made to start the movement.

—Kevin Systrom, cofounder of Instagram

One of the most interesting developments in Bitcoin has been start-up funding. Crowdfunding has taken the world by storm. It is full of success stories and industry-creating giants. Oculus, which was eventually purchased by Facebook for $2 billion and has singlehandedly resurrected the virtual reality industry, got its start on Kickstarter. Likewise, smartwatch company Pebble was so successful that companies ranging from LG to Samsung to Google and Apple got into the industry.

There is also equity-based crowdfunding, which is like normal crowdfunding except the funders receive shares of the company rather than a product or one of the rewards typical in crowd-funding campaigns. Although not feasible in the US due to stringent regulations, companies elsewhere have been crowdfunding projects and companies by selling off parts of the company to the crowdfunders. Essentially, it is crowdfunded investment capital. The funders of the Oculus Rift would have stood to gain a pretty penny had that company offered equity, rather than development kits that were quickly made obsolete, to their backers. (Oculus later announced early backers will receive a consumer-version virtual reality headset when it launches.) Uphold, which has been mentioned a few times already, ran an equity crowdfunding campaign and raised more than $9 million without being open to US customers.[1]

But those are the fiat world's solutions. In the cryptocurrency world, there is a far more direct method of funding businesses: asset tokens distributed on the blockchain. Asset tokens are tokens that represent ownership of something other than Bitcoin, such as shares in a company, that can be sent on the blockchain. One thing potential investors and start-up owners should keep in mind is that the space is currently full of scams and Ponzi schemes.

This shouldn't be a surprise. Equity funding using cryptocurrency is a new, barely understood technology with little to no regulation. The businesses that have so far been funded, with a few exceptions, are cryptocurrency businesses with a less-than-apparent source of income.

---

[1] Parsa, Tim. "Series B Closes with $9.6M Raised via Crowdcube and Venovate." Bitreserve. January 13, 2015. Accessed June 22, 2015. https://bitreserve.org/en/blog/posts/bitreserve/series-b-closes-with-9-6m-raised-via-crowdcube-and-venovate.

But the current situation might mean there is a serious opportunity here for legitimate businesses. Cryptofinanciers are tired of the schemes and scams that populate the network. If you are a legitimate business owner—let's say you own a pizza shop and are willing to post pictures proving it—you could give up a part (say five percent) of your restaurant's ownership in hopes of raising enough money to open a second restaurant. You would create a contract or some sort of legal document indicating the tokens you make represent five percent ownership in your company and then put them out on the market. Investors could evaluate your business plan, determine if they want to invest and then buy some of your tokens from you. You could pay investors back by paying dividends or giving them voting rights for future location decisions and the investors would be able to sell the tokens at any time on the free market.

But I am getting ahead of myself. Before you can fund your business or product with cryptocurrencies, you need to know what services are available and how successful other such projects have been.

There are four major platforms you can use to issue your own token that represents a small amount of ownership of your company: Counterparty, Omni/Mastercoin, Ethereum, and Nxt. There are others but they are either still in development or are a part of a small community and would limit the number of your potential investors.

Counterparty is built on the Bitcoin blockchain so your potential pool of investors includes everyone who uses Bitcoin. Nxt, on the other hand, has its own technology and community, which is significantly smaller than Bitcoin's. However, Nxt's asset exchange—its name for its token marketplace—is built right into its core client, while Counterparty requires a special wallet. Essentially, Counterparty gives you immediate access to a subset of the Bitcoin community while offering the potential to reach the rest of them, while Nxt gives you access to its entire community from the start, albeit one that is much smaller overall.

Omni/Mastercoin is an asset platform built on top of the Bitcoin blockchain. As with other cryptocurrency 2.0 projects, it allows for the creation, sale and trading of assets.

Ethereum recently launched and is becoming more accessible every day. It, too, can be used to fund a business but can additionally incorporate extra programming to create interesting projects. This is best left to those with experience, however.

Issuing an asset that offers some sort of reward to buyers essentially works the same on any platform. Let's return to the pizza place example. The reward here could be something like five percent of your total profits, or 25 percent of total cryptocurrency sales, or a "free" slice of pizza for every token redeemed in the store. You will get to choose the type of asset, how many exist, if you'll ever be able to create more, and if it is divisible. I highly suggest you make it divisible; buying and selling indivisible assets on the open market tends to be more difficult and will therefore turn off some investors.

You should then write a business plan explaining how you intend to use the money, why you are issuing an asset and how you expect to reward your investors. It will help to have a website set up for your business, one that proves your business exists and that your crowdfunding campaign is indeed run by you.

After that, make a few announcements: one on the message board of the platform you are using, one on its Reddit page, and one on either NXTforum or BitcoinTalk, depending on which platform you used.

You can do more than just raise money in this manner. You can also find out what your investors—and possibly most loyal customers—want next. Let's say your initial pizza place campaign was a rousing success and the second store likewise is doing really well. It is doing so well that you are now considering opening a third location.

But adding a third location will cost a significant amount of money, so your investors won't get their dividends until you are profitable again. On the other hand, if they go along with that plan, a third store has a chance to greatly increase their profits. You could let your token/asset holders vote on the subject.

A more lighthearted example might be letting your token holders vote on the next "pizza of the month" deal your restaurant will run. Voting on things such as weekly or monthly deals are great incentives beyond simple dividend possibilities. It is another way to raise money without running afoul of US securities regulations.

Crowdfunding platforms incorporate voting capabilities to get your customers more involved. Nxt has the most full-featured voting mechanism. You can set up different rules to regulate the vote, such as giving more weight to people who had made a bigger investment or giving each address an equal vote regardless of holdings.

Voting with Counterparty is less ideal but still possible. Let's say you named your token "PIZZA" and there are 100 PIZZA token holders. You issue a new token called "PIZZAVOTE" and issue it to "PIZZA" holders as a dividend. Then you'll need to set up a few Bitcoin addresses that the coins can be sent to, each representing a different vote. Token holders send their vote token to the address that represents the way they want to vote; you tally it up and make your decision based on the count (but remember the results will be publicly visible).

It should be noted there are concerns about the legality of issuing dividend-producing assets on an unregulated market, especially for businesses operating within the US. This has led most coin communities to carefully avoid the words "asset" and "dividend" in their marketing materials, as if that will provide them some cover if the Securities and Exchange Commission (SEC) comes knocking. I personally don't think the SEC cares what you call it; I think they are worried about whether you are using it to defraud investors. Although I would advise you to speak to a lawyer before making any commitments to the cryptocommunity you might not legally be able to keep, I doubt the SEC is going to be too concerned with legitimate businesses raising money in a transparent and open way, especially with so many illegitimate businesses doing the same thing. However, it is definitely illegal to sell ownership of your company in any form of share or stock. For business owners in the US, offering voting rights is a viable alternative.

Another alternative is to give away rewards similar to Kickstarter. The SEC doesn't care if you give away free pizza, or whatever product you sell, to "token" holders.

One of the many names Bitcoin has been given is "programmable money" and this describes a critical feature of Bitcoin and other cryptocurrencies. They are more often called "the currency of the Internet." This means something more profound than when we say a country has its own currency. The Internet is wholly digital; it doesn't exist anywhere and it also exists everywhere.

We have been pushing dollars and euros and yuan through very specified corridors. Bitcoin not only breaks down these boundaries but also can be repurposed for almost any use imaginable. The blockchain keeps things fair and the only other limit is the programmer's imagination and skill.

Bitcoin can help you launch your business and create new business models. And just as the Internet allows smaller artists to survive on donations from a few thousand dedicated fans, cryptocurrencies have the potential to create new self-sustaining mini-ecosystems. Raising money for businesses is only one of the things cryptocurrencies can help facilitate, and indeed some businesses might not be able to exist without them.

Section IV:
The Future of Bitcoin

Chapter 21:
Altcoins and Bitcoin 2.0 Projects

We're going to have millions of altcoins.

—Andreas Antonopoulos, April 2014

So far I have talked a lot about Bitcoin, its history, its uses, and its mechanics. But Bitcoin is far from the only digital currency in existence. While it is arguably the first workable digital currency and undoubtedly the most successful, there are more than a thousand different alternative currencies out there, hundreds of which are traded every day. A few of them seem to have at least a chance at a successful future.

Bitcoin is a risky investment, since no one can be sure that the digital currency revolution will be successful or that it will progress in a way that increases Bitcoin's value. Investing in an altcoin, any altcoin, is at least twice as risky. The investor is betting that the digital currency revolution as a whole will be successful. But he or she is also betting that it will be successful *enough* to increase the value not only of Bitcoin but also his or her altcoin of choice.

As is true in any speculative investment, investing isn't always the same as believing. There is money to be made in day trading. The long-term holders of various coins, however, are betting that the coin developers and marketers will be able to stay afloat in the sea of other altcoins and offer enough unique features that people will choose it over Bitcoin.

As Bitcoin became more popular, various developers decided to see if they could emulate its meteoric rise with their own currencies. In 2011, Namecoin launched as the first alternative Bitcoin derivative. It brought decentralized registration for the .bit name and allowed data to be stored easily on its blockchain. (Ordinarily, when you register a website, you go to an organization called ICANN—or more likely, you utilize a company such as GoDaddy.com, which goes to ICANN—and it links your server's IP address to your URL in a domain name system (DNS). Namecoin, in addition to being a cryptocurrency, is a distributed, decentralized DNS that runs on the Namecoin blockchain and isn't subject to ICANN or any other regulatory bodies.) Since that time, thousands of coins have been launched, the vast majority of which are near-worthless clones of more successful coins. Few have the innovation that Namecoin brought to the table in 2011.

There are far too many altcoins out there to be viable. My general advice is to stay away from altcoins altogether unless you are really interested in being on the cutting edge. The next few years, most predict, will be a massive bloodletting for altcoins. A lot of them are kept afloat purely by speculative trading and pump-and-dump tactics. They have no use in the long run and therefore are unlikely to survive.

The problem is that altcoins are too easy to create. Ars Technica published an article on this topic. Its author, Cyrus Farivar, created and released a coin to illustrate the ease of the process. He used a now-defunct service called Coingen.io. For 0.2BTC he was able to create a custom-made Scrypt coin named Arscoin.[1] (Scrypt is a popular algorithm for cryptocurrencies.) Farivar writes:

> [We] paid up, and waited. The process took just a few minutes. At the end of it, we had Windows and Linux apps, complete with a GUI and the source code. Arscoin was born—now we just had to mine some actual coins and find a way to spend them.

Compiling the source code and issuing software doesn't actually create any coins. Although the coins exist in theory, none can be created or used until a network is set up and the code is actually run. At the time, Arscoins only existed in the sense that an inactive piece of software said that 42 million of them could potentially be created. None of them actually had been. Farivar describes the process by which Arscoin turned from a hypothetical cryptocurrency into an actual one:

> I called Corallo, the Coingen creator, for some guidance. First, he said, I needed one of my colleagues to

---

[1] Farivar, Cyrus. "Behold Arscoin, Our Own Custom Cryptocurrency!" Ars Technica. March 5, 2014. Accessed June 21, 2015. http://arstechnica.com/business/2014/03/behold-arscoin-our-own-custom-cryptocurrency/.

install the app as well so that person could be added as a peer. Soon Peter Bright joined the grand experiment, allowing me to open the Arscoin-qt console and type: "addnode [Peter's IP address] add." Bam! Suddenly there was an Arscoin peer-to-peer network of two.

The next step was to begin mining with the command "setgenerate true." In the Windows version of the Arscoin app, a pop-up soon flashed in the taskbar to denote a successfully mined block. The reward? Fifty Arscoins. Now Arscoin was officially born.

While this might have been worthless mathematical crunching, the thrill of minting "coins" quickly attracted a host of other staffers. Our network of Arscoin nodes tripled in size. Once the group mined 120 blocks, those initial coins would reach "maturity" and could then be spent. With five peers, it took several hours to mine that many blocks.

At that point, we could send each other coins. Pasting in the long string of numbers and letters that served as someone's Arscoin wallet address was simple, and sending coins to others took only a few minutes to complete. Our worthless coins now had the rudiments of a worthless economy.

Worthless as these coins might have seemed, there was a demand for them, so they had a "more than zero" value. After the article was released, Ars Technica readers became interested in Arscoin and the media outlet suddenly had a fairly successful cryptocurrency on its hands. It launched a store where readers could spend their Arscoins. The store only sold flair—little images of decorative hats that would accompany usernames in the comments section of the website's articles—but it was something.

Instantly, Arscoin had three things very few altcoins manage to have: media attention, a community, and a use case. It lacked a few things as well, such as a competent developer staff, long-term plans to create a long-lasting economy, and a decentralized marketplace. But its flaws did not deter numerous Ars Technica readers who wanted decorative hats next to their names. Silly as it might sound, you could purchase the decorative hats only with Arscoins. Very few other altcoins can make the same claim. Even in the case of Bitcoin, there are few items or services other than the Dark Web markets that accept it exclusively.

Of course, success is subjective, but the currency received more attention than a cloned and self-proclaimed funny money could be expected to. (Cloned money involves copy-and-pasted code—a coin with no changes other than name and maybe a few easily modified variables such as total number of coins and block reward.) On April 11, 2014, the Ars Technica team killed Arscoin and all the computational power that had been put toward it went down the digital drain. The decorative hats followed soon after.

In an article describing this decision, writer Lee Hutchinson discussed some of the currency's milestones:

> As of [April 7, 2014], there has been a total of 1,103,600 Arscoins generated (though several blocks' worth were lost due to pool issues). About 81,600 of those coins are sitting undistributed on the pool server, mined by users who never configured automatic payouts for their wallets.

The Arscoin store has processed a total of 864 purchases—that's everything, counting first-time hat purchases, regretful hat repurchases, and colored usernames. These purchases amounted to a total of 572,565 Arscoins spent at the store.

Altogether, 3,005 users registered accounts on the pool server, and a total of 5,108 pool workers were created and used.[2]

Arscoin showed how easy it is to create an altcoin and, intentionally or not, illuminated the pure ridiculousness of the entire altcoin ecosystem. But this particular experiment does not mean there aren't coins with real uses that have a chance to become truly valuable someday.

Through the rest of this chapter, I cover the top altcoins by market cap size—excluding coins still in their ICO (initial coin offering) phase—along with other altcoins chosen because they were either successful in the past or have a unique feature I feel is worth mentioning. No coin developers have paid me to include them on this list, and I am not a significant holder of any of them. This is far from a comprehensive list of all the useful altcoins out there. It is simply my honest attempt to portray the general landscape of the altcoin market as concisely as is practical.

---

[2] Hutchinson, Lee. "Farewell to Arscoin: Preparing to Kill Our Cryptocurrency." Ars Technica. April 7, 2014. Accessed June 21, 2015. http://arstechnica.com/information-technology/2014/04/farewell-to-arscoin-preparing-to-kill-our-cryptocurrency/.

Litecoin

Algorithm: Scrypt
Mining Type: Proof-of-Work
Block Time: 2.5 minutes
Difficulty Re-target: 2016 blocks
Block Reward (current): 25 LTC
Reward Curve: Halves every 840,000 blocks
Total Number of LTC: 84 million

Litecoin is arguably the second most popular cryptocurrency after Bitcoin, judging by its level of acceptance and brand recognition. Created by Charlie Lee, it is technically a fork of the first Scrypt coin Tenebrix, which had a horrible distribution. Initially marketed as "silver to Bitcoin's gold," Litecoin was an attempt to head off the growing hardware and ASIC race of Bitcoin, in which miners are building mining equipment that is continually getting more complex. The idea was to use a CPU-minded algorithm with the intention of bringing mining back to home computers and away from specifically designed hardware.

For a while, it worked. Litecoin was and remains a more viable mining option for those looking to mine at home. It has, however, run into the same problems as Bitcoin, and mining at home is not recommended, though it remains far more feasible than mining Bitcoin.

ASICs designed to mine Scrypt were eventually released and as Litecoin became more popular, its difficulty followed a curve similar to that of Bitcoin. Even with its price dropping over the past few years, Litecoin's difficulty has continued to rise, and mining profitability is razor-thin even with cutting-edge hardware. Mining on a home computer is more likely to damage your hardware than net you any Litecoin. That said, if one has free or extremely cheap electricity, some home mining is possible. It is certainly more feasible than home mining Bitcoin but it is still not recommended for the average user.

Today, Litecoin is used much the same way that it was intended to be: just as Bitcoin, only cheaper. As I write, a Litecoin is worth $2.93. It is the most common trading pair (*i.e.*, currency other cryptocurrencies are traded against) outside of Bitcoin and fiat currencies. It is also accepted by a fair number of merchants, either through popular merchant processing companies such as Coin Merchants or independently on a merchant-by-merchant basis.

Charlie Lee, who started Litecoin, was also an early investor in Coinbase, perhaps the most popular US-based on-ramp to Bitcoin. His involvement with Coinbase has led to near-constant speculation that Coinbase will accept Litecoin at some point. Given the status of Coinbase as a payment processor and a bridge to the fiat world, adoption by Coinbase would be extremely beneficial to Litecoin. Other than the Charlie Lee connection, however, there are currently no indications that Coinbase will ever accept Litecoin.

From a technical standpoint, Litecoin is faster than Bitcoin. With the same block size as Bitcoin and a much shorter block time, the network is capable of performing more transactions per second than Bitcoin in its current form. Bitcoin's block size isn't set in stone and there is an ongoing debate over changing the size of the blocks, but for now, Litecoin remains faster.

Recently, Litecoin started merge mining (*i.e.*, mining two coins with the same algorithm at the same time) with Dogecoin. Both coins use Scrypt, so hashrates can be put toward both coins simultaneously. There was no downside for Litecoin miners and the merge helped secure the Dogecoin network by bringing Litecoin miners onto it.

Dogecoin

Algorithm: Scrypt with AuxPoW
Mining Type: Proof-of-Work
Block Time: 1 minute
Difficulty Re-target: Digishield (variable)
Block Reward (current): 10k Doge
Reward Curve: Halves every 840,000 blocks
Total Number of Doge: 100 billion [goal, variable]

If Litecoin is the most popular serious cryptocurrency, Dogecoin—pronounced either "Doggy Coin" or "Douje-Coin" depending on whom you ask—is the most "viral." Originally intended as a joke, Dogecoin ended up being a major hit with better-than-average staying power. The key to Dogecoin's early success was its mascot. A Shiba Inu dog that had become an Internet meme has served as the mascot for the currency since its inception. The coin itself was never meant to survive long-term from a technical perspective, as it offered extremely high rewards early on to benefit early adopters. It is arguable that Dogecoin was set up as a pump-and-dump itself.

This aspect hasn't stopped it from thriving as a currency. A coin's community can be extremely important and Dogecoin's community is top-notch. Great at natural, viral marketing, the community has worked extremely hard to keep the "joke" going.

Those who entered early profited greatly. Dogecoin, in addition to practically taking over the Internet with its "doge-speak," also gained some fame when it sponsored a NASCAR driver. Josh Wise drove with a Dogecoin Shiba Inu on his car after the community, relying entirely on donations, paid more than $55,000 to get the image on there.[3] I am not talking about a little logo next to the tailpipe, either. It was a mural painted on the hood of the car. Josh Wise was driving "the Dogecoin Car."

Later, in a story that would have made John Candy's ghost feel warm inside, the community helped sponsor the Jamaican Bobsled team, getting the team to the Sochi 2014 Winter Olympics.[4]

As I've mentioned, however, Dogecoin was never designed to survive long-term, so when it lasted longer than anyone—including its original developers—had expected, it ran into some issues. Dogecoin was designed to benefit the early adopters by making 90 percent of the mining rewards come early in the coin's creation. As the supply of Dogecoins dwindled, so did its mining reward, its hashrate and, ultimately, its security. With less mining reward, more miners decided to point their hardware at more profitable currencies. Although network difficulty is supposed to compensate for any declining interest in or value of a coin, Dogecoin's extreme drop-off of miner rewards could not be easily managed. Dogecoin had gained a large overall market cap

---

[3] "Dogecoin to Sponsor Josh Wise at Talladega." NASCAR.com. May 22, 2014. Accessed June 22, 2015. http://www.nascar.com/en_us/news-media/articles/2014/5/22/josh-wise-dogecoin-sponsorship-talladega-sprint-fan-vote.html.

[4] Davidson, Kavitha A. "Jamaican Bobsledders Ride Dogecoin Into Olympics." BloombergView.com. February 4, 2014. Accessed June 22, 2015. http://www.bloombergview.com/articles/2014-02-04/jamaican-bobsledders-ride-dogecoin-into-olympics.

and with its hashrate quickly dropping, a 51% attack became a real possibility.

The solution came by way of Litecoin. After much discussion in both communities, Litecoin decided to enable merged mining with Dogecoin. Despite the exceedingly small rewards available on the Dogecoin network, Litecoin miners still benefited from this decision. Since they use the same algorithm, both coins can be mined simultaneously without a decrease in mining of either.[5] What this did was enable Dogecoin's network to be secured by Litecoin's miners, and anyone looking to force a double-spend through a 51% attack would have to match both the Litecoin network's hashrate and that of Dogecoin. Afterward, merge mining became a popular feature in a lot of smaller cryptocurrencies.

Dogecoin isn't the future of Internet currency, as even its most adamant supporters admit. But that doesn't mean it doesn't have a place in the meantime. It has already passed all expectations and the rest of the cryptocurrency scene could learn a lot from Dogecoin's community and its successes.

Ripple/Stellar

Ripple Labs technically existed before Bitcoin itself.[6] It was originally a payment processor not all that different from PayPal.

---

[5] Higgins, Stan. "Dogecoin Community Celebrates as Merge Mining with Litecoin Begins." CoinDesk. September 11, 2014. Accessed June 22, 2015. http://www.coindesk.com/dogecoin-celebrates-litecoin-merge-mining/.

[6] Buterin, Vitalik. "Introducing Ripple." Bitcoin Magazine. February 26, 2013. Accessed June 22, 2015. https://bitcoinmagazine.com/3506/introducing-ripple/.

After Satoshi Nakamoto's white paper was published and Bitcoin's subsequent rise, the company decided to launch its own cryptocurrency, called Ripple.

Ripple is different than Bitcoin and most other currencies. Many in the community argue that it isn't a "true" cryptocurrency because of its centralized nature, and they might have a point. That doesn't change the fact that Ripple has proven to be very adept at working with the fiat world and has led the way in terms of interacting with banks and other aspects of the traditional financial industry.

Ripple was created by Mt. Gox founder Jeb McCaleb and Chris Larsen after McCaleb sold Mt. Gox to its former CEO Mark Karpelès. Ripple shares no code with Bitcoin and is designed to do a few things Bitcoin can't easily do without third-party software. How useful these features are is a matter of some debate, but they nevertheless have enabled Ripple to stand out.

Ripple works using a concept called gateways, which allows essentially any commodity to be purchased on Ripple's shared ledger. The gateways are individuals or companies who own a commodity and can issue what is essentially an IOU for that commodity. For example, a precious metals company could sell an IOU worth an ounce of gold. Anyone who purchases it on the Ripple network could, in theory, redeem that IOU for a physical ounce of gold at any of that company's physical locations.

That merchant could then partner with other trustworthy merchants around the world, creating a worldwide network where people could buy or sell gold digitally and exchange digital tokens for gold. This system would rely on trust, something that most post-Bitcoin digital currencies strive to eliminate. Bitcoin has been so successful precisely because it did away with the need to trust third parties. Ripple's gateway system is, in effect, a third-party system requiring users to honor the IOUs the gateways issue on the system. This is a trade-off but one that enables features facilitating the trading of virtually any commodity on the system. (I wrote more in Chapter 17 about the issues related to these trusted parties and how they work.)

No third party is required to send Ripple's own currency, which is also called a Ripple and whose currency code is XRP. As with Bitcoin and other cryptocurrencies, it can be sent to any other Ripple user anywhere in the world for less than a penny. But it is the distribution of that currency that worries some in the community and leads them to consider Ripple something other than a true cryptocurrency.

Ripple was completely pre-mined by Ripple Labs, meaning all the Ripple that will exist already exists and Ripple Labs owns most of it. Ripple Labs has promised to keep 20 billion Ripple for development and give away another 50 billion in as fair a way as possible, but ultimately this means Ripple Labs controls the currency. It holds enough Ripple that it could tank the price if it chose to. It is also unclear how much control it has over Ripple's public ledger since no one is securing the network through decentralized mining. Although it has given away a lot of Ripple, it still holds billions, and if Ripple the company disappeared tomorrow, it is not clear what would happen to its holdings. This pre-mine is also responsible for Ripple's overinflated market size. Just because a Ripple is worth a certain amount and there are 100 billion Ripples on the network, that does not mean the total network is worth that amount times 100 billion. If Ripple Labs sold all of its Ripple coins at once, the price would tank based on supply and demand. The true value of Ripple is its price versus how much has been sold, but this is a more difficult number to calculate.

According to Jeb McCaleb, such concerns were one reason why he left Ripple and started Stellar. Stellar essentially works the same as Ripple but attempts to add more transparency and a fairer distribution. It launched with Stripe investment (Stripe is a company that enables people to accept credit card and other payment methods, including Bitcoin, with their cell phones) and promised a more transparent distribution, but the launch was rife with issues and the currency has yet to match Ripple's success.

Despite, or perhaps because of, Ripple's rejection of many of the Bitcoin community's core philosophies, it has made some headway with traditional financial institutions. Fidor Bank uses Ripple, Saldo.mx enables US customers to pay their family members' bills in Mexico, and a few smaller banks in America have also announced projects with Ripple. This list might not make it sound as if Ripple is setting the world on fire, but it is still light-years ahead of most altcoins, which typically never even get a sniff of the fiat world.

Dash/Dark

Algorithm: X11
Mining Type: Proof-of-Work
Block Time: 2.5 minutes
Difficulty Re-target: 2016 blocks
Block Reward (current): $2222222/(((Difficulty+2600)/9)^2)$
Total number of Dash: ~22 million

Dash—not to be confused with Dashcoin—was originally called Darkcoin, but the creators decided to rebrand in an attempt to distance themselves from potential perceptions of a criminal connection. Dash is a privacy-minded cryptocurrency that intends to make the final jump from the pseudonymous nature of Bitcoin to the anonymous promise of electronic cash.

Dash attempts to do this by interacting with a master node, which is not much different than the nodes that run the Tor network (Tor is a network built in the Deep Web that is only accessible through its special browser, also called Tor. See Chapter 6 for more about Tor.) The basic idea is that every transaction is sent to a master node where it is grouped together with a bunch of other transactions and cryptographically signed into the blockchain. The outputs are blinded, so no outside observer can see who sent what to whom—only that a group of coins from various users went into a master node and the same number of coins came out and were passed on to other members. This technology, called Darksend, is based on the Bitcoin technology CoinJoin, which mixes Bitcoin transactions to hide their origin and destination.

Although it is inarguable that Dash is more anonymous than Bitcoin, it suffers from the same problem that plagues the Deep Web browser Tor: it depends on the nodes to be trustworthy. It is probably enough to obscure purchases from regular interested parties, but there is no guarantee the laundering process would be able to deter a dedicated and well-funded entity determined to figure out how the users are spending their Dash.

As is true of most "anonymous" cryptocurrencies, people often hyped the possibility that the dark markets would adopt Dash because of its increased privacy features. Even for those who have no interest in purchasing illegal goods, the thought that the dark markets would adopt Dash is tantalizing, as the demand created from an active underground market could increase over-all demand and help drive the price up, as it did with Bitcoin in the early days. That has yet to happen, however, as most if not all dark markets have continued to use the more highly adopted Bitcoin as their currency of choice.

Today, Dash is trying to distance itself from this perception. As its developers are quick to point out, wanting privacy is not a crime, and there are plenty of legitimate reasons to want to keep your financial transactions out of public view. Dash's biggest feature is still its increased privacy options, but it appears to be courting the "mainstream" crypto-crowd going forward.

NuBits

NuBits is an interesting coin because it ties itself to the currency much of the community claims to hate. NuBits is designed to cost a dollar, always. Currency controls? Price-pegging to an inflationary currency? Isn't this what people joined cryptocurrencies to get away from?

That might be the case but there is a desire for a cryptocurrency without volatility and NuBits provides this. It is still decentralized, since anyone can download a wallet with its blockchain and hold their own wealth on their own computer, but there is a lot of work going on behind the scenes to keep that price at a dollar.

NuBits uses bots to buy and sell NuBits on various exchanges to keep the price in check. This means that its price-pegging is dependent on developer support and it is impossible to know if they will be around forever, but they have—apart from one instance when the price dropped significantly below a dollar—done a fantastic job of keeping that price around where it should be.

NuBits is useful as a hedge against Bitcoin's price as well as a way to get into cryptocurrencies without risking your investment. Of course, price-pegging prevents any speculative investment but NuShares—another related cryptocurrency from NuBits' creators—have been created to give people a way to bet on the technology. It will be interesting to see if the price controls—which, according to the developers, act almost autonomously—will be able to keep the currency stable long-term.

Nxt

Algorithm: N/A uses SHA256 to sign
Type: Proof-of-Stake
Block Time: 1 minute
Minting Reward (current): 1%

Nxt, pronounced "Next," is a "Crypto 2.0" (*i.e.*, next-generation) coin that is among the most powerful of those available. It has one of the most active developer communities and its 2.0 features are among the most commonly used. Nxt features a decentralized marketplace for digital goods, a digital "token" or asset exchange, a monetary system that allows the easy creation of currencies secured on the Nxt blockchain, a messaging system, and an alias system. It is also the flagship coin in the SuperNET system, which combines several blockchains and allows them to communicate.

These features came out over time since the currency's 2013 release and new features are constantly added. Like Bitcoin's Satoshi Nakamoto, Nxt's creator chose to remain anonymous and went by the name BCNext before disappearing in a fashion similar to Nakamoto.

Although the Nxt community is one of the coin's strongest assets, it has also proven to be one of its biggest liabilities as well. Early on in its history, the community split for reasons that still aren't clear. This split led to the creation of two message boards, causing confusion for newcomers that persists to this day. There have also been a few scams involving members or former members of the community that further hurt the coin's reputation.

Nxt has also been subject to a few Bitcoin-style hacks. Although all these have had to do with exchange security or user error more than the security of the coin itself, Nxt is stored entirely online—and the lack of easily stored *offline* wallets is sometimes blamed for the issue. In 2014, one of Nxt's biggest exchanges, Bter, lost 50 million NXT.[7] The community considered a hard fork to reverse the effects of the hack but decided this wouldn't be fair to people who made legitimate transactions during the time between the hack and the hard fork. It was also thought this would set a bad precedent in the community.

Others point to Nxt's distribution as a problem. Nxt is a proof-of-stake coin, which means each account, as long as it is "minting," receives roughly one percent annual interest on its coins. Although it can be argued that Nxt's initial distribution is no worse than Bitcoin's, proof-of-stake coins continually reinforce

---

[7] DeMartino, Ian M. "Breaking: Bter Hacked, 50M NXT Stolen." CoinTelegraph. August 15, 2014. Accessed June 22, 2015. http://cointelegraph.com/news/112278/breaking-bter-hacked-50m-nxt-stolen.

the "rich get richer" dynamic by making Nxt creation dependent solely on how "rich" the wallet owner is. For this reason, initial distribution is a big concern in proof-of-stake coins. Still, Bitcoin's proof-of-work mechanism has not resulted in a free and equal coin creation mechanism either, and proof-of-stake has its advantages.

Ultimately, Nxt has survived these and other controversies because it is an extremely powerful and unique piece of technology. Many of the original holders of the coin have been distributing them through giveaways and bug bounty programs (*i.e.*, when software developers offer money to anyone who finds bugs in their programs), though perhaps not as quickly as others would like. Unlike most coins, which borrow heavily from Bitcoin's code, Nxt was built from the ground up with Javascript. Because of this, its developers have managed to create a very user-friendly user interface and powerful features that might not be as easy to implement in coins based on Bitcoin's code.

Nxt's developer community is among the best, along with Bitcoin, Ethereum, and Counterparty, and its asset exchange is a fun place for high-risk investments. Some features haven't been as successful. Its monetary system, for instance, is full of shovel-wear cryptocurrencies—*i.e.*, cryptocurrencies that bring no new features or value—that serve no purpose and are being bought by virtually no one. Likewise, its digital goods store is very impressive but users hardly ever see the listings change.

Despite these less successful features, Nxt is one of the few alternative currencies that has any footing in discussions about superseding Bitcoin. However, I don't think this prospect is likely, because I don't think any coin is likely to overcome Bitcoin.

Counterparty

Counterparty is another Bitcoin 2.0 project, but it works on the Bitcoin blockchain, giving it the security and hashing power of the Bitcoin network. It enables asset creation and smart contracts. Asset issuers can set a bunch of different parameters, including whether more of the asset can ever be created, and distribute dividends in the form of the asset, Counterparty or Bitcoin.

Counterparty was created through a proof-of-burn method, in which the people who wanted to receive Counterparty coins when it launched sent bitcoins to a verifiable unspendable address, taking those bitcoins out of the Bitcoin ecosystem forever. This was done to create a public perception of value. People, including the developers, had to spend money to get Counterparty. Although that might always be true with cryptocurrencies in the sense that people have to pay fair market value, that money generally goes to the miners. In the case of an unmineable currency (*i.e.*, one that can't be mined as Bitcoin can) such as Counterparty, that money would have gone to the developers. Proof-of-burn was seen as a way to distribute the coins fairly, while proving that the developers were dedicated enough to burn their own bitcoins in order to support the project.

This approach was controversial because there is a very limited number of bitcoins that will ever exist. Burning them to give the perception of value to a currency that might or might not exist long-term rubbed many Bitcoin enthusiasts the wrong way. Although, in theory, any burning of bitcoins should make the bitcoins remaining in the wild more valuable because there are now fewer of them to go around, cutting into that limited supply was not a universally loved idea.

Counterparty was later contracted by Overstock.com to build a "Bitcoin-like" stock market that would be hosted by Overstock and called Medici. Overstock's CEO, Patrick Byrne, is one of Bitcoin's largest supporters. Unfortunately, the Counterparty developers and Overstock split in February 2015, a mere four months after the announcement. Medici never shipped and Overstock has been developing its own stock market.

It is also worth noting that many of Counterparty's features have been ported to another platform that was built on the Dogecoin system, not surprisingly named Dogeparty.

Counterparty has a few systems built around it already and more are coming all the time.

Mastercoin/Omni

Like Counterparty, Mastercoin/Omni is also built on the Bitcoin blockchain. In January 2015, Mastercoin rebranded as Omni, partially to help separate it from controversy that plagued its launch and to indicate the project was turning over a new leaf.

Mastercoin/Omni was hired by Overstock.com to create a cryptocurrency-powered asset exchange but Overstock eventually decided to continue on with the project without the help of the Mastercoin/Omni developers.[8] There are, however, three projects built on the Omni/Mastercoin system that prove its usefulness: Maidsafe, Tether, and Factom.

---

[8] Rizzo, Pete. "Lead Developers Leave Overstock's Medici Project." CoinDesk. February 4, 2015. Accessed June 22, 2015. http://www.coindesk.com/lead-developers-leave-overstocks-medici-project/.

Maidsafe

Maidsafe is a decentralized Internet. Rather than storing websites and other files on one server that then serves the entire Internet, files are encrypted, split up and sent to computers around the world. The participants who donate unused portions of their hard drive to the network are awarded Maidsafe coins/tokens. In its current form, Maidsafe is more of a decentralized file storage service, which in itself is disruptive enough to be significant. If it succeeds in becoming a new Internet free of governmental control, it could massively change our future.

Tether

Tether is a token designed to allow people to hedge against Bitcoin's volatility. In this way, it is similar to NuBits but with more currencies—TetherUSD, for example, is tied to the US dollar.

Unlike NuBits, however, it is not meant to be spent and as an addition to Omni—itself an addition to Bitcoin—does not have its own blockchain. Rather, it is better used by day traders or anyone looking to get out of Bitcoin's volatility temporarily.

Factom

Factom is a document backup service that commits files to the Bitcoin blockchain in a cryptographically secure way. Passports, land titles and even wills can be stored in a completely secure and unmodifiable fashion. There is some question about whether a court would accept a backup copy from the blockchain as an original, but there should be no reason why they wouldn't, assuming the document had been properly notarized before being committed.

Peercoin

Algorithm: N/A
Mining Type: Proof-of-Stake
Block Time: 10 minutes
Reward (current): 1% annual

Peercoin was the first legitimate proof-of-stake coin. There was an earlier coin that Peercoin was forked from but it contained a massive hidden pre-mine. Pre-mines are unacceptable in all cryptocurrencies but are especially troubling in proof-of-stake coins. Proof-of-stake algorithms assign more value to stakers—proof-of-stake's version of miners—based on how many coins are held. Just as Bitcoin and proof-of-work coins give weight to hashing power—but as with Bitcoin, where if you control 51 percent of the network's hashing power you can change the blockchain— the same is true with proof-of-stake coins if one entity holds 51 percent of the coins currently being "staked" to secure the network.

As the first viable proof-of-stake coin, Peercoin used the same method later used by Nxt, Blackcoin and various others. Instead of mining, as with proof-of-work coins, Peercoin users "mint" new Peercoins at a one percent annual interest rate. Like miners, these minters secure the network. But unlike miners, they aren't in competition with each other and don't waste massive computational power, as proof-of-work coins arguably do. In fact, a full node and wallet can be run and stored on a lightweight system such as the Raspberry Pi microcomputer.

The Peercoin community is an innovative one that pioneered many advances. It has its own "2.0" projects, including Peershares, a system built on top of Peercoin that allows for token/asset distribution.

However, the coin has been stagnant for a while. Months elapse between each git commit and there has been no news for quite a while. It is easy to wonder what the future holds for the world's first proof-of-stake coin, especially given that later proof-of-stake coins have far more active developer communities.

Bytecoin/Monero

Algorithm: CryptoNote
Mining Type: Proof-of-Work
Block Time: 2 minutes
Difficulty Re-target: 1 block
Block Reward: variable based on difficulty

Bytecoin and Monero are CryptoNote coins, which means that instead of SHA-256 or Scrypt they use the CryptoNote algorithm. There are several other CryptoNote coins, all essentially the same, with some variation of parameters and branding. These two, however, are the most significant.

CryptoNote technology is not simply another algorithm. Instead, it uses key signatures to enable completely anonymous transactions, or at least transactions that are more anonymous than Bitcoin. It uses a technology known as ring signatures. This uses the mathematical equivalent of a picture to confirm that transactions are sent by the right person but this key can't be used to identify that person without outside information. Additionally, every transaction creates a new address, so only the sender knows where it is going.

Bytecoin (BCN)—not to be confused with Bytecoin (BTE), a long-dead direct Bitcoin clone— was the first implementation of CryptoNote technology. Its launch is still shrouded in mystery. Likely originating somewhere in Eastern Europe or Russia, the coin was supposedly running in secret in the Deep Web since 2012. This official story is highly doubted by most of the community and Bytecoin's past remains a blemish on CryptoNote's present. In addition, Bytecoin was heavily and secretly pre-mined, all but eliminating it from consideration for most Bitcoin users.

When Monero launched, it was a near-carbon copy of Bytecoin but it ditched the pre-mine that plagued Bytecoin. Although it is impossible to see the distribution of CryptoNote coins due to their anonymous nature, Monero is generally regarded as the more "fair" of the two coins, even if it didn't innovate right off the bat.

Namecoin

Algorithm: SHA256
Mining Type: Proof-of-Work
Block Time: 10 minutes
Difficulty Re-target: 2016 blocks

Block Reward (current): 25 NMC
Total Supply: 21 million

Namecoin was the first "Bitcoin 2.0" or "Cryptocurrency 2.0" project. It was released in April 2011 and was a novel solution to domain registration centralization and censorship issues that some on the Internet worry about.

A useful and usable system isn't all that is needed for a Bitcoin 2.0 project to be successful, however. Namecoin is largely considered a failure or at least something that never lived up to its potential. A decentralized domain registry, free from the regulations and censorship inherent in traditional systems, has use cases for journalists, activists and those on the legal fringes of the Internet. Yet the .bit domains that Namecoin gives users access to haven't been scooped up by many people outside of companies that have been sitting on the addresses, hoping to resell them later for profit. This is not unlike how companies and individuals squatted on .com web addresses in the early days of the Internet.

The combination of useful .bit domains being held by parking companies (*i.e.*, companies that buy up domain name registrations to sell to other companies) and the daunting requirement of having to download the Namecoin blockchain just to browse .bit sites has resulted in very little growth in numbers of people actually browsing .bit sites. Most hidden services would prefer to use Tor, which is probably safer in terms of privacy for those groups and has more reach. Namecoin might yet find its use. Although many have written it off, I wouldn't be so quick to do so. The combined altcoin market can't support the market size it currently holds. There just aren't enough currencies with useful functions or niches that Bitcoin can't already fill. This is speculation, but I believe it to be sound: the altcoin market will continue to shrink until the mass of useless and insufficiently useful coins die off. What exactly "dying off" means hasn't been defined by the community but I suspect this definition will be written soon.

When the smoke clears, be it from a slow bloodletting or a quick and definitive crash, the coins left standing will be the useful ones. I don't believe the price is an indicator of a coin's long-term viability. It sounds idealistic, but ultimately a coin's survival depends on three things: the dedication of its community, the talent of its developers and the appeal of its uniqueness.

Namecoin has a use most other coins don't. It was an early altcoin, so it has a large number of knowledgeable investors with backgrounds as developers who have an interest in seeing the technology survive.

Former Namecoin developer and advocate Michael Dean disagrees, calling the technology "dead." He believes the coin will never take off the way it should because, among other things, the developers didn't focus on adoption and usability:

> It's had nearly four years to catch on, and it has pretty much zero adoption. There are 100,000s of squatted domains, but only about 30 developed Dot-Bit sites. All of those are mirrors of Dot-Com or Dot-Net or Dot-Org sites (as they probably should be, to provide redundancy and protection against censorship), and about half of those 30 sites are mine.
>
> There are probably less than 5,000 people in the world set up to actually view Dot-Bit sites, based on downloads of MeowBit and FreeSpeechMe. There was

a lot of mining and trading of Namecoin, and a lot of squatting domains, but almost no building of domains or use of resolvers.

Dean makes a lot of good points and the developers' apparent insistence on the small over the big picture probably hurt the coin significantly. But long-term, it might not matter. Although his concerns about a hostile ICANN (the entity that currently handles domain name registrations on the Internet) takeover hold some validity, apart from that, I see Namecoin surviving until someone more capable attempts to revive it.

Namecoin ultimately holds the rights to .bit addresses, even if the useful ones have been bought out by parking companies. This is valuable because .bit isn't a bad domain name system; it is memorable and relates to a lot of companies. If and when .bit addresses are integrated into regular browsers, an uncensorable Internet will be exposed to the world and there likely will be a market for that, however small or large it might be.

Will this happen? I'm not sure. I wouldn't bet on it. But I also wouldn't be as quick to write off Namecoin as Dean seems to be. To be fair, he has been trying to get the coin off the ground for the past few years, while I am merely an outside observer. Even copycat coins are prevented from scooping up .bit addresses, so Namecoin is in the extremely rare position among crypto-currencies of being open source but also protected from being directly copied by a lesser coin. Someone else could make a similar uncensorable Internet, but they will have to think up another unused domain extension to do it.

Namecoin has underperformed in this era of altcoins, because the era is focused almost entirely on speculative trading. In the next era for altcoins, this won't matter. What matters is whether Namecoin has a reason to survive and it does. This doesn't mean it *will* survive but it has an advantage no other coin has. Some of its developers might have lost sight of that but I still think it is significant.

Blackcoin

Algorithm: N/A

Mining Type: Proof-of-Stake "3.0" (Short PoW/PoS hybrid period for initial distribution)

Block Time: 1 minute, 4 seconds

Block Reward: 1% annual

Maximum Blocksize: 1MB

Total Number: No limit; currently ~74.5 million + <1% annual interest

Blackcoin has been impressive due to the number of features it has brought to the cryptocurrency community, even if its innovations haven't been reflected in its price. Blackcoin's price has been on a downturn since its early 2014 high but its community doesn't appear to be going anywhere anytime soon.

Blackcoin has its own version of proof-of-stake (dubbed "Proof-of-Stake 3.0") that depends less on coinage than other cryptocurrencies and which aims to secure the network. Blackcoin's developers are also reportedly working on further improvements to the proof-of-stake method of securing cryptocurrencies.

Blackcoin's crowning jewels are BlackHalo and NightTrader, two pieces of software that had great potential. BlackHalo is a smart contract system with a double-deposit escrow system. NightTrader is a decentralized marketplace for digital goods, such as downloadable games and ebooks. They combine into a decentralized marketplace for digital goods with a working escrow system that doesn't depend on a middleman; BlackHalo acts as the escrow system. The double-deposit system was novel at the time it was created. It still has a long way to go from the user-experience point of view. Perhaps because of this and its insistence that users run a full Blackcoin node, adoption of the technology has been slow.

To make matters worse, BlackHalo's lead developer, David Zimbeck, was involved in the BTER/Baybit scandal, in which he, a notorious pump-and-dump group called BobSurplus and BTER created a coin and artificially pumped the coin's initial sale by inflating its price. Zimbeck maintains he was unaware of the plan until after the project went live but it has nevertheless done serious harm to his reputation and Blackcoin.[9]

Blackcoin itself, however, still has a dedicated community and a fairly competent developer team, with or without Zimbeck. It is not as large as Nxt's and doesn't come close to Bitcoin's massive community but the developers who are there have proven to be talented.

Blackcoin has made headway in China as well, with a significant number of the coin's nodes residing in that country.

The price of an altcoin matters only because if it gets too low, people will lose interest. Otherwise, there isn't much use in tracking the price outside of day trading. What matters is whether

---

[9] DeMartino, Ian M. "Chat Logs Allegedly Show Bter Creating and Pumping Its Own Coin." CoinTelegraph. January 3, 2015. Accessed June 22, 2015. http://cointelegraph. com/news/113238/chat-logs-allegedly-show-bter-creating-and-pumping-its-own-coin.

a coin can survive until the market settles itself. Currently it is oversaturated with legitimate and scam coins. Eventually this oversaturation will result in a crash of the altcoin ecosystem. The coins that survive will be in an advantageous position.

Blackcoin has a chance of doing this because its development team is talented enough to keep people hanging around for a while. It has a long road ahead of it, because as it turns out, even useless scam coins die hard.

Ethereum

Algorithm: Ethash
Mining Type: Proof-of-Work with plans to switch to new proof-of-stake method
Block Time: Around 20 seconds
Block Reward: 5 Ether per block
Maximum Blocksize: 1MB
Total Number: No limit

I conclude with perhaps the most exciting cryptocurrency since Bitcoin. Ethereum is more than a coin, describing itself thus: "Ethereum is a decentralized platform that runs smart contracts: applications that run exactly as programmed without any possibility of downtime, censorship, fraud or third party interference. Ethereum is how the Internet was supposed to work."

As with Nxt and CounterParty, it allows for asset/token creation. But more than that, Ethereum has its own programming language built in, which has resulted in some very exciting projects. These include Augur, a crowd-powered prediction market where people with the Augur coin are incentivized to vote on whether a prediction came true or not. (How this works and how it keeps people honest is beyond the scope of this chapter.)

There is a Bitcoin-like coin in Ethereum, called Ether, that makes the system run, secures the network and settles contracts.

What has really made headlines, however, is that major technology companies, banks and financial institutions around the world have announced they are working on projects using Ethereum. Details are thin at this point, but UBS and Barclays have both announced an interest in Ethereum, and Microsoft is offering Ethereum in some capacity on its cloud computing service, making it easy for developers to create Ethereum apps.

This support from the outside world is unheard of for cryptocurrencies not named Bitcoin and that, more than anything, is the biggest sign that Ethereum will have some success going forward. It has a long way to go before it becomes the next Bitcoin, which is still light-years ahead in support from both inside and outside the community.

Ethereum has proven itself head and shoulders above the rest of the altcoin world. Its product took far longer than expected to be released, and that caused many to write it off. But when it was, the mainstream world seemed to take notice. Other coins have powerful features, but only Ethereum has its own programming language. This doesn't mean a lot to people without programming experience, but it apparently means a lot to the large entities that have expressed interest in it.

A cryptocurrency's feature's usefulness is tied directly to the quality and quantity of the people using it. If no one is using an asset exchange or if only scammers are using it, it is not very useful.

The support for Ethereum from the outside world is, to me, a sign that the altcoin world is finally solidifying. Most altcoins will fail; in fact, most already have. There are simply too many of them. But a few might find niches and one or two might even be a part of our mainstream economy one day. I would suggest you don't invest anything more than pocket change into an altcoin with the possible exception of Ethereum. But this doesn't mean altcoins aren't worth paying attention to. Anonymous coins, asset-creating Bitcoin 2.0 coins, and intriguing technologies such as Ethereum will all play some role in our future economy.

Chapter 22:

Distributed Autonomous Corporations, Governance, and Niche Economies

I am passionate about bitcoin because I believe it is one of the most exciting inventions of the last two decades and is a platform for building de-centralized trusted applications for financial services, commerce and governance. Much more than just a currency, bitcoin is the Internet of Money. Currency is only the first app!

—Andreas Antonopoulos, January 15, 2015,
Reddit AMAA (Ask Me Almost Anything)

The future of Bitcoin is hard to predict. Advocates, myself included, would say Bitcoin *is* the future.

I've already covered most of Bitcoin's current projects. The immediate future will likely see the evolution of these tools, along with more user-friendly services and hopefully increased interoperability between different wallets and payment processors.

The ongoing debate over the block size limit might or might not have resolved itself by the time you read this, but it will have long-lasting implications for whether the Bitcoin blockchain's size limit will increase or for the need to develop sidechains. (Sidechains are a proposal to make Bitcoin usable by more people. They are types of blockchains made to keep track of transactions separately from the Bitcoin blockchain. The sidechain then adds transactions to the Bitcoin blockchain at once in a compressed form that can still be cryptographically checked.)

These issues will eventually work themselves out, neatly or otherwise, but Bitcoin will survive. It might be harmed as a result, it could even be set back years, but Bitcoin will continue. People are too invested in it for it not to move on. People who paid $800 for a bitcoin aren't going to let it go for eight cents. As long as Bitcoin has a price, the network can still function. It has had many obituaries written about it,[1] and it will again. But the network will survive, regardless of what happens to the price.

What might happen in the more distant future is a far more interesting question than what will happen in the near future.

In the grand scheme of things, five years is a blink of an eye, but in the cryptocurrency world, it is a lifetime. Andreas Antonopoulos said to give Bitcoin two years.[2] I don't agree with that assessment because I think Bitcoin can exist as a niche product for five or even 10 years and then explode when the right product or application is created. That won't be good

---

[1] Last, Jonathan V. "Bitcoin Is Dead." March 5, 2014. Accessed June 22, 2015. http://www.weeklystandard.com/blogs/bitcoin-dead_784187.html.

[2] Bundrick, Hal M. "Andreas Antonopoulos: 'Give Bitcoin Two Years.'" February 8, 2015. Accessed June 22, 2015. http://insidebitcoins.com/news/andreas-antonopoulos-give-bitcoin-two-years/29708.

news for the investors who are looking for returns this quarter or this year, but it could happen. Apple Pay and PayPal will never be as good as Bitcoin is for gambling, porn, and other gray- or black-market products. That isn't a popular thing to say—and I certainly think Bitcoin is useful for more than just that, even in its present form—but if all else fails, it always has that. Since it will always have that, people will always use it. As long as people are using it, there will be some coder, some tinkerer, who will make improvements and make more or better uses for it.

As long as that is happening, Bitcoin always has a chance.

But Antonopoulos's prediction does illustrate one point: things move quickly in the cryptocurrency space. Two years seems like an almost unfathomable amount of time for the people entrenched in it. I preach a bit more patience but the point remains: a lot will be determined by then. Predicting anything is tough with a new technology, because the changes are amplified drastically when the in-hindsight obvious uses are in place. Imagine trying to predict AltaVista, Geocities, and ICQ before web browsers existed, then imagine trying to predict Facebook, Reddit, and Google Earth in 2000 when AltaVista, Geocities, and ICQ were still Internet mainstays.

Given that I will likely be wrong at least as often as I am right, what kind of services do I see evolving in a cryptocurrency wonderland?

Amazing ones.

Altcoins are currently plagued by speculative investing. This drives everything in the space. If the price goes down, the community demands that the developers announce something. Every community in every coin seems to be waiting for that next big jump they are sure will be brought on by the next "revolution-ary" feature.

It usually fails to drive up the price—and then communities and developers alike can become discouraged.

I think the most important and interesting innovations to come from the altcoin space—both actual alternative cryptocurrencies and "coins" built on top of Bitcoin—will come from communities that realize chasing the price is a fruitless endeavor.

I talked earlier about Arscoin, which was made by the popular tech site Ars Technica. It was, in a vacuum, a really bad coin. It was centralized, used copy-and-pasted code, and was not well planned. But it never pretended to be what it wasn't and it had a use that a group of people cared about: it allowed them to buy little virtual hats to put next to their name in the comments, as well as change their name color.

That's it. That is all you could do with Arscoins besides send them to other Arscoin users. But it worked and it was far more popular than it otherwise would have had any right to be. The coin was eventually shut down because Ars Technica likely didn't want to spend resources and time managing a cryptocurrency, but the experiment still proved that having a function people actually want is a quick path to success.

This is different than a function people *say* they want to use. Everyone said they wanted a decentralized marketplace but how many people have been using the ones that are available? Maybe after the next Mt. Gox–like failure, people will see some more use for it, but what folks actually want are exchanges that are fast and full of features. What the mainstream tech community wants from a cryptocurrency and what the hardcore hobbyists think they want tends to vary drastically.

What could be done is best illustrated with a project that was probably a bit too ambitious and ahead of its time but was nevertheless a fascinating technology and concept.

LTBCoin, which was built using Counterparty, is not jumping up the charts. Its price is deflated and its transaction volume is low, but it was and remains an interesting concept. It was perhaps the first real attempt at creating a self-sustaining microeconomy using cryptocurrencies.

Not that its economy is "self-sustaining" right now, with a market cap of only a tad more than $30,000.[3] I don't think anyone is paying their rent with LTBCoins. But as a concept and future project, it is fascinating. Being built on the Counterparty platform means it is secured by the Bitcoin blockchain. If its popularity wanes, there is no need to worry about network security.

LTBCoin is the official token of Let's Talk Bitcoin. Let's Talk Bitcoin started out as a popular Bitcoin-focused podcast. As its popularity grew, the podcast added more shows and eventually decided to start the social experiment that is LTBCoin.

Coins are distributed to content creators and listeners/viewers on a set schedule. LTBCoin is capped at 510 million, and roughly five years after its 2014 debut, all of it will be distributed.

I have no idea where LTBCoin will be in 2019 but where it is now is interesting. Podcasts that are a part of the LTBCoin network give out a magic word every week. Listeners can then enter that magic word and get their supply of LTBCoins for the week. Those LTBCoins can be sold for Bitcoin or used to buy ad space on the LTBCoin network or to buy your own blog on the

---

[3] "Crypto-Currency Market Capitalizations – LTBCoin." Chart. CoinMarket Cap. Accessed June 22, 2015. http://coinmarketcap.com/assets/ltbcoin/.

network. You can also earn coins by submitting articles or running your own auctions.

Things have been quiet on the LTBCoin front at the time of this writing, but a new website is being developed that will hopefully bring in more viewers. This would give the coin value as the ad space that can be bought exclusively with it would become more valuable.

The idea itself is what is fascinating, though: a self-contained economy that has value because it offers something no other place can. I wrote on the concept back in 2014, pondering what a coin could do in the sports world.

The sports world, as you are likely aware, is full of passionate people. Each team has its own subculture—which is in the larger subculture of fans of that sport, which is in the still-larger subculture of all sports fans.

Teams also have the near-exclusive ability to make products unique to them that will be highly desirable to fans. It is as simple as having a player or coach sign something. Some teams have already flirted with a similar idea, creating branded products akin to frequent flyer miles. My 2014 piece was inspired by the New York Jets, who had just announced their plan for "Jets Points" that would be awarded to season ticket holders for showing up to games early, whenever the crowd reached certain noise levels or for watching the team's official postgame show. The Jets Points are meant to give more value to the hated and expensive Purchase Seat Licenses (PSL) that are required to buy season tickets. I wrote about how that could look as a cryptocurrency:

> The Jets could sell exclusive items that would have instant monetary value but could only be purchased

with [Jets Coin]. This would give Jets Coins (or whatever they end up being called) instant value. If a valuable piece of memorabilia was released, say a jersey worn in a game by [Hall of Fame Quarterback] Joe Namath, hundreds of thousands of Jets fans would want it, and would be willing to pay PSL owners for the Jets Coins needed to purchase it. Essentially, the Jets and their fans would have their own currency and it would be the ones that supported the team the most (monetarily) that would reap the benefits. But, it would also give Jets fans who live too far away, a new avenue to obtain memorabilia in a safe way, or to purchase once in a lifetime opportunities, like dinner with Jets owner, Woody Johnson.[4]

Suddenly a PSL is an investment not only because holders can sell tickets to games they don't want to attend but also because attending as many games as possible would reward you with a cryptocurrency. This currency would not only net you exclusive memorabilia but could also be sold on the open market to people who want that memorabilia. The actual Jets Points aren't transferable but a potential Jets Coin could be.

I believe more niche economies such as LTBCoin will spring up over time. Shortly before this book was finished, Uphold announced the Voxel, a cryptocurrency designed to be a currency for virtual reality content creation. What else does the future hold?

---

[4] DeMartino, Ian M. "How Bitcoin Could Change How We Interact With Sports." CoinTelegraph. April 13, 2014. Accessed June 22, 2015. http://cointelegraph.com/news/112268/op-ed-how-bitcoin-could-change-how-we-interact-with-sports.

One of the most heady concepts surrounding Bitcoin is the idea of decentralized governance. It is said that in a democracy people get to choose their government, but that isn't completely true and it especially isn't true in democratic republics such as the US. What people really mean is that they get to choose aspects of their government. A person can't vote to turn their government into the French government. In an ideal situation, they could vote to turn their government into something *resembling* the French government—or whatever government they prefer—but they are still usually stuck with the government they had.

Which is a shame, because the only thing people who live under oppressive regimes are guilty of is being born in the wrong place. Our world is becoming increasingly global and borders are becoming less meaningful over time. First, transportation broke them down. Cars and planes made crossing borders quicker than ever before. Next, the Internet broke down communications between borders, blurring the line further. Today, Bitcoin is blurring the financial separation between borders. In the future, blockchain governance might come close to eliminating those lines altogether.

Why can't I choose my government? I mean, *really* choose my government. I'm not a libertarian or an anarchist; I understand someone has to pay for roads and hospitals and, yes, even the military, so we will likely always be taxed by the government.

But couldn't everything else be an option? What if, rather than handing a portion of my check to the government for Social Security, I had it sent to a Bitcoin account instead? What if that Bitcoin account had hundreds of thousands of people contributing to it? A program could be written ensuring that I get that money back when I retire. I think a lot of people would trust that over the US government and its management of Social Security.

Voting mechanisms could be installed, creating a workable direct democracy arguably for the first time ever. Even insurance could be handled; if someone were injured on the job and had to stop working, the rest of the group could decide if he or she deserved their retirement early and how that retirement would be handled.

You might assume people would always vote "no" in that situation, but I have more faith in the human spirit than that. Besides, there would be competitor governments, and if it got out that Government A doesn't take care of its citizens when they fall on hard times, more people might decide to join Government B.

Competing systems could be built: one person could join a government that puts five percent of all contributions on the side for a social safety net, while other, more libertarian systems could contribute one percent or even zero percent.

The point is, people could choose the government they want. There will always be some obligation to your regional government because there are certain local and regional needs that can't be provided for by a global government. But there are countless tasks handled by the government that aren't on the local or regional level, and those services could be handled in a collaborative, volunteer way. Before Bitcoin, I was more socialist than libertarian. But I now foresee systems being built with cryptocurrencies that satisfy the individual freedoms of libertarian ideals and the social safety nets desired by more progressive people.

In a far-flung future, even local and regional needs could be handled on the blockchain. Individual towns could have their own blockchain and coin. Citizens could vote on how much money should go to schools, roads, police, and everything else in a direct way, right on their cell phones or computers or whatever strange technology they are using in the future. If that is ever going to happen, it will be decades from now—or perhaps in the more immediate future, in small communes as an experiment.

Another possibility arises as virtual reality grows alongside Bitcoin. Communities are already growing inside virtual reality's versions of chatrooms. It isn't unreasonable to predict that as virtual "places" become more permanent, rudimentary governments might arise. If that happens, running it on a blockchain makes perfect sense. Not to mention that these communities will eventually need a currency, and cryptocurrencies are uniquely designed to operate in the digital world.

It's not that traditional governments will go away completely; few are that optimistic. Nathan Wosnack is one of the cofounders of iNation—one of several companies working on this concept—and although he is hopeful for the future, he urges caution:

> Do I believe that government will get entirely out of the business of Deeds/Land titles, Education, Passports and Weddings? Of course not, they want to maintain their control. There is an agorist and more-libertarian move towards less trust and getting away from government run central systems, and more towards peer to peer, decentralized networks where information becomes democratized. Naturally with more security (encryption), document veracity of the blockchain, and lower overhead costs versus per-fee offered by alternative systems (like iNation), the government will have little choice but to accept that private competition is

entering in their governance space. We see it as happening first in the developed countries, and developing countries will eventually follow along.

In fact, first world citizens might find very little use for decentralized governments. To them, it might seem like an unnecessary luxury, like insurance for your insurance. But in countries where the social safety net is nonexistent, a decentralized safety net secured by math rather than bureaucrats or tyrants might find more use.

It could even serve as an "end of your government" insurance. Not sure Social Security is going to be around when you retire? Don't trust the bankers who promise that your 401(k) will work out in the end? If Bitcoin can stabilize in price, it might become a viable hedge against catastrophic governmental collapse.

The question of who will run these governments, who will be the kings and queens of the digital kingdoms, has yet to be determined. My prediction is they will become direct democracies that are set up with math and then just set free. Issues affecting the entire system, such as when to vote and what to vote on, could be determined automatically though a combination of user input and code. It is an interesting idea, but there are many steps between where we are now and that potential future. Still, other projects might bring a form of direct democracy to the people— even if not in governmental form.

Distributed autonomous corporations (DACs) are one of the more exciting concepts to come out of cryptocurrencies. The idea is to have a program operate on its own, with little-to-no human input once it's running, and have it turn a profit while running loose on the Internet.

There have been a few ideas put forth on what kind of corporations these could be. Some of the ideas proposed aren't the most savory but they still illustrate the point. An email spambot, for example, could easily be run in a distributed fashion on the computers of multiple users who had paid for its development by buying its own token or coin. It could then automatically distribute the profits it earns to its owners without having anyone approving or overseeing payment.

Ideally, there will be more useful programs than spambots. More complex proposals have included a bank, which would function both as a place to store cryptocurrencies and to go for a loan. The bank would look at a borrower's credit score, proof of income, and various other aspects before deciding to finance a loan. If a borrower doesn't pay back a loan, he or she could be blacklisted. The profits raised from these loans could be used to pay interest for the participants who put their money into this automated bank.

This would be an extremely complex undertaking and would likely require more complex AI than is currently available. However, in the future it is possible that an automatic program would be able to assess risk and verify identities without human input. It would also be an interesting case for the courts if a borrower of a large loan neglected to pay it back. Would a contract between a DAC and a person be considered valid? Would the bank participants have to go after him or her with a class-action lawsuit?

These will be interesting bridges to cross when we reach them.

Apart from spambots and banks, another interesting idea is a social network that runs in a distributed fashion and turns ad revenue into a cryptocurrency that is distributed to all the users.

It would be up to the owners of the network to put into the initial program how the network plans on turning a profit—but with a much lower overhead than traditional businesses, it might not be that difficult.

Another idea is publicly run, self-driving cars acting as a decentralized, Uber-like platform. A group of people could raise money by selling a coin, then use that money to buy a fleet of self-driving cars, design an app that calls the cars, and let them loose on a metropolitan area.

In the future, people might have multiple DACs that they own a small part of, and they might receive some residual income from them on a regular basis. This might help ease the employment issues that have been and will continue to be exacerbated by increasing automation.

It is a cliché, but technology has been moving at a breakneck pace. Bitcoin technology is no exception. Bitcoin is uniquely positioned among all the world's currencies to be integrated into—and to take advantage of—all the technological advances that are seemingly around the corner.

The financial freedom that Bitcoin provides will be as revolutionary as the educational and informational freedom provided by the Internet. If Bitcoin reaches its potential, billions of people will have their economic lives impacted by the growth of cryptocurrencies. They will gain an economic freedom that will enable them to climb the economic ladder in ways they never imagined possible. In short, Bitcoin will level the playing field between the financial elites and everyone else.

Index